# Spanish Traditional Ballads

# Romances viejos españoles

## A Dual-Language Book

Edited and Translated by
**STANLEY APPELBAUM**

DOVER PUBLICATIONS, INC.
Mineola, New York

## Bibliographical Note

This Dover edition, first published in 2003, contains the full Spanish texts of 53 anonymous ballads reprinted from standard editions (see the section of the Introduction entitled "Sources" for bibliographical details), plus a new translation of each by Stanley Appelbaum, who also made the selection, wrote the Introduction, and supplied the footnotes and the alphabetical lists.

## Library of Congress Cataloging-in-Publication Data

Spanish traditional ballads = Romances viejos españoles : a dual-language book / edited and translated by Stanley Appelbaum.
    p. cm.
Includes index.
ISBN 0-486-42694-7 (pbk.)
    1. Romances, Spanish—Translations into English. 2. Romances, Spanish. I. Title: Romances viejos españoles. II. Appelbaum, Stanley.

PQ6267.E4S63 2003
861'.03308—dc21

2003041461

Manufactured in the United States of America
Dover Publications, Inc., 31 East 2nd Street, Mineola, N.Y. 11501

# Contents

iv Contents

# INTRODUCTION

**Characteristics of the *Romance Viejo*.** All the selections in this anthology (numbered 1 to 53 merely for convenience of reference) are *romances viejos* (or *antiguos*): *romances* written and published by ca. 1580. The entire corpus of these works is known as the *romancero viejo*. A *romance* is the Spanish counterpart of the narrative ballads, medieval and later, in Germanic lands, especially England and Scandinavia.[1] The length of the *romance* fluctuates between a few lines and a few hundred. Each line normally contains sixteen syllables, with a distinct caesura at the syllabic midpoint; all the lines throughout assonate on the same vowel or the same pair of vowels.[2] Basically, this was the form of each assonating section of such heroic epics as the *Poema de mio Cid* (1150? 1200?).

Most likely, *romances* were originally carefully selected and ingeniously compressed fragments of the earlier epics, reworked and recited at a time when shorter works were in vogue and the effecs of lyric poetry were being felt even in the narrative tradition. They were performed by professional reciters *(juglares)*, chanted or sung to instruments (especially plucked or strummed strings). The popular subjects appear in a variety of versions (and with varying titles in publications). The *romance* is episodic, often featuring brusque transitions; it often

---

1. As opposed to the dance-originated Italian *ballata* and French *ballade*. The Spanish *romance* may well be a legacy from such Germanic invaders of Spain as the Visigoths; many investigators believe that the Germanic narrative-poem tradition also underlies the French and Spanish heroic epic poems *(chansons de geste; cantares de gesta)*. Even those brief *romances* which most resemble lyric poems are apt to contain some narrative residue, which may even be fleshed out more fully in variant versions of the same *romances*.    2. For example, the last two syllables of every line in the first selection have the vowels *a* and *o*, respectively: cuida*do*, ha*blo*, llanto, etc., the *a*-syllable bearing the word stress. The rare *romances* that have more than one set of assonances are almost always later combinations of originally independent poems. *Romances* are frequently published with each line broken into two lines of eight syllables each, only the even-numbered lines assonating. The longer lines, as in this volume, may possibly appear more daunting at first, but they are more characteristic of the genre and true to its history—not to mention that they make it possible to include twice as much material in the book! In this volume the caesura in each line is indicated by additional space.

contains much lively dialogue; and, like most oral poetry, it is charac-
terized by stock formulas ("you shall hear what he said," "day was about
to break") and stock epithets ("the brave Reinaldos of Montalván").

The chief subject matter of the *romances viejos* includes: Spanish
history and legend; material from the French *chansons de geste*
(which were much more numerous than their Spanish counterparts),
centuring around the fairly passive figure of Charlemagne, just as "the
matter of Britain" centers around King Arthur; Arthurian (or Breton)
material; Greco-Roman themes; biblical and religious themes; and
miscellaneous themes. Unlike narrative ballads elsewhere, these *ro-
mances* are basically realistic, containing very few supernatural ele-
ments; whatever their source, the stories have acquired a distinctive
Spanish milieu and Spanish values (such as point-of-honor).

Within the category "Spanish history and legend," there is material
derived directly from the older epic poems, and material from
(chiefly) 14th-century prose chronicles (some of which include pas-
sages that are obviously lifted directly from now lost epic poems);
there are *romances* apparently written (not long after the event) to
commemorate current events *(romances noticieros)*, but nevertheless
imaginative and exaggerated; and many *romances* concerning wars
with the Moors, especially during the final decades of the Reconquista
*(romances fronterizos,* "border ballads").

Many historians believe that the composition of *romances viejos*
began about the middle of the 14th century (some even place the ear-
liest ones in the 13th), but the language of the ones we possess is
Castilian of the 15th and 16th centuries. The earliest of the relatively
few manuscript copies of *romances* dates from only 1421. The first
printed versions occur as chapbooks *(pliegos sueltos,* generally rang-
ing between eight and 32 pages) in the first decade of the 16th cen-
tury. As for publication in volumes, some *romances* were included in
songbooks *(cancioneros)* by 1511, but it was almost mid-century be-
fore the first volume exclusively devoted to the genre appeared, the
undated *Cancionero de romances* (see the section "Sources" for de-
tails); the first book called a *romancero* was the one published by
Lorenzo Sepúlveda in Antwerp in 1551.

The language of the *romances viejos* is not forbidding, but it does
feature: some archaic vocabulary (and words used in antiquated or
special senses); some older word forms, usually closer to the original
etymology from Latin, such as *fablar* (later *hablar*); the paragogic *e*
(an *e* added to the end of a word to aid in the assonance scheme (such
as *Roldane* instead of *Roldán*); and an unusual use of tenses (most

strikingly, imperfects used instead of presents), obviously for the sake of easier assonance, though some Spanish critics detect "Byzantine" subtleties of meaning in some of these convolutions of tenses.

**Later *Romances*.** Though no later romances are included here, it is essential to give at least a hint of how this quintessentially Spanish genre, internationally acclaimed as a glory of Spanish literature, influenced subsequent composition. Some historians speak of a *romancero medio,* in the mid 16th century, a period when specific poets and editors began to convert this anonymous genre into something more erudite and more fashionable. Every historian speaks of a *romancero nuevo* period, very roughly 1550 to 1650, in which new *romances* were created on old models by such eminent poets as Lope de Vega, Góngora, and Quevedo, and in which rhetorical, burlesque, and *morisco*[3] *romances* appeared, and some older secular *romances* were rewritten *a lo divino* (on religious subjects).[4]

*Romances* were not vital to 18th-century Enlightenment literature, but the Romantic writers of the 19th century venerated and emulated the older *romancero.* In the 20th century, *romances* inspired some outstanding new work, especially the *Romancero gitano* (Gypsy Ballad-Book) of García Lorca (1928). The corpus of *romances* mentioned in this paragraph is called the *romancero moderno.*

Another extremely significant aspect of *romances* is the so-called *romancero tradicional,* the corpus of orally transmitted Spanish-language ballads collected as folksongs in the field from the late 19th century onward, not only on the Iberian peninsula, but throughout the former Spanish colonies and the Spanish "diaspora" (Sephardic Jews and others) in North Africa, the Balkans, and the Near East. Many of the *romances viejos* in this volume have *tradicional* variants. Moreover, *romances* have inspired other forms of Spanish-language narrative verse, such as the Mexican *corrido.*[5]

---

3. As opposed to the earlier *fronterizo* ballads about Moors, the newer *morisco* ballads emphasized romantic love and flashy "local color" (costumes, fiestas, etc.).  4. In the Golden Age, *romances* affected other genres of literature as well. In drama, *romance* prosody was one of the verse forms most consistently used in the course of a play, especially (but not exclusively) for messenger's narrations and speeches furnishing a historical exposition. Cervantes was enamored of *romances,* and they are so intimately interwoven into *Don Quixote* (as direct quotations, parodies, and other clear or subtle allusions) that it's not too much to say that the Spanish national novel can't be fully understood without a knowledge of the *romancero viejo.*  5. A particularly fascinating offshoot of *romances* is the 19th-century corpus of poems from the Philippines in Tagalog and other local languages, many based closely on Carolingian and other *romances viejos.*

**Sources.** As mentioned above, all the texts in this volume were first published in the 16th century. The specific sources are as follows:

The "undated" *Cancionero de romances:*[6] Nos. 14, 30, 32, 39, 42, 47, 50.

The *Cancionero de romances* of 1550:[7] Nos. 5, 7, 9, 10, 11, 12, 13, 16, 17, 23, 28, 31, 40, 44, 45, 46, 49, 51, 52, 53.

*Silva de varios romances:*[8] Nos. 1, 3, 6, 8, 15, 21, 27, 37.

*Rosa de Amores:*[9] No. 48.

*Rosa Española:*[10] Nos. 18, 19.

Pérez de Hita, *Guerras civiles de Granada:*[11] Nos. 22, 24.

Marcelino Menéndez y Pelayo, *Antología de poetas líricos castellanos* (1890–1908): No. 26 (reprinted from an unclear 16th-century source).

Ramón Menéndez Pidal, *El romancero español,* Columbia University Press, New York, 1910: No. 41.

---

6. *Cancionero de romances en qve estan recopilados la mayor parte de los romances castellanos que hasta agora se han compuesto* (Songbook of Ballads, in Which Are Gathered Most of the Castilian Ballads Written to Date), published by Martín Nucio, Antwerp, n.d. [between 1547 and 1549]. 7. *Cancionero de romances Nuevamente corregido, emendado y añadido en muchas partes* (Songbook of Ballads, Newly Corrected, Emended, and Expanded in Many Places), published by Martín Nucio, Antwerp, 1550. 8. *Primera parte de la Silua de varios romances En que estan recopilados la mayor parte de los romances Castellanos que hasta ahora se han compuesto, hay al fin algunas canciones, coplas graciosas y sentidas* (First Part of the Miscellany of Various Ballads, in Which Are Gathered Most of the Castilian Ballads Written to Date; at the End Are Some Humorous and Serious Songs and Verses), published by Esteban de Nájera, Zaragoza (Saragossa), 1550 [2nd part, 1550; 3rd part, 1551]. 9. *Rosa de Amores. Primera parte de Romances de Joan Timoneda, que tratan diversos, y muchos casos de amores. Dirigidos al discreto Lector* (Rose of Love. First Part of the Ballads of Juan Timoneda, Which Treat of Many Different Love Affairs. Addressed to the Wise Reader), edited and published by Juan de Timoneda, Valencia, 1573 (printed by Juan Navarro). 10. *Rosa Española. Segunda parte de Romances de Joan Timoneda, que tratan de hystorias de España. Dirigidos al prudente Lector* (Spanish Rose. Second Part of the Ballads of Juan Timoneda, Which Treat of Spanish History. Addressed to the Circumspect Reader), same publisher, printer, city, and year. (The other two ballad "Roses" of Timoneda's were *Rosa Gentil* [Pagan Rose], on Greco-Roman subjects, and *Rosa Real* [Royal Rose], on exploits of kings, princes, viceroys, and archbishops.) 11. Ginés Pérez de Hita, *Historia de los vandos de los Zegries y Abencerrajes cavalleros moros de Granada, de las Civiles guerras que vuo en ella, y batallas particulares que vuo en la Vega entre Moros y Christianos, hasta que el Rey Don Fernando Quinto la gano* (History of the Factions of the Zegris and Abencerrages, Moorish Knights of Granada, of the Civil Wars That Took Place There, and the Individual Combats Fought on the Plain Between Moors and Christians Until King Fernando V Conquered It) [first part], published by Ángelo Tabanco (printed by Miguel Jiménez Sánchez), Zaragoza, 1595.

From 16th-century chapbooks *(pliegos sueltos):* Nos. 2, 4, 20, 25, 29, 33, 34, 35, 36, 38, 43.[12]

**Commentary on the Poems Selected.** To save space, this commentary intentionally excludes: almost all place names (geography outside Spain in the *romances* tends to be quite fanciful); most personal names, except for the protagonists of the ballads; speculations on the specific literary sources of the subject matter of individual ballads; speculations on the specific time of original composition of individual ballads; details of the evolution of the legends behind individual ballads; the evolution of critical appreciation of the ballads.

Nos. 1–29, which concern Spanish history and national legends, and Moorish themes, are roughly chronological by subject matter (but no other way!).

Nos. 1–4: In the *Crónica sarracina* of Pedro del Corral, ca. 1430, the Muslim invasion of the 710s was said to have been instigated by the governor of Ceuta, whose daughter had been seduced by Rodrigo (Roderick), the last Visigothic king. "Cava" is said to mean "bad woman"; in pre-*romance* versions of the story, she's not merely an innocent victim. "Julián" may have been a historical figure, the chief of a Christian tribe in North Africa. The snake-pit penance appears to be a genuinely Germanic motif, with parallels in Old Norse literature and art.

No. 5: Of all the major epic and *romance* personalities, only Bernardo of El Carpio seems to lack any historical basis. His legend was formed in the 12th and 13th centuries as a nationalistic counterweight to the popularity of Charlemagne and his Twelve Peers; thus Bernardo is supposed to have lived in the late 8th and early 9th centuries. His chief feat (imaginary) was the routing of Charlemagne's rear guard, led by Roland, at Roncesvalles in 778 (actually done by Basques), but his legend also included insubordination to the king who had jailed his father. El Carpio was a castle in Asturias. El Encinal was the site of a battle against the Moors.

No. 6: Fernán González (ca. 930–970), Count of Castile, won his county's independence from Sancho II or Ramiro II of León; in the legend, he sold his horse and hawk to the king, who delayed payment, and when the price, mounting daily at a geometric rate, became astronomical, the King gave him Castile instead.

---

12. No. 20 may have been printed by Pedro de Castro in Salamanca, ca. 1541. Nos. 34 and 35 were printed by Pedro Malo, Barcelona, at the end of the 16th century. No. 36 was printed by Juan de Junta, Burgos, ca. 1535. No. 38, dated 1538, may also be a production of Junta in Burgos; a previous version of the ballad was published substantially earlier.

Nos. 7 & 8: The father of the Young Lords[13] of Lara, Gustos Gustioz, was a historical Spanish envoy to the Muslim court of Córdoba in the late 10th century. The wedding in No. 7 was between a female cousin of Fernán González and a man who had aided him in war (brother of the Young Lords' mother); Garci-Hernández was the son of Fernán González. Of the two games mentioned, *tablado* and *tablas,* the former was a physical, war-training sport (hurling javelins from horseback to topple a scaffolding on a tall pole), the latter was a board game like checkers, but with moves determined by dice-casting. Before the events in No. 8, the vengeful uncle of the Young Lords has betrayed them to the Moors, who have beheaded them and their tutor; their father, imprisoned by Al-Mansur, regent (not king) of Córdoba, is summoned to inspect the heads. The battle of Almenar occurred in 974. St. Cyprian's Day is variously given as the 14th or 16th of September. In the legend, Mudarra, son of "Gonzalo Gustos" and the Moorish woman, grows up to avenge the death of the half-brothers he never knew.

Nos. 9–12: A small sampling of the many *romances* (over 150) about the Cid, the national hero of Spain (died 1099), derived not only from the completely extant *Poema de mio Cid,* but also from lost epics about his haughty, devil-may-care youth *(mocedades).* Before the combined events of Nos. 9 and 10, the Cid has killed Lozano, father of Jimena, for slapping his own father; the king in question is Fernando I (1035–1065),[14] ruler of León, Castile, and Galicia. The king in No. 11 is Alfonso VI of León (1072–1109), who succeeded his murdered brother Sancho II of León (1065–1072). The harsh oath angered the king, who eventually exiled the Cid. No. 12: The Cid conquered the Moorish kingdom of Valencia in 1094.

No. 13: The king is Alfonso VIII of Castile (1158–1214), who won the battle of Las Navas de Tolosa, the greatest single Christian victory of the Reconquista, in 1212.

No. 14: Actually, two kings are involved. The one in lines 1–10 (assonating in *-e-a*) is Fernando III "el Santo" (1217–1252).[15] The rest of the poem does actually concern Fernando IV (1295–1312); the Carvajal brothers probably did kill a nobleman.

No. 15: The prior Fernán Rodríguez de Valbuena rebelled at Consuegra (province of Toledo) in 1328 against a minister of King

---

13. An *infante* was, strictly speaking, a prince other than the crown prince *(príncipe),* but the term was sometimes applied to other noblemen.    14. All years given for kings are the years of their reign.    15. From this point on, the kings mentioned ruled over León and Castile jointly.

Alfonso XI (1312–1350). The Don Juan previously executed by the king was the nobleman known as El Tuerto ("the one-eyed").

No. 16: Strictly speaking, this is an event in Portuguese history, but all historical names have been changed in this *romance*. The heroine was really the celebrated "queen after her death," Inés de Castro, wife of Prince Pedro, who reigned as Pedro I from 1357 to 1367 (she had been killed in 1355). The place name "Giromena" stands for Jurumanha.

Nos. 17 & 18: The king is Pedro I "el Cruel" (1350–1369). He killed his brother, the Master of the military-religious Order of Santiago, in 1358; "Coimbra" is not the famous Portuguese university town, but Jumilla (province of Murcia). María de Padilla was Pedro's mistress; Blanche (of Bourbon), his unloved and imprisoned queen.

Nos. 19–29 are chiefly concerned with the last 80 years of the wars against the Moors in Andalusia.

No. 19: This defeat of the Christians at Montejícar took place on May 11, 1410. Jaén had been in Christian hands since 1246.

No. 20: Antequera was conquered on September 16, 1410, after a five-month siege, by Prince Fernando "de Antequera," who later reigned over Aragon from 1412 to 1416.

No. 21: The event follows closely on that in No. 20. Granada was the last remaining Moorish stronghold, finally taken only after a prolonged, costly campaign lasting from 1481 to 1492, but fought over even earlier (see also Nos. 22–29). St. John's Day is June 24 ("midsummer").

No. 22: The Spanish king asking the questions is Juan II (1406–1454); the Moor who replies is Yusuf, Aben Alamao (or Alamar), with whom the king made a peaceable visit to the site of Granada in 1431. The poetic conceit of wooing a city like a woman is borrowed from Arabic literature.

No. 23: The bishop referred to may be Gonzalo de Zúñiga, bishop of Jaén, who died in 1456 (though he doesn't seem to have been captured). There may very well be some confusion between two different bishops, and the event may ultimately be identical to the one in No. 19. St. Anthony's Day is January 17th.

No. 24:[16] Santa Fe was a tent city established outside Granada in 1490 as Christian headquarters by Fernando "el Católico"

---

16. Because some of the events in Nos. 24–29 have been variously interpreted, and historical occurrences may have been confused by the poets or reciters to some extent, the chronological sequence-by-events may not be correct for these six ballads concerning the Granada campaign.

(1479–1516; the Ferdinand married to Isabel[la]);[17] it was 'walled in" by a cloth painted to look like masonry. The narrative, however, is possibly a mangled version of an event of 1448. The *donceles* were an elite military body of former pages. All the people named occur in an earlier chronicle. Garcilaso de la Vega was the father of the renowned Renaissance poet of the same name (1501 or 1503–1536). In a way, Nos. 24–26 form a little trilogy about Manuel Ponce de León, brother of the Duke of Cádiz; the lion adventure of No. 26 is mentioned in No. 24.

Nos. 25 & 26: More about Manuel Ponce de León. The event in No. 25 may just possibly have occurred in 1491. No. 26 was probably the source of Schiller's famous poem "Der Handschuh" (The Glove).

No. 27: The Master of the military-religious Order of Calatrava who won such renown in the Granada campaign was Rodrigo Téllez Girón (1458–1482), a prominent character (at the age of 18) in Lope de Vega's play *Fuenteovejuna*.

No. 28: A *romance* of muddled origins. Ordiales, a servant of the Duke of Medina Sidonia, was killed in 1448, the year in which a Juan Sayavedra was taken prisoner by the Moors; but some historians have connected the adventure described with the Master of Calatrava and with Alonso de Aguilar.

No. 29: Alonso de Aguilar, also known as Alfonso Fernández de Córdoba, was a brother of Gonzalo Fernández de Córdoba y Herrera (of the Aguilar family; 1453–1515), who negotiated the surrender of Granada and later gained the nickname Gran Capitán for his military successes in Italy in 1496.

Nos. 30–42, concerning Charlemagne and his paladins, are not historical events, but are ultimately derived from French epics of chivalry and other courtly narratives, though the poets or reciters of the Spanish *romances* didn't always make the connection (and added inventions of their own).[18]

No. 30: The names Garinus and Garin occur in French epics. For the *tablado*, see the comment on No. 7. This *romance* is cited in *Don Quixote*.

17. He was Fernando II of Aragon, Fernando V of Castile.   18. The names of the chief characters have been so thoroughly assimilated into Spanish literature that their Spanish forms have been retained in the English translation. Naturally, however, Carlos = Charles (Charlemagne); Roldán = Roland (the Orlando of the later Italian epic poems); Oliveros = Olivier; Reinaldos de Montalván = Renaud de Montauban (the later Italian Rinaldo); Alda = Aude; and Urgel Danés = Ogier le Danois. Other names are discussed individually.

No. 31: Roland's fiancée Aude was a sister of Olivier.

No. 32: The love affair between Claros and the princess recalls the legendary one between Eginhard, Charlemagne's secretary, and the emperor's daughter Emma, or Enilde; there may even be a connection with No. 41. The surprising speech of the page is magnificent, and the princess is refreshingly active and fiery.

No. 33: This is even a closer parallel to the Emma and Eginhard story, and the characters' names are obviously related to the German ones. The motif of the sword separating the lovers occurs in the *Nibelungenlied,* the *Tristan* literature, and elsewhere. This *romance* is especially widespread in folksong variants *(romances tradicionales),* in which the hero's name sometimes appears as Erinerdo.

Nos. 34 and 35: Two *romances* printed separately in 16th-century sources, but really continuous. The name of Gaiferos may be derived from that of Waifarius, a duke of Aquitaine (died 769) whose adventures inspired narrative poems in Latin and several vernacular languages.

No. 36: This completely separate Gaiferos adventure is most famous for providing the plot of Maese Pedro's puppet performance in *Don Quixote* (Part Two, Chapter 26), which in turn inspired Falla's 1923 opera *El retablo de Maese Pedro.* The name of the place where Gaiferos finds his wife—Sansueña—is probably a version of Sachsen (Saxony, or Saxons), via the French form *Saisnes.*

No. 37: Valdovinos is a form of Baudoin (or Baudouin), who appears as a nephew of Charlemagne in some French sources. In the epic *La chevalerie Ogier,* Charlot (here Carloto) kills a son, not a nephew, of Ogier, who flees to Italy (Mantua and Milan are possibly associated with Charlemagne's [historical] annexation of Lombardy). The fate of Charlot varies greatly in versions of this ballad and in its sources.

No. 38: This poem has been called overlong, dull, and unpoetic (it does have irregular verses, vague syntax, and illogicalities great and small), but it was the most popular *romance* in the 16th century, the one most frequently reprinted in chapbooks, and the foremost *romance* scholar, Ramón Menéndez Pidal, called it "the greatest narrative effort bequeathed to us by the reciters of Carolingian themes, a true *cantar de gesta* in miniature." The count's title is printed as *dIrlos* in some sources, and "of [the city] Irlos" is clearly the proper rendering of "Dirlos." The just barely prevented remarriage of a woman not really widowed is a common theme in European folklore.

No. 39: Based on the French verse epic *Aïol* (12th & 13th

centuries). Another *romance,* not in this anthology, "Romance del conde Grimaltos y su hijo" (also based on *Aïol*), supplies the background of No. 39: Grimaltos, who has risen from page to Charlemagne's son-in-law and viceroy of León, is envied by Tomillas, who accuses him of treason, causing his exile; his wife gives birth while they are in a wild forest (*montes;* hence the child's name, Montesinos); they live with a hermit for fifteen years, during which time Grimaltos gives Montesinos thorough training as a knight; on St. John's Day father and son ascend a mountain with a view of Paris; the father's subsequent speech is the beginning of No. 39. The epic *Aïol* is much longer, and Aïol (the Montesinos character) has many more adventures before he can rest on his laurels.

No. 40: This *romance* is probably a total invention by Spanish poets imbued with Carolingian themes. A *palmero* is specifically a pilgrim returning (with palm leaves) from the Holy Land.

No. 41: The name Melisenda may be a corruption of Belissant, a daughter of Charlemagne in the French verse epic *Ami et Amile* (ca. 1200). Her beloved, Ayuelos, may bear the same name as the French hero Aïol (see comment to No. 39). The situation resembles those in Nos. 32 and 33.

No. 42: Is the Princess Sevilla here the same woman as Valdovinos's wife in No. 37? (A 19th-century Philippine adapter of *romances* thought so.) She is in the city of Sansueña, like Gaiferos's wife in No. 36.

Nos. 43–45 have Greco-Roman subject matter.[19]

No. 43: A not too distorted account of the Trojan War. The imprisonment of Paris is modeled on that of Guarinos in No. 30.

No. 44: In the original Roman legend, Lucrece (Lucretia) was raped by Sextus, the *son* of King Tarquin (Tarquinius Superbus).

No. 45: The ancient Roman poet Vergil was the hero of many a medieval legend, often as a wizard, sometimes as a lover.

No. 46: This Arthurian *romance* is quoted in Part One, Chapter 13, of *Don Quixote,* and parodied in Part One, Chapter 2, when the whores at the inn remove the Don's makeshift armor.

No. 47: This *romance novelesco* (nonhistorical story ballad) was already being imitated by the mid-15th century, and folksong versions of it have been collected in Portugal.

No. 48: This ballad has several early literary parallels in France and

---

19. The translations of Nos. 43–46 (Greco-Roman and Arthurian ballads) use the normal English forms of the characters' names, for the sake of clarity.

Italy. Among its widespread folklore motifs are: multiple births as an indication of adultery, and the baby set adrift in a small vessel (cf. Moses).

No. 49: This is one of the few known *romances* with a distinctly supernatural element, a spell cast by fairies. Some of the numerous folksong versions turn it into a *caballero burlado* story (an amorous knight disappointed by a wily rural girl); in some versions the girl proves to be the knight's sister.

No. 50: This short version is the most famous, universally admired for the aura of mystery it generates. In longer versions, Arnaldos finds his servants on the boat when he boards it, and falls asleep for seven years (the singing sailor is an enticing demon). The hero's name has been connected with Herla, another name of the Norse god Woden, and with that of Compte Arnau, who, is a Catalan myth, escapes from hell to inform his wife of his sins.

Nos. 51–53 are lyrical romances (whether intrinsically so, or because they're in a fragmentary state).

No. 51: This has been traced back to a "spring song" known in the 13th century.

No. 52: This ballad already appears in songbooks published early in the 16th century. *Frida* is an old form of *fría* (cool; from Latin *frigida*).

No. 53: A genuine old folksong seems to be incorporated into this ballad.

**The Nature of This Edition.** This anthology includes *romances viejos* of various length, ones that are representative of the major groups and subgroups in scholarly classifications, and a number of the most famous and influential examples.

The form of the Spanish text reflects the general practice of present-day Spanish editors (as opposed to outright modernizers): the punctuation is modern, but the spelling is only discreetly modernized,[20] and old forms like *fablar* and *parescer* (for *hablar* and *parecer*) are retained,[21] with no attempt at perfect consistency throughout the volume. Each poem is complete (for the version selected).

The translation is absolutely complete, confronting each difficulty and ambiguity squarely. Many Spanish dictionaries, glossaries, and

---

20. That is (generally speaking), modernization has been introduced where an archaic spelling is merely a hindrance to recognition and the pronunciation is not basically affected. For instance, a novice may very well be perplexed by *vuo*, which has been regularly respelled as the much more familiar *hubo* (past tense of *haber*).
21. Obviously, the meter doesn't permit the modernization of such forms as *vido, fer,* or *lloredes* into *vio, hacer,* and *lloréis*, which have a different syllable count.

commentaries have been consulted in the pursuit of maximum accuracy, with an eye out for semantic changes that have occurred over the centuries. The English is formal, but never falsely archaizing. As far as the difference in syntax between Spanish and English permits, the translation hews closely to the sequence of the original, being strictly line-for-line 99 percent of the time, and hemistich[22] by hemistich most of the time.

---

22. Half-line.

# Spanish Traditional Ballads

## Romances viejos españoles

# Historia de España

## 1. Seducción de la Cava

Amores trata Rodrigo,   descubierto ha su cuidado;
a la Cava lo decía,   de quien era enamorado;
miraba su lindo rostro,   miraba su rostro alindado,
sus lindas y blancas manos   él se las está loando:
—Querría que me entendieses   por la vía que te hablo:
darte hía mi corazón   y estaría al tu mandado.
La Cava, como es discreta,   a burlas lo había echado;
el rey hace juramento   que de veras se lo ha hablado;
todavía lo disimula   y burlando se ha excusado.
El rey va a tener la siesta   y en un retrete se ha entrado;
con un paje de los suyos   por la Cava ha enviado.
La Cava, muy descuidada,   cumplió luego su mandado.
El rey, luego que la vido,   hale de recio apretado,
haciéndole mil ofertas,   si ella hacía su rogado.
Ella nunca hacerlo quiso,   por cuanto él le ha mandado,
y así el rey lo hizo por fuerza   con ella, y contra su grado.
La Cava se fue enojada,   y en su cámara se ha entrado.
No sabe si lo decir,   o si lo tener callado.
Cada día gime y llora,   su hermosura va gastando.
Una doncella, su amiga,   mucho en ello había mirado,
y hablóle de esta manera,   de esta suerte le ha hablado:
—Agora siento, la Cava,   mi corazón engañado,
en no me decir lo que sientes   de tu tristeza y tu llanto.
La Cava no se lo dice,   mas al fin se lo ha otorgado.
Dice cómo el rey Rodrigo   la ha por fuerza deshonrado,
y por que más bien lo crea,   háselo luego mostrado.
La doncella, que lo vido,   tal consejo le ha dado:
—Escríbeselo a tu padre,   tu deshonra demonstrando.

# History of Spain

## 1. Rodrigo Seduces La Cava

Rodrigo is in love,   he has revealed his preoccupation;
he told it to La Cava,   with whom he was infatuated;
he gazed on her lovely face,   he gazed on her beautiful face,
he kept on praising   her lovely white hands:
"I want you to understand me   from the way I talk to you:
I would give you my heart   and would be at your beck and call."
Since La Cava was prudent,   she thought he was joking;
the king swore   that he had said it in earnest;
yet, he concealed his passion,   apologizing lightheartedly.
The king went to take a nap,   entering a small private room;
through one of his pages   he sent for La Cava.
La Cava, quite unsuspecting,   obeyed his order at once.
As soon as the king saw her,   he embraced her tightly,
making her a thousand offers   if she did what he asked.
She absolutely refused,   however much he commanded her to,
and so the king took her   by force against her will.
La Cava was distressed,   and entered her chamber.
She didn't know whether to report it   or keep silent about it.
Every day she moaned and wept,   ruining her beauty.
A young lady, her friend,   had observed this closely,
and spoke to her thus,   spoke to her in this fashion:
"Now, La Cava, I feel   that my heart is disappointed,
since you won't tell me how you feel   in your sorrow and tears."
La Cava didn't tell her,   but at last she permitted her to know.
She told how King Rodrigo   had dishonored her by force,
and to make her believe it,   she at once showed her condition.
Seeing this, the young lady   gave her the following advice:
"Write your father about it,   declaring your dishonor."

3

La Cava lo hizo luego,    como se lo ha aconsejado,
y da la carta a un doncel    que de la Cava es criado.
Embarcárase en Tarifa    y en Ceuta la hubo llevado,
donde era su padre, el conde,    y en sus manos la hubo dado.
Su madre, como lo supo,    grande llanto ha comenzado.
El conde la consolaba    con que la haría bien vengado
de la deshonra tan grande    que el rey les había causado.

## 2. Visión del rey Rodrigo

Los vientos eran contrarios,    la luna estaba crecida,
los peces daban gemidos    por el mal tiempo que hacía,
cuando el buen rey don Rodrigo    junto a la Cava dormía
dentro de una rica tienda    de oro bien guarnecida.
Trescientas cuerdas de plata    que la tienda sostenían;
dentro había cien doncellas    vestidas a maravilla:
las cincuenta están tañendo    con muy extraña armonía,
las cincuenta están cantando    con muy dulce melodía.
Allí habló una doncella    que Fortuna se decía:
—Si duermes, rey don Rodrigo,    despierta por cortesía,
y verás tus malos hados,    tu peor postrimería,
y verás tus gentes muertas,    y tu batalla rompida,
y tus villas y ciudades    destruidas en un día;
tus castillos fortalezas    otro señor los regía.
Si me pides quién lo ha hecho,    yo muy bien te lo diría:
ese conde don Julián    por amores de su hija,
porque se la deshonraste    y más de ella no tenía;
juramento viene echando    que te ha de costar la vida.
Despertó muy congojado    con aquella voz que oía,
con cara triste y penosa    de esta suerte respondía:
—Mercedes a ti, Fortuna,    de esta tu mensajería.
Estando en esto ha llegado    uno que nueva traía
cómo el conde don Julián    las tierras le destruía.

## 3. La derrota de don Rodrigo

Las huestes de don Rodrigo    desmayaban y huían,
cuando en la octava batalla    sus enemigos vencían.
Rodrigo deja sus tiendas    y del real se salía;

La Cava did so at once,    as she had been counseled,
and gave the letter to a young man    from among her servants.
He boarded ship at Tarifa    and brought it to Ceuta,
where the count, her father, was,    and placed it in his hands.
When her mother learned the facts,    she began to weep bitterly.
The count consoled her,    saying he'd avenge her well
for that great dishonor    the king had caused them.


## 2. King Rodrigo's Vision

The winds blew every way at once,    the moon was full,
the fish uttered moans    because of the stormy weather,
when good King Rodrigo    slept beside La Cava
within a rich tent    well trimmed with gold.
Three hundred silver cords    held up the tent;
inside were a hundred maidens    marvelously dressed:
fifty played instruments    with a very strange harmony,
fifty were singing    with a very sweet melody.
Then there spoke a maiden    named Fortune:
"If you're asleep, King Rodrigo,    please wake up,
and you'll see your evil fate    and your even worse end,
and you'll see your people dead,    and your army dispersed,
and your towns and cities    destroyed in one day;
your castles and fortresses    governed by another lord.
If you ask me who has done this,    I shall tell you clearly:
Count Julián    for love of his daughter,
because you dishonored her,    and he had no other but her;
he has sworn an oath    that it will cost you your life."
He awoke in great distress    at that voice he had heard;
with a sad, troubled face    he replied in this manner:
"Thank you, Fortune,    for this message of yours."
At this moment there arrived    one bearing news
of how Count Julián    was ravaging his lands.


## 3. Rodrigo's Defeat

Rodrigo's forces    lost heart and fled
when his enemies won    the eighth battle.
Rodrigo left his tents    and abandoned his camp;

solo va el desventurado,    que no lleva compañía,
el caballo de cansado    ya mudar no se podía,
camina por donde quiere,    que no le estorba la vía.
El rey va tan desmayado    que sentido no tenía;
muerto va de sed y hambre    que de verle era mancilla,
iba tan tinto de sangre    que una brasa parecía.
Las armas lleva abolladas, que eran de gran pedrería,
la espada lleva hecha sierra    de los golpes que tenía,
el almete, de abollado,    en la cabeza se le hundía,
la cara lleva hinchada    del trabajo que sufría.
Subióse encima de un cerro,    el más alto que veía;
desde allí mira su gente    cómo iba de vencida;
de allí mira sus banderas    y estandartes que tenía,
cómo están todos pisados    que la tierra los cubría;
mira por los capitanes,    que ninguno parecía;
mira el campo tinto en sangre,    la cual arroyos corría.
El triste, de ver aquesto,    gran mancilla en sí tenía;
llorando de los sus ojos    de esta manera decía:
—Ayer era rey de España,    hoy no lo soy de una villa;
ayer villas y castillos,    hoy ninguno poseía;
ayer tenía criados    y gente que me servía,
hoy no tengo una almena    que pueda decir que es mía.
Desdichada fue la hora,    desdichado fue aquel día
en que nací y heredé    la tan grande señoría,
pues lo había de perder    todo junto y en un día!
¡Oh muerte!, ¿por qué no vienes    y llevas esta alma mía
de aqueste cuerpo mezquino,    pues se te agradecería?


## 4. La penitencia de don Rodrigo

Después que el rey don Rodrigo    a España perdido había,
íbase desesperado    por donde más le placía;
métese por las montañas,    las más espesas que vía,
porque no le hallen los moros    que en su seguimiento iban.
Topado ha con un pastor    que su ganado traía,
díjole: —Dime, buen hombre,    lo que preguntarte quería:
si hay por aquí poblado    o alguna casería
donde pueda descansar,    que gran fatiga traía.
El pastor respondió luego    que en balde la buscaría,
porque en todo aquel desierto    sola una ermita había,

the unlucky man was alone,   without company;
his horse was so weary   it could no longer move;
it journeyed wherever it liked,   not keeping to the road.
The king was so disheartened   that he felt nothing;
he was so racked by thirst and hunger,   he was pitiful to behold;
he was so reddened with blood,   he looked like a live coal.
the armor he wore was dented,   though it was rich with gems;
his sword resembled a saw,   it had received so many blows;
his helmet was so dented,   it slid down his head;
his face was swollen   from the toils he had undergone.
He climbed to the top of a hill,   the highest one he saw;
from there he viewed his people   retreating in defeat;
from there he viewed his banners   and the standards he had,
how they were all trampled   so that they were covered with earth;
he looked for his captains,   but none was in sight;
he looked at the field red with blood,   which flowed in streams.
Seeing this, the sad man   felt great pity for himself;
with tears in his eyes,   he spoke in this manner:
"Yesterday I was king of Spain,   today not even of one town;
yesterday I had towns and castles,   today I possess none;
yesterday I had servants   and people who served me,
today I don't have one merlon   I can call my own.
Unlucky was the hour,   unlucky was that day
when I was born and inherited   such a great realm,
since I was fated to lose it   all at once and in one day!
O death, why don't you come   and take this soul of mine
out of this wretched body,   since I'd thank you for it?"

## 4. Rodrigo's Penance

After King Rodrigo   had lost Spain,
he traveled in despair   wherever he liked;
he entered the mountains,   the most densely forested he could find,
to avoid being discovered by the Moors   who were pursuing him.
He came across a shepherd   leading his flock,
and said: "Tell me, good man,   what I wish to ask you:
is there an inhabited place around here,   or some farmhouse,
where I can rest,   for I am greatly fatigued?"
The shepherd replied at once   that he'd seek one in vain,
because in all that wilderness   there was just one hermitage,

donde estaba un ermitaño    que hacía muy santa vida.
El rey fue alegre de esto    por allí acabar su vida;
pidió al hombre que le diese    de comer, si algo tenía.
El pastor sacó un zurrón,    que siempre en él pan traía;
diole de él y de un tasajo    que acaso allí echado había;
el pan era muy moreno,    al rey muy mal le sabía,
las lágrimas se le salen,    detener no las podía,
acordándose en su tiempo    los manjares que comía.
Después que hubo descansado    por la ermita le pedía;
el pastor le enseñó luego    por donde no erraría;
el rey le dio una cadena    y un anillo que traía,
joyas son de gran valor,    que el rey en mucho tenía.
Comenzando a caminar,    ya cerca el sol se ponía,
llegado es a la ermita    que el pastor dicho le había.
Él, dando gracias a Dios,    luego a rezar se metía;
después que hubo rezado    para el ermitaño se iba,
hombre es de autoridad    que bien se le parecía.
Preguntóle el ermitaño    cómo allí fue su venida;
el rey, los ojos llorosos,    aquesto le respondía:
—El desdichado Rodrigo    yo soy, que rey ser solía;
véngome a hacer penitencia    contigo en tu compañía;
no recibas pesadumbre,    por Dios y Santa María.
El ermitaño se espanta,    por consolarlo decía:
—Vos cierto habeis elegido    camino cual convenía
para vuestra salvación,    que Dios os perdonaría.
El ermitaño ruega a Dios    por si le revelaría
la penitencia que diese    al rey, que le convenía.
Fuele luego revelado    de parte de Dios un día
que le meta en una tumba    con una culebra viva
y esto tome en penitencia    por el mal que hecho había.
El ermitaño al rey    muy alegre se volvía,
contóselo todo al rey    como pasado le había.
El rey, de esto muy gozoso,    luego en obra lo ponía:
métese como Dios manda    para allí acabar su vida.
El ermitaño muy santo    mírale al tercero día,
dice:—¿Cómo os va, buen rey?    ¿Vaos bien con la compañía?
—Hasta ora no me ha tocado,    porque Dios no lo querría;
ruega por mí, el ermitaño,    porque acabe bien mi vida.
El ermitaño lloraba,    gran compasión le tenía,
comenzóle a consolar    y esforzar cuanto podía.
Después vuelve el ermitaño    a ver si ya muerto había;

in which dwelt a hermit    of very holy ways.
The king was glad of that,    so he could end his days there;
he asked the man to give him    something to eat if he had it.
The shepherd took out a pouch    in which he always had some bread;
he gave him some, and some jerked meat    he had happened to put in it;
the bread was very dark,    the king hated the taste of it;
tears came to his eyes,    which he couldn't hold back,
as he recalled the days    when he had eaten fine meals.
After he had rested,    he asked the way to the hermitage;
at once the shepherd showed it,    so that he wouldn't go astray;
the king gave him a chain    and a ring that he wore,
jewels of great value    that the king thought highly of.
When he began walking,    the sun was almost setting;
he reached the hermitage    the shepherd had told him of.
Giving thanks to God,    he started praying at once;
after praying,    he went up to the hermit,
a man of great authority,    as you could tell from his looks.
The hermit asked him    how he had come there;
the king, tears in his eyes,    made this reply:
"The unlucky Rodrigo    am I, who once was king;
I have come to do penance    with you, in your company;
may it not grieve you,    for the love of God and St. Mary."
The hermit stood in awe;    to comfort him he said:
"You have surely chosen    the proper path
to your salvation,    for God will forgive you."
The hermit asked God    to reveal to him
the penance he should impose    on the king that would be appropriate.
Then it was revealed to him    by God one day
that he should put him in a tomb    with a live serpent,
and that this should be his penance    for the wrong he had done.
Very happy, the hermit    addressed the king
and told the king everything    that had occurred with him.
Overjoyed by this, the king    at once complied with his words:
he followed God's commands    to end his days in that tomb.
The very saintly hermit    observed him on the third day,
saying: "How are you, good king?    Getting along with your companion?"
"Up to now it hasn't touched me,    because it wasn't God's will;
pray for me, hermit,    so that my life will end well."
The hermit wept,    feeling great compassion for him,
and began to comfort him    and encourage him as much as he could.
Afterward, the hermit returned    to see if he was already dead;

halló que estaba rezando   y que gemía y plañía;
preguntóle cómo estaba.   —Dios es en la ayuda mía,
respondió el buen rey Rodrigo,   la culebra me comía;
cómeme ya por la parte   que todo lo merecía,
por donde fue el principio   de la mi muy gran desdicha.
El ermitaño lo esfuerza,   el buen rey allí moría.
Aquí acabó el rey Rodrigo,   al cielo derecho se iba.


## 5. Entrevista de Bernardo con el rey

Con cartas y mensajeros   el rey al Carpio envió;
Bernardo, como es discreto,   de traición se receló;
las cartas echó en el suelo   y al mensajero habló:
—Mensajero eres, amigo,   no mereces culpa, no,
mas al rey que acá te envía   dígasle tú esta razón:
que no lo estimo yo a él   ni aun a cuantos con él son;
mas por ver lo que me quiere   todavía allá iré yo.
Y mandó juntar los suyos,   de esta suerte les habló:
—Cuatrocientos sois, los míos,   los que comedes mi pan:
los ciento irán al Carpio,   para el Carpio guardar,
los ciento por los caminos,   que a nadie dejan pasar;
doscientos iréis conmigo   para con el rey hablar;
si mala me la dijere,   peor se la he de tornar.
Por sus jornadas contadas   a la corte fue a llegar:
—Dios os mantenga, buen rey,   y a cuantos con vos están.
—Mal vengades vos, Bernardo,   traidor, hijo de mal padre,
dite yo el Carpio en tenencia,   tú tómaslo en heredad.
—Mentides, el rey, mentides,   que no dices la verdad,
que si yo fuese traidor,   a vos os cabría en parte;
acordárseos debía   de aquella del Encinal,
cuando gentes extranjeras   allí os trataron tan mal,
que os mataron el caballo   y aun a vos querían matar;
Bernardo, como traidor,   de entre ellos os fue a sacar.
Allí me disteis el Carpio   de juro y de heredad,
prometístesme a mi padre,   no me guardaste verdad.
—Prendedlo, mis caballeros,   que igualado se me ha.
—Aquí, aquí los mis doscientos,   los que comedes mi pan,
que hoy era venido el día   que honra habemos de ganar.
El rey, de que aquesto viera,   de esta suerte fue a hablar:
—¿Qué ha sido aquesto, Bernardo,   que así enojado te has?

he found him praying,    moaning and weeping;
he asked him how he was.    "God is aiding me,"
replied good king Rodrigo,    "the serpent is eating me;
it's already eating the part of me    that deserved all the punishment,
and which was the source    of my very great misfortune."
The hermit encouraged him;    the good king died there.
Here ended King Rodrigo's life,    and he went straight to heaven.


## 5. Bernardo's Audience with the King

With letters and messengers    the king sent to El Carpio;
Bernardo, who was circumspect,    suspected treachery;
he threw the letters on the ground    and said to the messenger:
"You're a messenger, my friend,    and you deserve no blame, no,
but to the king who sends you here    make this declaration:
that I have no esteem for him    or for any who are with him;
but to see what he wants of me    I shall go there all the same."
And he ordered his men to assemble,    and spoke to them as follows:
"There are four hundred of you, my men,    who eat my bread:
a hundred shall go to El Carpio,    to guard El Carpio;
a hundred shall patrol the roads,    allowing no one to pass;
two hundred of you will come with me    to speak with the king;
if he speaks evil to me,    it will go all the worse for him."
On the day assigned    he arrived at the court:
"God keep you, good king,    and all those with you!"
"Evilly come, Bernardo,    traitor, son of an evil father!
I gave you El Carpio in usufruct,    you have taken it in perpetuity."
"You lie, king, you lie,    and speak untruth,
for if I were a traitor,    you would be partly to blame;
you ought to remember    the battle at El Encinal,
when foreign men    mishandled you so badly there,
killing your horse    and trying to kill you, too;
Bernardo, the so-called traitor,    rescued you from their midst.
It was then you gave me El Carpio    as my absolute legal possession;
you promised to release my father,    but you didn't keep your word."
"Seize him, my knights!    He has put himself on an equal footing with me."
"To me, to me, my two hundred,    you that eat my bread,
for today the day has come    when we are to win honor!"
When the king saw this,    he spoke as follows:
"What's all this, Bernardo?    What has made you so angry?

¿lo que hombre dice de burla    de veras vas a tomar?
Yo te do el Carpio, Bernardo,    de juro y de heredad.
—Aquesas burlas, el rey,    no son burlas de burlar;
llamásteme de traidor,    traidor, hijo de mal padre;
el Carpio yo no lo quiero,    bien lo podeis vos guardar,
que cuando yo lo quisiere,    muy bien lo sabré ganar.

## 6. Romance del conde Fernán González

Preso está Fernán González,    el buen conde castellano;
prendiólo don Sancho Ordoñez,    porque no le ha tributado,
En una torre en León    lo tienen a buen recaudo.
Rogaban por él al rey    muchas personas de estado,
y también por él rogaba    ese monje fray Pelayo;
mas el rey, con grande enojo,    nunca quisiera soltallo.
Sabiéndolo la condesa,    determina ir a sacallo:
cabalgando en una mula,    como siempre lo ha usado,
consigo lleva dos dueñas,    y dos escuderos ancianos.
Lleva en su retaguardia    trescientos hijosdalgo
armados de todas armas,    cada uno buen caballo.
Todos llevan hecho voto    de morir en demandarlo,
y de no volver a Burgos    hasta morir o librarlo.
Caminan para León    contino por despoblado:
mas cerca de la ciudad    en un monte se han entrado.
La condesa, como es sabia,    mandó ensillar un caballo,
y mandóle a un escudero    que al conde quede aguardando,
y que en siendo salido    se lo dé, y le ponga en salvo.
La condesa con las dueñas    en la ciudad se ha entrado:
como viene de camino,    vase derecho al palacio.
Así como el rey la vido,    a ella se ha levantado:
—¿Adónde bueno, condesa?    —Señor, voy a Santiago,
y víneme por aquí    para besaros las manos.
Suplícoos me deis licencia    para al conde visitar.
—Que me place, dijo el rey,    pláceme de voluntad.
Llévenla luego a la torre    donde el conde preso está.
Por amor de la condesa    las prisiones quitádole han.
Desde rato que llegó,    la condesa le fue a hablar:
—Levantáos luego, señor,    no es tiempo de echado estar:
y vestíos estas mis ropas,    y tocáos vos mis tocados,
y junto con esas dueñas    os salís acompañado,

What someone says as a joke,    will you take it seriously?
I give you El Carpio, Bernardo,    as an absolute legal possession."
"Those jokes, king,    aren't jokes to laugh about;
you called me a traitor,    a traitor and son of an evil father;
I don't want El Carpio,    you can keep it,
because whenever I want it    I'll know very well how to get it."

# 6. Ballad of Count Fernán González

Fernán González is in prison,    that good count of Castile;
he was arrested by Sancho Ordoñez    for refusing to pay tribute.
In a tower in León    he is kept under heavy guard.
Many persons of high rank    have interceded for him with the king,
and that monk Friar Pelayo    has interceded for him, too,
but the king, in his great anger,    has never consented to release him.
Knowing this, the countess    has resolved to go and rescue him:
riding a she-mule,    as she has always done,
she takes two ladies with her    and two elderly squires.
As a rear guard she takes    three hundred noblemen
in full armor,    each one a good cavalryman.
They have all made a vow    to die in their quest of him,
and not to return to Burgos    until they are dead or he is free.
They journey to León,    crossing uninhabited land the whole way,
but near the city    they have entered a forest.
Since the countess is wise,    she has ordered a horse to be saddled,
and has ordered a squire    to remain in waiting for the count,
and, once he has left prison,    to give it to him and put him in safety.
The countess and the ladies    have entered the city:
just as she has come from her trip,    she goes directly to the palace.
As soon as the king saw her,    he rose to greet her:
"Where are you heading, countess?"    "Sire, I'm going to Santiago,
and I came this way    to kiss your hands.
I beseech you, permit me    to visit the count."
"I agree," said the king,    "I agree with pleasure."
At once she is led to the tower    where the count is imprisoned.
For love of the countess    they have removed his fetters.
The moment she arrived,    the countess spoke:
"Arise at once, my lord,    this is no time for lying down:
and put on these clothes of mine,    and put on my headgear,
and together with these ladies    depart in their company;

y en saliendo, que salgáis,    hallaréis vuestro caballo;
iros heis para el monte,    do está la gente aguardando.
Yo me quedaré aquí    hasta ver vuestro mandado.
Al conde le pareció    que era bien aconsejado;
vístese las ropas de ella,    largas tocas se ha tocado.
Las dueñas son avisadas,    a las guardas han llamado;
las guardas estaban prestas,    quitan de presto el candado;
salen las dueñas, y el conde;    nadie los habia mirado.
Dijo una dueña a las guardas    que la andaban rodeando:
—Por tener larga jornada    hemos madrugado tanto.
Y así se partieron de ellas    sin sospecha ni cuidado.
Luego que fuera salieron,    halló el conde su caballo,
el cual tomó su camino    para el monte señalado.
Las dueñas y el escudero    hasta el día han aguardado:
subídose han a la torre    do la condesa ha quedado.
Las guardas, desque las vieron,    mucho se han maravillado.
—Decí, ¿a qué subís, señoras,    háseos acá olvidado algo?
—Abrí, veréis lo que queda,    porque llevemos recaudo.
Como las guardas abrieron,    a la condesa han hallado.
Como la condesa vido    que las dueñas han tornado:
—Id, decíd al señor rey,    que aquí estoy a su mandado,
que haga en mí la justicia,    que el conde ya está librado.
Como aquesto supo el rey,    hallóse muy espantado:
tuvo en mucho a la condesa,    saber hacer tal engaño.
Luego la manda sacar,    y dalle todo recaudo,
y envióla luego al conde:    muchos la han acompañado.
El conde, desque la vido,    holgóse en extremo grado,
enviado ha decir al rey,    que pues tan bien lo ha mirado,
que le mandase pagar    la del azor y el caballo,
si no, que lo pediría    con la espada en la mano.
Todo por el rey sabido,    su consejo ha tomado;
sumaba tanto la paga,    que no pudo numerallo;
así que, todo bien visto,    fue por el rey acordado
de le soltar el tributo    que el conde le era obligado.
De esta manera el buen conde    a Castilla ha libertado.


## 7. "A Calatrava la Vieja"

A Calatrava la Vieja    la combaten castellanos;
por cima de Guadiana    derribaron tres pedazos:

and when you leave this place    you will find your horse;
you will go to the forest,    where your people await you.
I shall remain here    until learning your orders."
It appeared to the count    to be good advice;
he puts on her clothes    and her long headgear.
The ladies are sensible,    they have called the guards;
the guards were quick,    they quickly remove the padlock;
the ladies leave, so does the count;    no one has observed them.
One lady said to the guards    who were all around them:
"Because we have a long day's ride ahead    we are starting out this early."
And so the guards left them    without suspicions or afterthoughts.
As soon as they were outside,    the count found his horse,
which made its way    to the forest that was indicated.
The ladies and the squire    have waited until daylight:
they have gone up to the tower    where the countess has remained.
When the guards saw them,    they were greatly surprised.
"Tell us, why have you come up, ladies,    have you forgotten something here?"
"Open, and you'll see what's still here    that makes us have this care."
When the guards opened the cell,    they found the countess.
When the countess saw    that the ladies were back:
"Go tell the king    that I await his orders here;
let him punish me,    for by now the count is free."
When the king learned of this,    he was thunderstruck:
he felt high regard for the countess    for being able to play such a trick.
At once he ordered her released    and given every attention,
and at once he sent her to the count;    many escorted her.
When the count saw her,    he was extremely happy;
he sent word to the king    that, since he had shown him such esteem,
he should bid him be paid    for his hawk and his horse;
otherwise he'd request payment    sword in hand.
When the king learned all this,    he met with his council;
the payment amounted to so much    that it couldn't be counted;
so that, in view of all the facts,    it was resolved by the king
to free him from the tribute    that the count was obliged to pay him.
In this way the good count    liberated Castile.

## 7. "Calatrava la Vieja"

Calatrava la Vieja    was being attacked by Castilians;
on top of Guadiana    they made three breaches in the wall:

por los dos salen los moros,    por el uno entran cristianos.
Allá dentro de la plaza    fueron a armar un tablado,
que aquel que lo derribare    ganará de oro un escaño.
Este don Rodrigo de Lara    —que ése lo había ganado—,
de Garci-Hernández sobrino    y de doña Sancha hermano,
al conde Garci-Hernández    se lo llevó presentado,
que le trate casamiento    con aquesa doña Lambra.
Ya se trata casamiento    —¡hecho fue en hora menguada!—
doña Lambra de Bureba    con don Rodrigo de Lara.
Las bodas fueron en Burgos,    las tornabodas en Salas;
en bodas y tornabodas    pasaron siete semanas.
Tantas vienen de las gentes    que no caben por las plazas
y aún faltaban por venir    los siete infantes de Lara.
Helos, helos por do vienen    con toda la su compaña.
Saliólos a recebir    la su madre doña Sancha:
—Bien vengades, los mis hijos;    buena sea vuestra llegada.
Allá iredes a posar    a esa cal de Cantarranas;
hallaréis las mesas puestas,    viandas aparejadas.
Desque hayáis comido, hijos,    no salgades a las plazas,
porque las gentes son muchas:    trábanse muchas barrajas.
Desque todos han comido,    van a bohordar a la plaza;
no salen los siete infantes,    su madre se lo mandara.
Mas, desque hubieron comido,    siéntanse a jugar las tablas.
Tiran unos, tiran otros;    ninguno bien bohordaba.
Allí salió un caballero    de los de Córdoba la llana.
Bohordó hacia el tablado    y una vara bien tirara.
Allí hablara la novia,    de esta manera hablara:
—Amad, señoras, amad    cada una en su lugar,
que más vale un caballero    de los de Córdoba la llana
que no veinte ni treinta    de los de la casa de Lara.
Oídolo había doña Sancha,    desta manera hablara:
—No digáis eso, señora;    no digades tal palabra,
porque aun hoy os desposaron    con don Rodrigo de Lara.
—Mas calláis, vos, doña Sancha;    no debéis ser escuchada,
que siete hijos paristes    como puerca encenagada.
Oído lo había el ayo    que a los infantes criaba;
de allí se había salido,    triste se fue a su posada.
Halló que estaban jugando    los infantes a las tablas,
si no era el menor de ellos:    Gonzalo González se llama.
Recostado lo halló    de pechos en una baranda.
—¿Cómo venís triste, amo?;    decí: ¿quién os enojara?

through two the Moors fled,    through one the Christians entered.
There on the main square    they set up scaffolding for a contest;
the man who'd topple it    would win a golden bench.
That Don Rodrigo of Lara    (for he won it),
nephew of Garci-Hernández    and brother of Doña Sancha,
made a gift of it    to Count Garci-Hernández,
asking him to arrange his wedding    to Doña Lambra.
Now the wedding is arranged    (it was done in an evil hour!)
between Lambra of Bureba    and Rodrigo of Lara.
The wedding was at Burgos,    the groom's festivities at Salas;
between the bride's and the groom's celebrations,    it lasted seven weeks.
So many people came    that there was no room for them in the squares,
and the seven young lords of Lara    had still to show up.
Behold, behold them coming    with all their followers!
Their mother, Doña Sancha,    went out to greet them:
"Welcome, my sons,    may your coming be lucky!
Go take lodgings there    in Cantarranas Street;
you'll find the tables set,    the food in readiness.
After eating, sons,    don't go out to the square,
because there are many people    and many quarrels begin."
After all the people had eaten,    they went to the square to hurl javelins;
the seven young lords didn't go out,    in obedience to their mother,
but, after eating,    they sat down at a board game.
In the square, various men hurled;    none knocked down the scaffolding.
Then a knight rode out,    one of those from Córdoba of the plain.
He hurled at the scaffolding    and threw a javelin skillfully.
Then the bride spoke,    she spoke in this manner:
"Ladies, love! Each of you,    love where you will,
for a knight    among those from Córdoba of the plain
is better than twenty or thirty    of those from the house of Lara."
This was heard by Doña Sancha,    who spoke as follows:
"Don't say that, my lady,    don't utter such a word,
because this very day you've been wed    to Rodrigo of Lara."
"You keep still, Doña Sancha,    you don't deserve a hearing,
because you gave birth to seven sons    like a muddy sow."
This was heard by the tutor    who was raising the young lords;
he left that place    and went to their lodgings sadly.
He found the young lords    playing draughts,
except the youngest of them,    named Gonzalo González.
He found him lying    face-down on a railing.
"Why are you sad, tutor?"    he asked. "Who has vexed you?"

Tanto le rogó Gonzalo    que el ayo se lo contara:
—Mas mucho os ruego, mi hijo,    que no salgáis a la plaza.
No lo quiso hacer Gonzalo,    mas antes tomó una lanza;
caballero en un caballo    vase derecho a la plaza.
Vido estar el tablado    que nadie lo derribara.
Enderezóse en la silla,    con él en el suelo daba.
Desque lo hubo derribado,    desta manera hablara:
—Amade, putas, amad,    cada una en su lugar,
que más vale un caballero    de los de la casa de Lara
que cuarenta ni cincuenta    de los de Córdoba la llana.
Doña Lambra, que esto oyera,    bajóse muy enojada;
sin aguardar a los suyos    fuese para su posada;
halló en ella a Rodrigo,    desta manera le habla.


## 8. "Pártese el moro Alicante"

Pártese el moro Alicante    víspera de sant Cebrián;
ocho cabezas llevaba,    todas de hombres de alta sangre.
Sábelo el rey Almanzor,    a recibírselo sale;
aunque perdió muchos moros,    piensa en esto bien ganar.
Manda hacer un tablado    para mejor las mirar,
mandó traer un cristiano    que estaba en captividad.
Como ante sí lo trujeron    empezóle de hablar,
dijole: —Gonzalo Gustos,    mira quién conocerás;
que lidiaron mis poderes    en el campo de Almenar:
sacaron ocho cabezas,    todas son de gran linaje.
Respondió Gonzalo Gustos:    Presto os diré la verdad.
Y limpiándoles la sangre,    asaz se fuera a turbar;
dijo llorando agramente:    —¡Conóscolas por mi mal!
la una es de mi carillo,    ¡las otras me duelen más!
de los infantes de Lara    son, mis hijos naturales.
Así razona con ellos,    como si vivos hablasen:
—¡Dios os salve, el mi compadre,    el mi amigo leal!
¿Adónde son los mis hijos    que yo os quise encomendar?
Muerto sois como buen hombre,    como hombre de fiar.
Tomara otra cabeza,    del hijo mayor de edad:
—Sálveos Dios, Diego González,    hombre de muy gran bondad,
del conde Fernán González    alférez el principal:
a vos amaba yo mucho,    que me habíades de heredar.
Alimpiándola con lágrimas    volviérala a su lugar,

Gonzalo kept asking    until his tutor told him:
"But I urge you, my son,    not to go out to the square."
Gonzalo refused to obey;    instead, he took a lance;
mounted on a horse,    he headed straight for the square.
He saw the scaffolding standing    which no one had toppled.
He sat up straight on his saddle,    and knocked it to the ground.
After toppling it,    he spoke as follows:
"Whores, love! Each of you,    love where you will,
for a knight    among those from the house of Lara
is better than forty or fifty    of those from Córdoba of the plain."
Doña Lambra, who heard this,    went down in great anger;
without awaiting her followers    she went to her lodgings;
there she found Rodrigo,    she spoke to him as follows. [poem ends here]

## 8. "The Moor Alicante Departs"

The Moor Alicante departs    on the eve of St. Cyprian's Day;
he carries eight heads,    all of men of noble birth.
King Almanzor learns of it    and goes out to greet him;
though he has lost many Moors,    he considers this a great gain.
He orders a platform erected    in order to have a better look at them;
he orders a Christian brought,    one whom he holds in captivity.
When they brought him before him,    the king started to speak,
saying: "Gonzalo Gustos,    look and see if you recognize anyone;
for my forces fought    in the field of Almenar:
they won eight heads,    all of men of ancient ancestry."
Gonzalo Gustos replied:    "I shall soon tell you the truth."
And, wiping the blood off them,    he became severely troubled;
weeping bitterly, he said:    "I know them, to my misfortune!
One is that of my friend, the tutor;    the others give me greater sorrow!
They are those of the lords of Lara,    my flesh-and-blood sons."
He addresses them thus,    as if speaking to living men:
"God save you, my comrade,    my faithful friend!
Where are my sons    whom I entrusted to you?
You died like a good man,    a trustworthy man."
He picked up another head,    that of his eldest son:
"God save you, Diego González,    man of very great goodness,
chief standard-bearer    of Count Fernán González:
I loved you very much,    for you were to be my heir."
Cleansing the head with tears,    he returned it to its place,

y toma la del segundo,     Martín Gómez que llamaban:
—Dios os perdone, el mi hijo,   hijo que mucho preciaba;
jugador era de tablas     el mejor de toda España,
mesurado caballero,     muy buen hablador en plaza.
Y dejándola llorando,     la del tercero tomaba:
—Hijo Suero Gustos,     todo el mundo os estimaba;
el rey os tuviera en mucho,     sólo para la su caza:
gran caballero esforzado,     muy buen bracero a ventaja.
¡Ruy Gómez vuestro tío     estas bodas ordenera!
Y tomando la del cuarto,     lasamente la miraba:
—¡Oh hijo Fernán González,   (nombre del mejor de España,
del buen conde de Castilla,     aquel que vos baptizara)
matador de puerco espín,     amigo de gran compaña!
nunca con gente de poco     os vieran en alianza.
Tomó la de Ruy Gómez,     de corazón la abrazaba:
—¡Hijo mío, hijo mío!     ¿quién como vos se hallara?
nunca le oyeron mentira,     nunca por oro ni plata;
animoso, buen guerrero,     muy gran feridor de espada,
que a quien dábades de lleno     tullido o muerto quedaba.
Tomando la del menor,     el dolor se le doblara:
—¡Hijo Gonzalo González!     ¡Los ojos de doña Sancha!
¡Qué nuevas irán a ella     que a vos más que a todos ama!
Tan apuesto de persona,     decidor bueno entre damas,
repartidor en su haber,     aventajado en la lanza.
¡Mejor fuera la mi muerte     que ver tan triste jornada!
Al duelo que el viejo hace,     toda Córdoba lloraba.
El rey Almanzor cuidoso     consigo se lo llevaba,
y mandó a una morica     lo sirviese muy de gana.
Esta le torna en prisiones,     y con hambre le curaba.
Hermana era del rey,     doncella moza y lozana;
con ésta Gonzalo Gustos     vino a perder su saña,
que de ella le nació un hijo     que a los hermanos vengara.

## 9. Romance de Jimena Gómez

Día era de los Reyes,     día era señalado,
cuando dueñas y doncellas     al rey piden aguinaldo,
sino es Jimena Gómez,     hija del conde Lozano,

and picked up that of his second son,   named Martín Gómez:
"God forgive you, my son,   son whom I highly esteemed;
you were a player of draughts,   the best in all of Spain,
a temperate knight,   a very good public speaker."
Leaving that head tearfully,   he picked up that of the third:
"My son Suero Gustos,   everybody respected you;
the king thought highly of you,   merely as a member of his hunt:
a great, valiant knight,   an excellent spear-hurler.
Ruy Gómez, your uncle,   arranged this 'marriage'!"
And, taking up that of the fourth,   he looked at it, feeling faint:
"O my son Fernán González   (the name of the best man in Spain,
the good Count of Castile,   who baptized you),
slayer of wild boars,   friend of lofty company!
You were never seen associated   with unworthy people."
He picked up that of Ruy Gómez,   and hugged it ardently:
"My son, my son!   Who else like you can be found?
No one ever heard you lie,   either for gold or for silver;
courageous, a good warrior,   a very great swordsman;
anyone that you hit squarely   was left crippled or dead."
Taking up that of the youngest son,   he felt redoubled sorrow:
"My son Gonzalo González!   The darling of Doña Sancha!
What news will she receive,   she who loves you best of all?
So neat in your person,   good at conversing with ladies,
generous in sharing your wealth,   excellent with the lance.
I should have died   sooner than seeing so sad a day!"
The old man's lamentations   made all of Córdoba weep.
King Almanzor, concerned for him,   took him along
and ordered a Moorish lass   to serve him cheerfully.
She sent him back to prison   and gave him a hunger cure.[1]
She was a sister of the king,   a young, vigorous maiden;
with her, Gonzalo Gustos   came to lose his fury,
so that she bore him a son   who was to avenge his brothers.

## 9. Ballad of Jimena Gómez

It was Epiphany,   it was that special day
when ladies and damsels   ask the king for Christmas gifts,
except for Jimena Gómez,   daughter of Count Lozano,

---

1. An eminent Spanish scholar emended *hambre* to *amor* ("a love cure").

que puesta delante el rey    de esta manera ha hablado:
—Con mancilla vivo, rey,    con ella vive mi madre;
cada día que amanece    veo quien mató a mi padre,
caballero en un caballo    y en su mano un gavilán;
otra vez con un halcón    que trae para cazar;
por hacerme más enojo,    cébalo en mi palomar,
con sangre de mis palomas    ensangrentó mi brial.
Enviéselo a decir,    envióme a amenazar
que me cortará mis haldas    por vergonzoso lugar,
me forzará mis doncellas,    casadas y por casar,
matarame un pajecico    so haldas de mi brial.
Rey que no hace justicia    no debía de reinar,
ni cabalgar en caballo,    ni espuela de oro calzar,
ni comer pan a manteles,    ni con la reina holgar,
ni oír misa en sagrado,    porque no merece más.
El rey, de que esto oyera,    comenzara de hablar:
—¡Oh, válame Dios del cielo!    ¡Quiérame Dios consejar!
Si yo prendo o mato al Cid,    mis cortes se volverán,
y si no hago justicia    mi alma lo pagará.
—Tente las tus cortes, rey,    no te las revuelva nadie:
al Cid que mató a mi padre    dámelo tú por igual,
que quien tanto mal me hizo    sé que algún bien me hará.
Entonces dijera el rey,    bien oiréis lo que dirá:
—Siempre lo oí decir,    y agora veo que es verdad,
que el seso de las mujeres    que no era natural:
hasta aquí pidió justicia,    ya quiere con él casar.
Yo lo haré de buen grado,    de muy buena voluntad;
mandarle quiero una carta,    mandarle quiero llamare.
Las palabras no son dichas,    la carta camino vae,
mensajero que la lleva    dado la había a su padre.
—Malas mañas habéis, conde,    no vos las puedo quitare,
que cartas que el rey vos manda    no me las queréis mostrare.
—No era nada, mi hijo,    sino que vades allae.
Quedaos aquí, hijo,    yo iré en vuestro lugare.
—Nunca Dios a tal quisiese    ni Santa María lo mande,
sino que adonde vos fueredes    que vaya yo adelante.

who stood before the king    and addressed him as follows:
"King, I live with a blot on my honor,    and so does my mother:
each day that dawns    I see the killer of my father
mounted on a horse    with a sparrow hawk on his fist,
or other times with a falcon    that he carries for the hunt;
to give me greater grief,    he feeds it from my dovecot;
with the blood of my doves    he has bloodied my silk gown.
I sent him a complaint,    he sent me back a threat:
he'd cut my skirts    where they cover my shame;[2]
he'd ravish my handmaids,    the married and the single;
and he'd kill one of my little pages    beneath the skirts of my gown.[3]
A king who doesn't mete out justice    doesn't deserve to reign,
or to ride a horse,    or wear golden spurs,
or eat at a covered table,    or sleep with the queen,
or hear Mass in church,    because he doesn't merit it."
When the king heard this,    he began to speak:
"Oh, may God in heaven stand by me!    May God counsel me!
If I imprison or kill the Cid,    my assembly will rebel,
and if I fail to do justice,    my soul will pay the penalty."
"Keep your assembly, king,    let no one make them rebel:
the Cid who killed my father,    give him to me as a husband,
for I know that the man who harmed me so    will do me some good."
Then the king spoke,    you shall hear what he had to say:
"I've always heard tell,    and now I see it's true,
that women's minds    were unnatural:
up to now she demanded justice,    now she wants to marry him.
I'll arrange it gladly,    with the greatest pleasure;
I shall send him a letter,    I shall summon him here."
Before he finished speaking,    the letter was on its way;
the messenger who bore it    gave it to the Cid's father.
"You have bad manners, count,    which I can't rid you of:
letters sent you by the king    you refuse to show to me."
"It was nothing, my son,    except that you are to go there.
Remain here, my son,    I shall go in your place."
"May God never consent to that,    nor St. Mary command it!
Rather, wherever you go,    let me precede you!"

2. A punishment for prostitutes.    3. An inviolable place of sanctuary.

## 10. Romance del Cid Ruy Díaz

Cabalga Diego Laínez    al buen rey besar la mano;
consigo se los llevaba    los trescientos hijosdalgo;
entre ellos iba Rodrigo,    el soberbio castellano.
Todos cabalgan a mula,    sólo Rodrigo a caballo,
todos visten oro y seda,    Rodrigo va bien armado,
todos espadas ceñidas,    Rodrigo estoque dorado,
todos con sendas varicas,    Rodrigo lanza en la mano,
todos guantes olorosos,    Rodrigo guante mallado,
todos sombreros muy ricos,    Rodrigo casco afilado
y encima del casco lleva    un bonete colorado.
Andando por su camino,    unos con otros hablando,
allegados son a Burgos,    con el rey se han encontrado.
Los que vienen con el rey    entre sí van razonando;
unos lo dicen de quedo,    otros lo van preguntando:
—Aquí viene, entre esta gente,    quien mató al conde Lozano.
Como lo oyera Rodrigo    en hito los ha mirado,
con alta y soberbia voz    de esta manera ha hablado:
—Si hay alguno entre vosotros,    su pariente o adeudado,
que se pese de su muerte    salga luego a demandarlo,
yo se lo defenderé,    quiera pie, quiera caballo.
Todos responden a una:    —Demándelo su pecado.
Todos se apearon juntos    para al rey besar la mano,
Rodrigo se quedó solo,    encima de su caballo;
entonces habló su padre,    bien oiréis lo que ha hablado:
—Apeaos vos, mi hijo,    besaréis al rey la mano
porque él es vuestro señor,    vos, hijo, sois su vasallo.
Desque Rodrigo esto oyó,    sintiose más agraviado,
las palabras que responde    son de hombre muy enojado:
—Si otro me lo dijera,    ya me lo hubiera pagado,
mas por mandarlo vos, padre,    yo lo haré de buen grado.
Ya se apeaba Rodrigo    para al rey besar la mano;
al hincar de la rodilla    el estoque se ha arrancado;
espantose de esto el rey    y dijo como turbado:
—Quítate Rodrigo allá,    quítateme allá, diablo,
que tienes el gesto de hombre    y los hechos de león bravo.
Como Rodrigo esto oyó,    aprisa pide el caballo;
con una voz alterada    contra el rey así ha hablado:
—Por besar mano de rey    no me tengo por honrado,
porque la besó mi padre    me tengo por afrentado.

# 10. Ballad of the Cid, Ruy Díaz

Diego Laínez is riding    to kiss the good king's hand;
with him he has taken    the three hundred noblemen;
among them is Rodrigo,    the haughty Castilian.
All ride mules,    Rodrigo alone is on horseback;
all wear gold and silk,    Rodrigo is in full armor;
all have swords girded on,    Rodrigo a gilded rapier;
all have one short spear,    Rodrigo holds a lance;
all wear scented gloves,    Rodrigo a mailed gauntlet;
all have very costly hats,    Rodrigo a pointed helmet,
and over the helmet he wears    a red bonnet.
Going their way,    talking with one another,
they have reached Burgos,    they have met the king.
The men accompanying the king    are having a discussion;
some speak their piece quietly,    others declare to the king:
"Among these people who come here    is the killer of Count Lozano."
When Rodrigo heard this,    he glared at them;
with a loud, haughty voice    he spoke in this manner:
"If there's anyone among you,    his relative or kinsman,
who is aggrieved by his death,    let him step out at once to challenge me;
I shall defend my cause against him    either on foot or on horse."
They all replied together:    "Let his devil fight with him!"
All of them dismounted    to kiss the king's hand;
only Rodrigo remained    seated on his horse;
then his father spoke,    you shall hear what he said:
"Dismount, my son,    you shall kiss the king's hand
because he is your lord,    and you, son, are his vassal."
When Rodrigo heard this,    he felt grievously affronted;
the words he spoke in reply    were those of a very angry man:
"Had anyone else said that to me,    I would have paid him back,
but since the order comes from you, father,    I shall obey willingly."
Now Rodrigo dismounted    to kiss the king's hand;
when he knelt down,    his rapier jumped out;
this frightened the king,    who said, as if upset:
"Out of my sight, Rodrigo;    away with you, you devil,
for you have the face of a man    but the actions of a wild lion!"
When Rodrigo heard this,    he quickly asked for his horse;
with an irate voice    he spoke thus to the king:
"To kiss a king's hand    I do not consider an honor;
because my father kissed it    I consider myself insulted."

En diciendo estas palabras    salido se ha del palacio,
consigo se los tornaba    los trescientos hijosdalgo.
Si bien vinieron vestidos,    volvieron mejor armados,
y si vinieron en mulas,    todos vuelven en caballos.

## 11. Romance del juramento que tomó el Cid al rey don Alonso

En Santa Águeda de Burgos,    do juran los hijosdalgo,
le toman jura a Alonso    por la muerte de su hermano;
tomábasela el buen Cid,    ese buen Cid castellano,
sobre un cerrojo de hierro    y una ballesta de palo
y con unos evangelios    y un crucifijo en la mano.
Las palabras son tan fuertes    que al buen rey ponen espanto.
—Villanos te maten, Alonso,    villanos, que no hidalgos,
de las Asturias de Oviedo,    que no sean castellanos;
mátente con aguijadas,    no con lanzas ni con dardos;
con cuchillos cachicuernos,    no con puñales dorados;
abarcas traigan calzadas,    que no zapatos con lazo;
capas traigan aguaderas,    no de contray ni frisado;
con camisones de estopa,    no de holanda ni labrados;
caballeros vengan en burras,    que no en mulas ni en caballos;
frenos traigan de cordel,    que no cueros fogueados.
Mátente por las aradas,    que no en villas ni en poblado,
sáquente el corazón    por el siniestro costado,
si no dijeres la verdad    de lo que te fuere preguntado,
si fuiste, o consentiste    en la muerte de tu hermano.
Las juras eran tan fuertes    que el rey no las ha otorgado.
Allí habló un caballero    que del rey es más privado:
—Haced la jura, buen rey,    no tengáis de eso cuidado,
que nunca fue rey traidor,    ni papa descomulgado.
Jurado había el rey    que en tal nunca se ha hallado;
pero allí hablara el rey    malamente y enojado:
—Muy mal me conjuras, Cid,    Cid, muy mal me has conjurado,
mas hoy me tomas la jura,    mañana me besarás la mano.
—Por besar mano de rey    no me tengo por honrado,
porque la besó mi padre    me tengo por afrentado.
—Vete de mis tierras, Cid,    mal caballero probado,

Saying those words,   he left the palace grounds;
with him he led back   the three hundred noblemen.
If they came in peaceful garb,   they came again in armor;
if they came on mules,   they all came again on horseback.

## 11. Ballad of the Oath Exacted by the Cid from King Alfonso

In St. Agatha's of Burgos,   where noblemen take oaths,
an oath is exacted from Alfonso   about his brother's death;
it was exacted from him by the good Cid,   the good Cid of Castile,
upon an iron door bolt   and a wooden crossbow,
and with several Gospels   and a crucifix in his hand.
The terms are so harsh   that they frighten the good king.
"May commoners kill you, Alfonso,   commoners and not noblemen,
from Oviedo in Asturias,   and not from Castile;
may they kill you with ox goads,   not with lances or javelins;
with horn-handled knives,   not with gilded daggers;
may they wear peasant sandals,   not laced shoes;
may they wear waterproof capes,   not fine Flemish wool or silk,
burlap smocks,   not of Holland cloth or embroidery;
may they be riding on donkeys,   not on mules or horses;
may they have bridles of rope,   not of hardened[4] leather.
May they kill you in the fields,   not in a town or peopled place;
may they tear out your heart   through your left side,
if you don't tell the truth   about what you will be asked:
whether you took part in, or agreed to,   your brother's death."
The oath was so harsh   that the king didn't consent to it.
Then a knight spoke up,   the man closest to the king's heart:
"Take the oath, good king,   and don't worry about it,
because no king was ever called a traitor,   nor any pope excommunicated."
The king swore   that he had never been involved in such things;
but then the king spoke   in malice and anger:
"You exact a very bad oath, Cid,   Cid, you have exacted a very bad oath,
but today you take the oath from me,   tomorrow you'll kiss my hand."
"To kiss a king's hand   I do not consider an honor;
because my father kissed it   I consider myself insulted."
"Depart from my lands, Cid,   proven to be a bad knight,

---

4. Or: "cleaned by fire."

y no vengas más a ellas    dende este día en un año.
—Pláceme, dijo el buen Cid,    pláceme, dijo, de grado,
por ser la primera cosa    que mandas en tu reinado.
Tú me destierras por uno,    yo me destierro por cuatro.
Ya se parte el buen Cid,    sin al rey besar la mano,
con trescientos caballeros,    todos eran hijosdalgo;
todos son hombres mancebos,    ninguno no había cano;
todos llevan lanza en puño    y el hierro acicalado,
y llevan sendas adargas    con borlas de colorado.
Mas no le faltó al buen Cid    adonde asentar su campo.


## 12. Romance del rey moro que perdió Valencia

Helo, helo, por do viene    el moro por la calzada,
caballero a la jineta    encima una yegua baya,
borceguíes marroquíes    y espuela de oro calzada,
una adarga ante los pechos    y en su mano una azagaya.
Mirando estaba a Valencia,    cómo está tan bien cercada:
—¡Oh, Valencia, oh Valencia,    de mal fuego seas quemada!
Primero fuiste de moros    que de cristianos ganada.
Si la lanza no me miente,    a moros serás tornada;
aquel perro de aquel Cid    prenderélo por la barba,
su mujer, doña Jimena,    será de mí cautivada,
su hija, Urraca Hernando,    será mi enamorada,
después de yo harto de ella    la entregaré a mi compaña.
El buen Cid no está tan lejos,    que todo bien lo escuchaba.
—Venid vos acá, mi hija,    mi hija doña Urraca;
dejad las ropas continas    y vestid ropas de pascua.
Aquel moro hi-de-perro    detenédmelo en palabras,
mientras yo ensillo a Babieca    y me ciño la mi espada.
La doncella, muy hermosa,    se paró a una ventana;
el moro, desque la vido,    de esta suerte le hablara:
—Alá te guarde, señora,    mi señora doña Urraca.
—Así haga a vos, señor,    buena sea vuestra llegada.
Siete años ha, rey, siete,    que soy vuestra enamorada.
—Otros tanto ha, señora,    que os tengo dentro en mi alma.
Ellos estando en aquesto    el buen Cid que asomaba.
—Adiós, adiós, mi señora,    la mi linda enamorada,

and don't come back to them    for a year from this date."
"Agreed," said the good Cid,    "agreed," he said, "and gladly,
since it is the first order    you have issued in your reign.
You exile me for one year,    I exile myself for four."
Now the good Cid departs,    without kissing the king's hand,
taking three hundred knights,    all of them noblemen,
all of them young men,    none with a gray hair;
each one bears a lance in his fist,    and a burnished sword,
and carries a shield    with red tassels.
But the good Cid had no lack of space    to pitch his camp in.

## 12. Ballad of the Moorish King Who Lost Valencia

Behold him, behold the Moor    coming down the road,
riding with short stirrups    on a bay mare,
wearing morocco half-boots    and golden spurs,
a shield before his breast    and an assegai in his hand.
He was looking at Valencia,    how closely it was besieged:
"O Valencia, O Valencia,    may you be burned with evil fire!
You were won by Moors before    you were won by Christians.
If my lance isn't lying to me,    you will be restored to the Moors;
that dog of a Cid    I shall seize by the beard;[5]
his wife, Doña Jimena,    will become my captive;
his daughter, Urraca Hernando,    will become my mistress;
after I'm tired of her    I'll hand her over to my soldiery."
The good Cid is not very far away,    and has heard all this clearly.
"Come here, my daughter,    my daughter Doña Urraca;
leave off your everyday garments    and put on holiday garb.
That whoreson Moor,    detain him for me with words,
while I saddle Babieca    and gird on my sword."
The maiden, very beautiful,    appeared at a window;
as soon as the Moor saw her,    he addressed her as follows:
"May Allah keep you, lady,    my lady Urraca!"
"So may He do to you, sir;    may your coming be lucky!
For seven years, king, seven,    I've been in love with you."
"For just so many, lady,    I've kept you in my soul."
When they were thus engaged,    the good Cid appeared.
"Farewell, farewell, my lady,    my pretty sweetheart,

5. A terrible insult.

que del caballo Babieca    yo bien oigo la patada.
Do la yegua pone el pie,    Babieca pone la pata.
Allí hablara el caballo,    bien oiréis lo que hablaba:
—¡Reventar debía la madre    que a su hijo no esperaba!
Siete vueltas la rodea    alrededor de una jara;
la yegua, que era ligera,    muy adelante pasaba
hasta llegar cabe un río    adonde una barca estaba.
El moro, desque la vido,    con ella bien se holgaba,
grandes gritos da al barquero    que le allegase la barca;
el barquero es diligente,    túvosela aparejada,
embarcó muy presto en ella,    que no se detuvo nada.
Estando el moro embarcado,    el buen Cid que llegó al agua,
y por ver al moro en salvo,    de tristeza reventaba;
mas con la furia que tiene,    una lanza le arrojaba,
y dijo: —Recoged, mi yerno,    arrecogedme esa lanza,
que quizás tiempo vendrá    que os será bien demandada.

## 13. Romance de los cinco maravedís que pidió el rey

En esa ciudad de Burgos    en cortes se habían juntado
el rey que venció las Navas    con todos los hijosdalgo.
Habló con don Diego el rey,    con él se había aconsejado,
que era señor de Vizcaya,    de todos el más privado:
—Consejédesme, don Diego,    que estoy muy necesitado,
que con las guerras que he hecho    gran dinero me ha faltado;
quería llegarme a Cuenca,    no tengo lo necesario;
si os pareciese, don Diego,    por mí fuese demandado
que cinco maravedís    me peche cada hidalgo.
—Grave cosa me parece,    le respondiera el de Haro,
que querades vos, señor,    al libre her tributario,
mas por lo mucho que os quiero    de mí sereis ayudado,
porque yo soy principal,    de mí os será pagado.
Siendo juntos en las cortes    el rey se lo había hablado.
Levantado está don Diego,    como ya estaba acordado:
—Justo es lo que el rey pide,    por nadie le sea negado,
mis cinco maravedís    helos aquí de buen grado.
Don Nuño, conde de Lara,    mucho mal se había enojado;
pospuesto todo temor,    de esta manera ha hablado:

for I clearly hear the hoofbeats    of the steed Babieca."
Where the mare sets foot    Babieca sets his hoof.
Then the steed spoke,    you shall hear what he said:
"May that mother burst    who doesn't await her son!"
He pursues her seven circuits    around a thicket of scrub;[6]
the mare, who was nimble,    passed far ahead
until arriving near a river    where there was a boat.
When the Moor saw it,    it gladdened his heart;
he shouted loudly to the boatman    to pull up the boat to him;
the boatman is diligent,    he got it ready for him;
he boarded it very quickly,    making no delay.
The Moor already in the boat,    the good Cid reached the river
and, seeing the Moor in safety,    was bursting with grief;
but with the rage that was in him    he hurled a lance at him,
saying: "Save this, son-in-law,    save this lance for me,
for perhaps a time will come    when I shall ask it back from you!"

## 13. Ballad of the Five Maravedis Requested by the King

In the city of Burgos    the assembly had been gathered
of the king who won at Las Navas    and all his noblemen.
The king spoke with Don Diego,    he had taken counsel with him;
he was the lord of Biscay    and the king's closest adviser:
"Counsel me, Don Diego,    for I am in great need,
since with the wars I have waged    I lack a vast sum of money;
I wanted to go to Cuenca,    and I don't have the wherewithal;
if you approved, Don Diego,    I'd issue an order
for every nobleman to pay me    a tax of five maravedis."
"It seems a heavy thing,"    replied the man of Haro,
"that you should wish, sire,    to exact tribute from free men,
but because I love you so,    you will have my aid;
because of my eminent position,    it will be paid to you by me."
When the assembly was held,    the king made his request of them.
Don Diego arose,    as they had agreed upon earlier:
"The king's request is just;    let nobody refuse it;
here are my five maravedis,    which I pay gladly."
Nuño, the Count of Lara,    had become very angry;
setting aside all fear,    he spoke in this manner:

---

6. Specifically, "rockrose," but often used generically.

—Aquellos donde venimos    nunca tal pecho han pagado,
nos, menos lo pagaremos,    ni al rey tal será dado;
el que quisiere pagarle    quede aquí como villano,
váyase luego tras mí    el que fuere hijodalgo.
Todos se salen tras él,    de tres mil, tres han quedado.
En el campo de la Glera    todos allí se han juntado,
el pecho que el rey demanda    en las lanzas lo han atado
y envíanle a decir    que el tributo está llegado,
que envíe sus cogedores,    que luego será pagado,
mas que si él va en persona    no será del acatado,
pero que enviase aquellos    de quien fue aconsejado.
Cuando esto oyera el rey,    y que solo se ha quedado,
volvióse para don Diego,    consejo le ha demandado.
Don Diego, como sagaz,    este consejo le ha dado:
—Desterrédesme, señor,    como que yo lo he causado,
y así cobraréis la gracia    de los vuestros hijosdalgo.
Otorgó el rey el consejo:    a decir les ha enviado
que quien le dio tal consejo    será muy bien castigado,
que hidalgos de Castilla    no son para haber pechado.
Muy alegres fueron todos.    Todo se hubo apaciaguado.
Desterraron a don Diego    por lo que no había pecado,
mas dende a pocos días    a Castilla fue tornado.
El bien de la libertad    por ningún precio es comprado.


## 14. Romance del rey don Fernando cuarto

Válasme, nuestra señora,    cual dicen, de la Ribera,
donde el buen rey don Fernando    tuvo la su cuarentena.
Desde el miércoles corvillo    hasta el jueves de la Cena,
que el rey no se hizo la barba,    ni peinó la su cabeza.
Una silla era su cama,    un canto por cabecera,
los cuarenta pobres comen    cada día a la su mesa;
de lo que a los pobres sobra    el rey hace la su cena,
con vara de oro en su mano,    bien hace servir la mesa.
Dícenle los caballeros:    —¿Dónde irás tener la fiesta?
—A Jaén, dice, señores,    con mi señora la reina.
Despues que estuvo en Jaén,    y la fiesta hubo pasado,
pártese para Alcaudete,    ese castillo nombrado:
el pie tiene en el estribo,    que aun no se había apeado,
cuando le daban querella    de dos hombres hijosdalgos,

"People where we come from    have never paid such a tax;
we won't pay it, either,    nor will it be given to the king;
that man who wishes to pay him,    let him stay here as a commoner;
anyone who's a nobleman,    let him leave at once after me!"
They all left after him;    out of three thousand, three remained.
In the field of La Glera,    there they all gathered.
The tax that the king requested    they tied to their lances,
and they sent word to him    that the tribute had arrived;
let him send his collectors    and he'd be paid at once;
further: if he came in person,    they'd take no heed of him;
rather, let him send those    who gave him that advice.
When the king heard this,    and found himself left alone,
he turned to Don Diego    and asked him for counsel.
Don Diego, being a wise man,    gave him this advice:
"Banish me, sire,    as the one who brought this about,
and thus you'll regain the favor    of your noblemen."
The king approved of the advice:    he sent word to them
that the man who had so advised him    would be severely punished,
for noblemen of Castile    aren't meant to be taxed.
Everyone was very happy.    They had all been calmed down.
Don Diego was banished    for a crime he never committed,
but within a few days    he was brought back to Castile.
The benefit of freedom    can't be purchased at any price.

## 14. Ballad of King Fernando IV

Stand by me, Our Lady,    the Virgin called "of La Ribera,"
where good king Fernando    held his Lent!
From Ash Wednesday    until Holy Thursday
the king didn't trim his beard    or comb his hair.
His bed was a chair,    his pillow a stone;
forty paupers ate    at his table daily;
from the paupers' leavings    the king made his meal;
a golden scepter in his hand,    he waited on the table.
His knights said:    "Where will you celebrate the feast?"
"At Jaén, my lords," he said,    "with the queen, my wife."
After his stay in Jaén,    after the holy days were over,
he left for Alcaudete,    that famous castle:
his foot was still in the stirrup,    he had not yet dismounted,
when a complaint was lodged with him    about two noblemen,

y la querella le daban    dos hombres como villanos:
abarcas traen calzadas    y aguijadas en las manos.
—Justicia, justicia, rey,    pues que somos tus vasallos,
de don Pedro Carvajal    y de don Alonso su hermano,
que nos corren nuestras tierras    y nos roban el ganado
y nos fuerzan las mujeres    a tuerto y desaguisado;
comíannos la cebada    sin después querer pagallo,
hacen otras desvergüenzas    que vergüenza era contallo.
—Yo haré de ello justicia,    tornáos a vuestro ganado.
Manda pregonar el rey    y por todo su reinado,
que cualquier que los hallase    le daría buen hallazgo.
Hallólos el almirante,    allá en Medina del Campo,
comprando muy ricas armas,    jaeces para caballos.
—Presos, presos, caballeros,    presos, presos, hijosdalgo.
—No por vos, el almirante,    si de otro no es mandado.
—Estad presos, caballeros,    que del rey traigo recaudo.
—Plácenos, el almirante,    por complir el su mandado.
Por las sus jornadas ciertas    en Jaén habian entrado.
—Manténgate Dios, el rey.    —Mal vengades, hijosdalgo.
Mándales cortar los pies,    mándales cortar las manos,
y mándalos despeñar    de aquella peña de Martos.
Allí hablara el uno de ellos,    el menor y más osado:
—¿Por qué nos matas, el rey,    por qué haces tal mandado?
Querellámonos, el rey,    al juez que es soberano,
que dentro de treinta días    con nosotros seas en plazo;
y ponemos por testigos    a San Pedro y a San Pablo;
ponemos por escribano    al apóstol Santiago."
El rey, no mirando en ello,    hizo complir su mandado
por la falsa información    que los villanos le han dado;
y muertos los Carvajales,    que lo habían emplazado,
antes de los treinta días    él se fallara muy malo,
y desque fueron cumplidos,    en el postrer dia del plazo,
fue muerto dentro en León,    do la sentencia hubo dado.

## 15. Romance del prior de San Juan

Don Rodrigo de Padilla,    aquel que Dios perdonase,
tomara al rey por la mano    y apartólo en puridad:
—Un castillo está en Consuegra    que en el mundo no lo hay tal:
más vale para vos, el rey,    que para el prior de San Juan.

and the complainants were   two men resembling peasants:
they wore sandals on their feet   and held goads in their hands.
"Justice, justice, king,   since we are your subjects,
on Don Pedro Carvajal   and his brother Don Alonso;
for they raid our lands   and steal our livestock
and ravish our wives   unjustly and illegally;
they eat our barley   and refuse to pay for it later,
and commit other acts so shameless   it would shame us to tell them."
"I shall see justice done in this,   return to your herds."
The king orders a proclamation   made throughout his kingdom
that to anyone who found them   he'd give a good reward.
The captain found them   there in Medina del Campo
buying very costly armor   and horse trappings.
"You're under arrest, knights,   under arrest, noblemen!"
"Not by you, captain,   unless someone else has ordered it!"
"You're under arrest, knights,   for I have the king's authorization."
"We agree, captain,   to comply with his orders."
On the day assigned   they entered Jaén.
"God keep you, king!"   "You are evilly come, noblemen."
He ordered their feet cut off,   he ordered their hands cut off,
and ordered that they be thrown   off the cliff of Martos.
Then one of them spoke up,   the younger, bolder one:
"Why do you kill us, king,   why do you give such an order?
We lodge a complaint, king,   with that Judge who is sovereign,
and ask that in thirty days   you be summoned to appear with us;
and as witnesses we call   St. Peter and St. Paul;
as scribe we assign   the apostle St. James."
The king, paying no heed to this,   had his orders carried out
on the basis of the false report   that the peasants had given him;
after the death of the Carvajal brothers,   who had summoned him to court,
before thirty days had passed   he fell gravely ill,
and when they were completed,   on the day of expiry,
he died at León,   where he had handed down the sentence.


## 15. Ballad of the Prior of San Juan

Don Rodrigo de Padilla,   may God forgive him,
took the king by the hand   and drew him aside in privacy:
"There's a castle at Consuegra   which has no equal in the world:
it's more suitable for you, king,   than for the prior of San Juan.

Convidédesle, el buen rey,     convidédesle a cenar,
la cena que vos le diésedes     fuese como en Toro a don Juan:
que le cortes la cabeza     sin ninguna piedad:
desque se la hayáis cortado,     en tenencia me la dad.
Ellos en aquesto estando,     el prior llegado ha.
—Mantenga Dios a tu Alteza,     y a tu corona real.
—Bien vengáis vos, el prior,     el buen prior de San Juan.
Digádesme, el prior,     digádesme la verdad:
¿el castillo de Consuegra,     digades, por quién está?
—El castillo con la villa     está todo a tu mandar.
—Pues convídoos, el prior,     para conmigo a cenar.
—Pláceme, dijo el prior,     de muy buena voluntad.
Déme licencia tu Alteza,     licencia me quiera dar,
mensajeros nuevos tengo,     irlos quiero aposentar.
—Vais con Dios, el buen prior,     luego vos queráis tornar.
Vase para la cocina,     donde el cocinero está,
así hablaba con él     como si fuera su igual:
—Tomades estos mis vestidos,     los tuyos me quieras dar;
ya después de medio día     saliéseste a pasear.
Vase a la caballeriza     donde el macho suele estar.
—De tres me has escapado,     con esta cuatro serán,
y si de ésta me escapas,     de oro te haré herrar.
Presto le echó la silla,     comienza de caminar.
Media noche era por filo,     los gallos quieren cantar,
cuando entra por Toledo,     por Toledo, esa ciudad.
Antes que el gallo cantase     a Consuegra fue a llegar.
Halló las guardas velando,     empiézales de hablar:
—Digádesme, veladores,     digádesme la verdad:
¿el castillo de Consuegra,     digades, por quién está?
—El castillo con la villa     por el prior de San Juan.
—Pues abrádesme las puertas,     catalde aquí donde está.
La guarda desque lo vido     abriólas de par en par.
—Tomédesme allá este macho,     y dél me queráis curar:
dejadme a mí la vela,     porque yo quiero velar.
¡Velá, velá, veladores,     que rabia os quiera matar!
que quien a buen señor sirve,     este galardón le dan.
Y él estando en aquesto     el buen rey llegado ha:

Invite him, good king,   invite him to dine;
let the dinner you give him    be like the one you gave Don Juan at Toro:
cut off his head   without any mercy!
After you've cut it off,    give it to me to keep."
While they were conversing,   the prior arrived.
"May God preserve Your Highness    and your royal crown!"
"Welcome to you, prior,    good prior of San Juan!
Tell me, prior,   tell me truly:
tell me, on whose side    is the castle of Consuegra?"
"The castle and the town    are completely at your disposal."
"Then I invite you, prior,    to dine with me."
"Gladly," said the prior,    "with all my heart.
Give me leave now, Highness,    please give me leave;
I have new messengers,[7]   and I wish to give them lodging."
"Go with God, good prior,    but come back right away."
He goes to the kitchen,    where the cook is,
and speaks to him    as to an equal:
"Take these clothes of mine    and give me yours;
after midday   go out for a stroll."
He goes to the stable    where his mule usually is.
"You've gotten me out of three scrapes,    thisi will be the fourth,
and if you get me out of this one,    I'll shoe you with gold."
Quickly he saddled him,    and set out on his journey.
It was the stroke of midnight,    the cocks were about to crow,[8]
when he entered Toledo,    the city of Toledo.
Before the cock crew,    he had reached Consuegra.
He found the guards on duty,    he began to address them:
"Tell me, guards,   tell me truly:
tell me, on whose side    is the castle of Consuegra?"
"The castle and the town    are with the prior of San Juan."
"Then open the gates for me,    see: here he is before you!"
When the guard saw this,    he opened them wide.
"Take this mule over there for me,    and tend to him well:
leave the watch to me,    because I want to stand guard.
Stand guard, stand guard, guards,    may you die of rabies!
For the man who serves a good master    receives a reward like this."
And while he was standing guard,    the good king arrived;

---

7. In another version, this half-line reads in Spanish: *monjes nuevos son venidos* ("new friars [friars of the Order of St. John] have arrived").   8. Apparently, medieval Spanish roosters could be relied upon to announce midnight, 3 A.M., and dawn accurately.

halló a los guardas velando,    comiénzales de hablar:
—Digádesme, veladores,    que Dios os quiera guardar:
¿el castillo de Consuegra,    digades, por quién está?
—El castillo con la villa,    por el prior de San Juan.
—Pues abrádesme las puertas,    catalde aquí donde está.
—Afuera, afuera, el buen rey,    que el prior llegado ha.
—¡Macho rucio, macho rucio,    muermo te quiera matar!
¡siete caballos me cuestas,    y con este ocho serán!
Abridme, el buen prior,    allá me dejéis entrar;
por mi corona te juro    de nunca te hacer mal.
—Harélo, eso, el buen rey,    que ahora en mi mano está.

## 16. Romance de doña Isabel de Liar

Yo me estando en Giromena    a mi placer y holgar,
subiérame a un mirador    por más descanso tomar;
por los campos de Monvela    caballeros vi asomar,
ellos no vienen de guerra,    ni menos vienen de paz,
vienen en buenos caballos,    lanzas y adargas traen.
Desque yo los vi, mezquina,    parémelos a mirare,
conociera al uno de ellos    en el cuerpo y cabalgar:
don Rodrigo de Chavela,    que llaman del Marichale,
primo hermano de la reina,    mi enemigo era mortale.
Desque yo, triste, le viera,    luego vi mala señale.
Tomé mis hijos conmigo    y subíme al homenaje;
ya que yo iba a subir,    ellos en mi sala estane;
don Rodrigo es el primero,    y los otros tras él vane.
—Sálveos Dios, doña Isabel,    —Caballeros, bien vengades.
—¿Conocédesnos, señora,    pues así vais a hablare?
—Ya os conozco, don Rodrigo,    ya os conozco por mi male.
¿A qué era vuestra venida?    ¿Quién os ha enviado acae?
—Perdonédesme, señora,    por lo que os quiero hablare:
sabed que la reina, mi prima,    acá enviado me hae,
porque ella es muy mal casada    y esta culpa en vos estae,
porque el rey tiene en vos hijos    y en ella nunca los hae,
siendo, como sois, su amiga,    y ella mujer naturale,
manda que murais, señora,    paciencia queráis prestare.
Respondió doña Isabel    con muy gran honestidade:
—Siempre fuisteis, don Rodrigo,    en toda mi contrariedade;
si vos queredes, señor,    bien sabedes la verdade:

he found the guards on duty,   he began to address them:
"Tell me, guards,   may God keep you,
tell me, on whose side   is the castle of Consuegra?"
"The castle and the town   are with the prior of San Juan."
"Then open the gates for me,   see: here he is before you!"
"Away, away, good king,   for the prior has already come!"
"Gray mule, gray mule,   may you die of glanders!
You've cost me seven horses,   and this will be the eighth!
Open the gates, good prior,   and let me enter in;
on my crown I swear to you   never to do you harm."
"I will, good king,   because now it lies with me to do so."

## 16. Ballad of Doña Isabel de Liar

While I was at Giromena   enjoying myself at my ease,
I ascended to a balcony   to take more pleasure;
on the fields of Monvela   I saw horsemen appear;
they weren't coming for war,   but weren't coming in peace, either;
they were riding good horses   and bearing lances and shields.
When I, wretched woman, saw them,   I stopped to observe them;
I recognized one of them   by his physique and his way of riding:
Don Rodrigo de Chavela,   called "of El Marichal,"
first cousin to the queen,   and my mortal enemy.
When I, sad woman, saw him,   I immediately took it as a bad sign.
I went to get my children   and ascended to the castle keep;
by the time I was ascending   they were in my great hall;
Don Rodrigo was the first,   and the others followed him.
"God save you, Doña Isabel!"   "Welcome, knights!"
"Do you know us, my lady,   that you address us thus?"
"I know you, Don Rodrigo,   I know you to my misfortune.
What is the cause of your coming?   Who has sent you here?"
"Forgive me, my lady,   for what I'm about to tell you:
know that the queen, my cousin,   has sent me here
because her marriage is very unhappy   and you are to blame,
since you have borne the king children   and she never has,
though you are only his mistress   and she his lawful wife;
she orders that you die, my lady,   please show fortitude."
Doña Isabel replied   with very great decorum:
"Don Rodrigo, you've always been   dead set against me;
if you wished, sir,   you'd acknowledge the truth:

que el rey me pidió mi amor,    y yo no se le quise dare,
temiendo más a mi honra,    que no sus reinos mandare.
Desque vio que no quería,    mis padres fuera a mandare;
ellos tampoco quisieron,    por la su honra guardare.
Desque todo aquesto vido,    por fuerza me fue a tomare,
trújome a esta fortaleza,    do estoy en este lugare,
tres años he estado en ella    fuera de mi voluntade,
y si el rey tiene en mí hijos,    plugo a Dios y a su bondade,
y si no los ha en la reina    es así su voluntade.
¿Por qué me habeis de dar muerte,    pues que no merezco male?
Una merced os pido, señores,    no me la queráis negare:
desterréisme de estos reinos,    que en ellos no estaré mase;
irme ha yo para Castilla,    o a Aragón más adelante
y si aquesto no bastare,    a Francia me iré a morare.
—Perdonédesnos, señora,    que no se puede hacer mase;
aquí está el duque de Bavia    y el marqués de Villareale
y aquí está el obispo de Oporto,    que os viene a confesare;
cabe vos está el verdugo    que os había de degollare,
y aun aqueste pajecico    la cabeza ha de llevare.
Respondió doña Isabel    con muy gran honestidade:
—Bien parece que soy sola,    no tengo quién me guardare,
ni tengo padre ni madre,    pues no me dejan hablare,
y el rey no está en esta tierra,    que era ido allende el mare,
mas desque él sea venido,    la mi muerte vengaráe.
—Acabedes ya, señora,    acabedes ya de hablare.
Tomadla, señor obispo,    y metedla a confesare.
Mientras en la confesión,    todos tres hablando estane
si era bien hecho o mal hecho    esta dama degollare:
los dos dicen que no muera,    que en ella culpa no hae,
don Rodrigo es tan cruel,    dice que la ha de matare.
Sale de la confesión    con sus tres hijos delante:
el uno dos años tiene,    el otro para ellos vae,
y el otro era de teta,    dándole sale a mamare,
toda cubierta de negro,    lástima es de la mirare.
—Adiós, adiós, hijos míos,    hoy os quedaréis sin madre;
caballeros de alta sangre,    por mis hijos queráis mirare,
que al fin son hijos de rey,    aunque son de baja madre.
Tiéndenla en un repostero    para haberla de degollare;
así murió esta señora,    sin merecer ningún mal.

the king requested my love,   but I refused it,
more regardful of my honor    than desirous of sharing his rule.
When he saw I was unwilling,   he sent for my parents;
they refused, as well,   in order to preserve their honor.
When he saw all this,   he took me by force
and brought me to this fortress,   where I stay in this place;
I've been here three years    against my will,
and if the king has children by me,   it so pleased God and His kindness,
and if he has none by the queen,   such is His will.
Why must you kill me,   since I deserve no bad treatment?
I ask one favor of you, lords,   don't refuse it:
banish me from this realm,   in which I shall no longer stay;
I shall go to Castile   or even farther, to Aragon,
and if that's not enough,   I'll go and live in France."
"Forgive us, my lady,   nothing more can be done;
the Duke of Bavia is here   and the Marquess of Villareal,
and the bishop of Oporto has come   to hear your confession.
Beside you is the executioner   who is to behead you,
and even this little page,   who is to carry your head."
Doña Isabel replied   with very great decorum:
"It's clear that I'm alone,   with no one to defend me;
I don't have a father or mother,   since they don't let me speak,
and the king isn't in this land,   he has gone across the sea;
but as soon as he returns,   he will avenge my death."
"Enough now, my lady,   enough talking!
My lord bishop, take her   and hear her confession."
While she was making confession,   all three were arguing
whether it was a good deed or bad   to behead that lady:
two said she shouldn't die,   because she was blameless,
but Don Rodrigo was so cruel,   he insisted she must be killed.
She left the room where she made confession,   her three children in front of her;
one was two years old,   the other approaching that age,
and the third was a suckling   whom she nursed as she walked;
she was dressed all in black,   and was pitiful to behold.
"Farewell, farewell, my children,   today you will be left motherless;
knights of lofty descent,   please look after my children,
for, after all, they are royal children   though their mother is of low birth."
They stretched her out on an armorial cloth   to behead her;
thus died that lady,   who hadn't merited any bad treatment.

## 17. Romance de don Fadrique

Yo me estaba allá en Coimbra,    que yo me la hube ganado,
cuando me vinieron cartas    del rey don Pedro, mi hermano,
que fuese a ver los torneos    que en Sevilla se han armado.
Yo, Maestre sin ventura,    yo, Maestre desdichado,
tomara trece de mula,    venticinco de caballo,
todos con cadenas de oro,    de jubones de brocado.
Jornada de quince días    en ocho la había andado.
A la pasada de un río,    pasándole por el vado,
cayó mi mula conmigo,    perdí mi puñal dorado,
ahogáraseme un paje,    de los míos más privados,
criado era en mi sala    y de mí muy regalado.
Con todas estas desdichas    a Sevilla hube llegado.
A la puerta Macarena    encontré con un ordenado,
ordenado de evangelio,    que misa no había cantado.
—Manténgate Dios, Maestre,    Maestre, bien seáis llegado.
Hoy te ha nacido hijo,    hoy cumples ventiún año,
si te plugiese, Maestre,    volvamos a bautizarlo,
que yo sería el padrino,    tú, Maestre, el ahijado.
Allí hablara el Maestre,    bien oiréis lo que ha hablado:
—No me lo mandéis, señor,    padre, no queráis mandarlo,
que voy a ver qué me quiere    el rey don Pedro, mi hermano.
Di de espuelas a mi mula,    en Sevilla me hube entrado.
De que no vi tela puesta,    ni vi caballero armado,
fuime para los palacios    del rey don Pedro, mi hermano.
En entrando por las puertas,    las puertas me habían cerrado;
quitáronme la mi espada,    la que traía a mi lado,
quitáronme mi compañía,    la que me había acompañado.
Los míos, de que esto vieron,    de traición me han avisado
que me saliese yo fuera    que ellos me pondrían en salvo.
Yo, como estaba sin culpa,    de nada hube curado.
Fuime para el aposento    del rey don Pedro, mi hermano.
—Mantengaos Dios, el rey,    y a todos de cabo a cabo.
—Mal hora vengáis, Maestre,    Maestre, mal seais llegado.
Nunca nos venís a ver    sino una vez en el año,
y ésta que venís, Maestre,    es por fuerza o por mandado.
Vuestra cabeza, Maestre,    mandada está en aguinaldo.

## 17. Ballad of Don Fadrique

I was there in Coimbra,    which I had conquered,
when I received letters    from King Pedro, my brother,
inviting me to the tourneys    being held in Seville.
I, a luckless Master,    I, an unfortunate Master,
took along thirteen on muleback,    twenty-five on horseback,
all with golden chains    and embroidered doublets.
A journey of two weeks    I accomplished in one.
While crossing a river,    passing through the ford,
my mule fell with me    and I lost my gilded dagger;
one of my pages drowned,    one of those closest to my heart;
he had been raised in my great hall,    very pampered by me.
With all these misfortunes    I reached Seville.
At the Macarena gate    I met a churchman,
a deacon    who had never sung mass.
"God keep you, Master;    Master, welcome!
A son was born to you today,    today is your twenty-first birthday;
if it so please you, Master,    let's go and baptize him;
I'll be his godfather,    and you, Master, a fellow sponsor."[9]
Then the Master spoke,    you shall hear what he said:
"Don't ask this of me, sir;    Father, please don't ask it,
for I'm going to see what King Pedro,    my brother, wants of me."
I spurred my mule,    I entered Seville.
Seeing no place curtained off for a tourney,    or any armed knight,
I went to the palace    of King Pedro, my brother.
When I entered the gates,    the gates were locked behind me;
they took away my sword,    which I wore at my side;
they took away my men    who had escorted me.
When my people saw this,    they warned me of treachery,
asking me to go outside,    where they'd put me in safety.
Since I was blameless,    I paid no mind to all that.
I went to the room    of King Pedro, my brother.
"God keep you, king,    and all who are here!"
"Evilly come, Master!    Master, you are unwelcome.
You never come to see us    except once a year,
and now that you've come, Master,    it's by force or by orders.
Your head, Master,    has been ordered as a holiday gift."

---

9. A conjectural rendering of *ahijado*, which normally means "godson" (when it doesn't mean "adopted son" or "protégé").

—¿Por qué es aqueso, buen rey?    nunca os hice desaguisado,
ni os dejé yo en la lid    ni con moros peleando.
—Venid acá, mis porteros,    hágase lo que mandado.
Aún no lo hubo bien dicho,    la cabeza le han cortado;
a doña María de Padilla    en un plato la ha enviado.
Así hablaba con ella,    como si estuviera sano,
las palabras que le dice    de esta suerte está hablando:
—Aquí pagaréis, traidor,    lo de antaño y lo de hogaño,
el mal consejo que diste    al rey don Pedro, tu hermano.
Asióla por los cabellos,    echádosela a un alano;
el alano es del Maestre,    púsola sobre un estrado,
a los aullidos que daba    atronó todo el palacio.
Allí demandara el rey:    —¿Quién hace mal a ese alano?
Allí respondieron todos    a los cuales ha pesado:
—Con la cabeza lo ha, señor,    del Maestre, vuestro hermano.
Allí hablara una su tía,    que tía era de entrambos:
—Cuán mal lo mirastes, rey,    rey, qué mal lo habéis mirado.
Por una mala mujer    habéis muerto un tal hermano.
Aún no lo había bien dicho    cuando ya le había pesado.
Fuese para doña María,    de esta suerte le ha hablado:
—Prendedla, mis caballeros,    ponédmela a buen recaudo,
que yo le daré tal castigo    que a todos sea sonado.
En cárceles muy oscuras    allí la había aprisionado,
él mismo le da a comer,    él mismo con la su mano,
no se fía de ninguno,    sino de un paje que ha criado.


## 18. Romance del rey don Pedro el Cruel

Por los campos de Jerez    a caza va el rey don Pedro;
en llegando a una laguna,    allí quiso ver un vuelo.
Vido volar una garza,    disparóle un sacre nuevo,
remontárale un neblí,    a sus pies cayera muerto.
A sus pies cayó el neblí,    túvolo por mal agüero.
Tanto volaba la garza,    parece llegar al cielo.
Por donde la garza sube    vio bajar un bulto negro;
mientras más se acerca el bulto,    más temor le va poniendo,
con el abajarse tanto,    parece llegar al suelo
delante de su caballo,    a cinco pasos de trecho.
De él salió un pastorcico,    sale llorando y gimiendo,
la cabeza desgreñada,    revuelto trae el cabello,

"Why is that, good king?   I never offended you;
nor did I desert you in combat    or when fighting Moors."
"Come here, doorkeepers,    let my orders be carried out!"
Before he had finishd speaking,    they cut off his brother's head;
he sent it on a platter    to Doña María de Padilla.
She addressed it thus,    as if he were alive,
the words she said to it    were framed in this fashion:
"Traitor, here you shall pay    for what you did in the past and this year,
the bad advice you gave    King Pedro, your brother."
She grasped it by the hair    and threw it to a mastiff;
the mastiff was the Master's,    he put it on a dais;
the howls he uttered    deafened the whole palace.
Then the king asked:    "Who's hurting that mastiff?"
Then everyone replied,    all those who felt any grief:
"Sire, it's because of the head    of the Master, your brother."
Then an aunt of his spoke up,    who was aunt to both:
"How badly you've acted, king!    King, how badly you've acted!
For the sake of an evil woman    you've killed a brother like that!"
Before she finished speaking,    he already felt grief.
He went to Doña María,    he addressed her as follows:
"Seize her, my knights,    and put her under heavy guard,
for I will give her such a punishment    that it will be talked about everywhere!"
In a very dark dungeon    he imprisoned her;
he himself fed her,    he himself with his own hand;
he trusted no one else    except one page whom he had raised.

## 18. Ballad of King Pedro the Cruel

In the fields of Jerez    King Pedro went hunting;
reaching a small lake    he wanted to try out his hawks.
He saw a heron flying    and dispatched a new gerfalcon after it;
a peregrine falcon crossed its path    and fell dead at his feet.
The falcon fell at his feet;    he took this as a bad omen.
The heron flew so high,    it seemed to reach heaven.
Where the heron ascended    he saw a dark shape descend;
the closer the shape came,    the more it frightened him;
it descended so low,    it seemed to reach the ground
in front of his horse,    at a distance of five paces.
From it there emerged a young shepherd,    weeping and moaning,
his head tousled,    his hair disheveled,

con los pies llenos de abrojos    y el cuerpo lleno de vello;
en su mano una culebra,    y en la otra un puñal sangriento,
en el hombro una mortaja,    una calavera al cuello;
a su lado, de traílla,    traía un perro negro,
los aullidos que daba    a todos ponían gran miedo;
y a grandes voces decía:    —Morirás, el rey don Pedro,
que mataste sin justicia    los mejores de tu reino:
mataste tu propio hermano,    el Maestre, sin consejo,
y desterraste a tu madre,    a Dios darás cuenta de ello.
Tienes presa a doña Blanca,    enojaste a Dios por ello,
que si tornas a quererla    darte ha Dios un heredero,
y si no, por cierto sepas    te vendrá desmán por ello:
serán malas las tus hijas    por tu culpa y mal gobierno,
y tu hermano don Enrique    te habrá de heredar el reino,
morirás a puñaladas,    tu casa será el infierno.
Todo esto recontado,    despareció el bulto negro.

## 19. "Ya se salen de Jaén"

Ya se salen de Jaén    los trescientos hijosdalgo:
mozos codiciosos de honra,    pero más enamorados.
Por amor de sus amigas,    todos van juramentados
de llegar hasta Granada    y correrles todo el campo
y no dar vuelta sin traer    algún moro en aguinaldo.
Un lunes por la mañana    parten todos muy lozanos,
con lanzas y con adargas    muy ricamente aderezados.
Todos visten oro y seda;    todos, puñales dorados.
¡Muy bravos caballos llevan    a la jineta ensillados!
Los jaeces son azules    de plata y oro broslados;
las reatas son listones    que sus damas les han dado.
Los mozos más orgullosos    son don Juan Ponce y su hermano;
y también Pedro de Torres,    Diego Gil y su cuñado.
En medio de todos iban    cuatro viejos muy ancianos;
éstos van diciendo a todos:    —Perdémonos de livianos,
en querer ir a probar    donde hay moriscos doblados.
Cuando esto oyó don Juan,    con gran enojo ha hablado:
—No debían ir en guerra    los hombres viejos cansados,
porque estorban los ardides    y pónenles embarazos.
Si en Jaén queréis quedar,    quedaréis más descansados.
Allí respondieron todos    de valientes y esforzados:

his feet full of thistle points    and his body shaggy with hair;
in one hand a serpent,    in the other a bloody dagger,
on his shoulder a shroud,    on his neck a skull;
at his side, on a leash,    he had a black dog,
whose howling    struck great fear in all;
and loudly he cried:    "You shall die, King Pedro,
for you unjustly killed    the best men in your realm:
you killed your own brother,    the Master, unwisely,
and you exiled your mother;    you shall account to God for that.
You're keeping Doña Blanca prisoner;    you vexed God by that,
for if you restore your love to her,    God will give you an heir,
but if not, know for a certainty    that it will bring you misfortune:
your daughters will have evil ways    thanks to you and your bad guidance,
and your brother Don Enrique    will inherit the realm from you;
you will die by dagger blows,    and hell will be your home."
Having made that declaration,    the black shape vanished.

## 19. "Now There Sally Forth from Jaén"

Now there sally forth from Jaén    the three hundred noblemen,
young men ambitious for honor,    but incited even more by love.
For love of their sweethearts    they have all sworn
to reach Granada    and raid all its territory,
not returning without bringing    some Moor as a gift.
One Monday morning    they all set out most gallantly,
with lances and shields,    most richly adorned.
All wear gold and silk;    all have gilded daggers.
They ride very spirited horses    saddled with short stirrups.
The trappings are blue,    embroidered with silver and gold;
the single-file straps are silk ribbons    their ladies have given them.
The proudest young men    are Juan Ponce and his brother;
and also Pedro de Torres,    Diego Gil, and his brother-in-law.
In the midst of them all rode    four very old men;
they said to them all:    "We'll be lost out of thoughtlessness
if we try to venture    where the Moors are twice our number."
When Don Juan heard this,    he said in great anger:
"Tired old men    shouldn't go to war,
because they impede the brave    and are an obstacle to them.
If you want to stay in Jaén,    you'll relax more."
Then they all replied    as valiant, courageous men:

—No lo mande Dios del cielo    que de miedo nos volvamos,
que no queremos perder    la honra que hemos ganado.
Llegados son a Granada,    dado han vuelta a todo el campo.
Ya que llevaban la presa,    de moros hueste ha somado:
más de seis mil son de guerra,    que los estaban mirando.
Ven tocar los atambores,    ven pendones campeando,
ven poner los escuadrones,    los de pie y los de caballo,
vieron mil moros mancebos,    tanto albornoz colorado;
vieron tanta yegua overa,    tanto caballo alazano,
tanta lanza con dos fierros,    tanto del fierro acerado,
tantos pendones azules    y de lunas plateados;
con tanta adarga ante pechos,    cada cual muy bien armado.
Los de Jaén esto viendo,    como mozos hijosdalgo,
parescióles que el huir    les sería mal contado.
Aborreciendo las vidas    por no vivir deshonrados,
comenzaron a llamar    a voz alta ¡Santiago!
y entráronse por los moros    con ánimo peleando.
Más han muerto de dos mil,    como leones rabiando;
mas cargaron tantos moros    que pocos han escapado.
Doscientos y treinta y seis    han muerto y aprisionado,
por no seguir ni creer    los mozos a los ancianos.


## 20. Romance del moro de Antequera

De Antequera sale un moro,    de Antequera, aquesa villa,
cartas llevaba en su mano,    cartas de mensajería,
escritas iban con sangre,    y no por falta de tinta,
el moro que las llevaba    ciento y veinte años había.
Ciento y veinte años el moro,    de doscientos parecía,
la barba llevaba blanca    muy larga hasta la cinta,
con la cabeza pelada,    la calva le relucía;
toca llevaba tocada,    muy grande precio valía,
la mora que la labrara    por su amiga la tenía.
Caballero en una yegua    que grande precio valía,
no por falta de caballos,    que hartos él se tenía;
alhareme en su cabeza    con borlas de seda fina.
Siete celadas le echaron,    de todas se escabullía;
por los cabos de Archidona    a grandes voces decía:
—Si supieres, el rey moro,    mi triste mensajería
mesarías tus cabellos    y la tu barba vellida.

"God in heaven forbid    that we should turn back in fear,
for we don't want to lose    the honor we've won."
They reached Granada    and rode all around the field.
While they were carrying off their booty,    a Moorish force appeared:
over six thousand warriors    observing them.
They see drums beaten,    they see pennants waving,
they see squadrons drawn up,    men on foot and on horse,
they saw a thousand young Moors    and many a red burnoose;
they saw many a peach-colored mare    and many a chestnut stallion,
many a two-pointed lance,    many a cutting sword,
many a blue pennant    with crescents worked in silver;
with shields before their breasts,    all were in good armor.
Seeing this, those from Jaén,    like the young nobles they were,
deemed that running away    would be held against them.
Counting life as nought    to avoid a life of dishonor,
they began to shout    "Santiago!" at the top of their voice,
and they clashed with the Moors,    fighting bravely.
They killed over two thousand,    raging like lions;
but so many Moors charged them    that very few escaped.
Two hundred thirty-six    were killed or captured,
because the young didn't obey    and trust their elders.

## 20. Ballad of the Moor of Antequera

From Antequera a Moor departs,    from the town of Antequera,
bearing a letter in his hand,    a letter with a message;
it was written in blood,    and not for lack of ink;
the Moor who bore it    was a hundred twenty years old.
A hundred and twenty the Moor,    and he looked like two hundred;
his beard was white    and very long, to his waist;
his head clean shaven,    and its baldness gleaming;
the headgear he wore    was worth a great deal;
the Moorish woman who had woven it    was his sweetheart.
He rode a mare    that was worth a great deal,
not for lack of stallions,    for he had plenty;
the turban on his head    had tassels of fine silk.
Seven ambushes were laid for him,    he slipped away from all;
just outside Archidona    he called loudly:
"If you knew, Moorish king,    my sad message,
you'd tear your hair    and your beautiful beard!"

Tales lástimas haciendo    llega a la puerta de Elvira;
vase para los palacios    donde el rey moro vivía.
Encontrado ha con el rey    que del Alhambra salía
con doscientos de a caballo,    los mejores que tenía.
Ante el rey, cuando le halla,    tales palabras decía:
—Mantenga Dios a tu alteza,    salve Dios tu señoría.
—Bien vengas, el moro viejo,    días ha que te atendía.
¿Qué nuevas me traes, el moro,    de Antequera esa mi villa?
—No te las diré, el buen rey,    si no me otorgas la vida.
—Dímelas, el moro viejo,    que otorgada te sería.
—Las nuevas que, rey, sabrás    no son nuevas de alegría:
que ese infante don Fernando    cercada tiene tu villa.
Muchos caballeros suyos    la combaten cada día:
aquese Juan de Velasco    y el que Henríquez se decía,
el de Rojas y Narváez,    caballeros de valía.
De día le dan combate,    de noche hacen la mina;
los moros que estaban dentro    cueros de vaca comían,
si no socorres, el rey,    tu villa se perdería.

## 21. "La mañana de San Juan"

La mañana de San Juan    al tiempo que alboreaba,
gran fiesta hacen los moros    por la vega de Granada.
Revolviendo sus caballos    y jugando de las lanzas,
ricos pendones en ellas    broslados por sus amadas,
ricas marlotas vestidas    tejidas de oro y grana.
El moro que amores tiene    señales de ello mostraba,
y el que no tenía amores    allí no escaramuzaba.
Las damas moras los miran    de las torres del Alhambra,
también se los mira el rey    de dentro de la Alcazaba.
Dando voces vino un moro    con la cara ensangrentada:
—Con tu licencia, el rey,    te daré una nueva mala:
el infante don Fernando    tiene a Antequera ganada;
muchos moros deja muertos,    yo soy quien mejor librara,
siete lanzadas yo traigo,    el cuerpo todo me pasan,
los que conmigo escaparon    en Archidona quedaban.
Con la tal nueva el rey    la cara se le demudaba;
manda juntar sus trompetas    que toquen todas el arma,
manda juntar a los suyos,    hace muy gran cabalgada,
y a las puertas de Alcalá,    que la Real se llamaba,

Making similar lament, he reached the Elvira gate;
he headed for the palace where the Moorish king lived.
He came across the king leaving the Alhambra
with two hundred mounted men, the best he had.
To the king, upon finding him, he spoke these words:
"God keep Your Highness, God keep Your Lordship!"
"Welcome, ancient Moor, I've been awaiting you for days.
What news do you bring me, Moor, from my town of Antequera?"
"I won't tell it, good king, unless you promise me my life."
"Tell it, ancient Moor, for I grant it to you."
"The news you'll hear, king, isn't happy news:
for Prince Fernando is besieging your town.
Many of his knights assail it every day:
Juan de Velasco and the man called Henríquez,
De Rojas and Narváez, valiant knights.
In the daytime they attack, at night they dig tunnels;
the Moors who are inside are eating cowhides;
if you don't help, king, your town will be lost."

## 21. "On the Morning of St. John's Day"

On the morning of St. John's Day, when dawn was breaking,
the Moors held a great celebration in the plain of Granada;
turning their horses round and round, and playing games with their lances,
which bore costly pennants embroidered by their sweethearts,
they wore costly tunics woven with gold and scarlet.
Any Moor who loved a woman bore her tokens in his attire;
those not in love stayed away from that contest.
The Moorish ladies watched them from the towers of the Alhambra;
the king watched them, too, from inside the citadel.
A Moor arrived shouting; his face was bloodied:
"By your leave, king, I'll give you some bad news:
Prince Fernando has conquered Antequera;
he has left many Moors dead, I'm the one who got off most lightly;
I bear seven lance wounds that completely pierced my body;
those who escaped with me are staying at Archidona."
At that news the king's face turned pale;
he bids all his trumpeters assemble to sound the alarm;
he bids his troops assemble, they ride out in numbers,
and, at the gates of Alcalá called "la Real,"

los cristianos y los moros    una escaramuza traban.
Los cristianos eran muchos,    mas llevaban orden mala,
los moros, que son de guerra,    dádoles han mala carga,
de ellos matan, de ellos prenden,    de ellos toman en celada.
Con la victoria, los moros    van la vuelta de Granada;
a grandes voces decían:    —¡La victoria ya es cobrada!

## 22. Romance de Abenámar

—¡Abenámar, Abenámar,    moro de la morería,
el día que tú naciste    grandes señales había!
Estaba la mar en calma,    la luna estaba crecida,
moro que en tal signo nace    no debe decir mentira.
Allí respondiera el moro,    bien oiréis lo que diría:
—Yo te la diré, señor,    aunque me cueste la vida,
porque soy hijo de un moro    y una cristiana cautiva;
siendo yo niño y muchacho    mi madre me lo decía
que mentira no dijese,    que era grande villanía;
por tanto pregunta, rey,    que la verdad te diría.
—Yo te agradezco, Abenámar,    aquesa tu cortesía.
¿Qué castillos son aquéllos?    ¡Altos son y relucían!
—El Alhambra era, señor,    y la otra la mezquita,
los otros los Alixares,    labrados a maravilla.
El moro que los labraba    cien doblas ganaba al día,
y el día que no los labra,    otras tantas se perdía.
El otro es Generalife,    huerta que par no tenía,
el otro Torres Bermejas,    castillo de gran valía.
Allí habló el rey don Juan,    bien oiréis lo que decía:
—Si tú quisieses, Granada,    contigo me casaría;
daréte en arras y dote    a Córdoba y a Sevilla.
—Casada soy, rey don Juan,    casada soy, que no viuda;
el moro que a mí me tiene    muy grande bien me quería.

## 23. Romance del obispo don Gonzalo

Un día de San Antón,    ese día señalado,
se salían de San Juan    cuatrocientos hijosdalgo.
Las señas que ellos llevaban    es pendón rabo de gallo;
por capitán se lo llevan    al obispo don Gonzalo,

the Christians and the Moors engage in a skirmish.
The Christians had more men but fought in disorder;
the Moors, on a warlike footing, charged them disastrously;
some they killed, some they captured, some they caught in ambush.
Winning the victory, the Moors returned to Granada,
shouting loudly: "Now the victory has been gained!"

## 22. Ballad of Abenámar

"Abenámar, Abenámar, Moor of Moors' land,
on the day you were born there were portentous signs!
The sea was becalmed, the moon was full;
a Moor born under such signs should not tell a lie."
Then the Moor replied, you shall hear what he said:
"I shall tell you truly, sire, though it cost me my life;
for I am the son of a Moorish man and a captive Christian woman;
when I was a child and a lad, my mother would tell me
never to lie, since it was despicable conduct;
therefore, ask, king, for I shall tell you the truth."
"I thank you, Abenámar, for this courtesy of yours.
What castles are those? They are lofty and radiant!"
"It is the Alhambra, sire, and that other is the mosque,
the others are the Alixares, marvelously constructed.
The Moor who constructed them earned a hundred doubloons each day;
each day he didn't work he lost that amount.
The other is Generalife, a garden that has no equal;
that other, Torres Bermejas, a castle of great value."
The King Juan spoke up, you shall hear what he said:
"If you were willing, Granada, I would marry you;
as bride gift and dowry I'll give you Córdoba and Seville."
"I'm already married, King Juan, married and not a widow;
the Moor who possesses me loves me very dearly."

## 23. Ballad of Bishop Gonzalo

One St. Anthony's Day, that special day,
there rode out from San Juan four hundred noblemen.
The standards they bore were a cock's-tail pennant;
as captain they had Bishop Gonzalo,

armado de todas armas,    encima de un buen caballo;
íbase para La Guarda,    ese castillo nombrado;
sáleselo a recibir    don Rodrigo, ese hidalgo.
—Por Dios os ruego, obispo,    que no pasedes el vado,
porque los moros son muchos    que a La Guarda habían llegado;
muerto me han tres caballeros,    de que mucho me ha pesado:
el uno era mi primo,    y el otro era mi hermano,
y el otro era un paje mío,    que en mi casa se ha criado.
Demos la vuelta, señores,    demos la vuelta a enterrarlos,
haremos a Dios servicio    y honraremos los cristianos.
Ellos estando en aquesto,    llegó don Diego de Haro:
—Adelante, caballeros,    que me llevan el ganado;
si de algún villano fuera    ya lo hubiérades quitado,
empero, alguno está aquí    a quien place de mi daño;
no cabe decir quién es,    que es el del roquete blanco.
El obispo, que lo oyera,    dio de espuelas al caballo.
El caballo era ligero    y saltado había un vallado,
mas al salir de una cuesta,    a la asomada de un llano,
vido mucha adarga blanca,    mucho albornoz colorado
y muchos hierros de lanzas    que relucen en el campo.
Metido se había por ellos,    como león denodado;
de tres batallas de moros    las dos ha desbaratado,
mediante la buena ayuda    que en los suyos ha hallado;
aunque algunos de ellos mueren,    eterna fama han ganado.
Todos pasan adelante,    ninguno atrás se ha quedado;
siguiendo a su capitán,    el cobarde es esforzado.
Honra ganan los cristianos,    los moros pierden el campo:
diez moros pierden la vida    por la muerte de un cristiano,
si alguno de ellos escapa,    es por uña de caballo.
Por su mucha valentía    toda la prez han cobrado.
Así, con esta victoria    como señores del campo,
se vuelven para Jaén    con la honra que han ganado.

## 24. "Cercada está Santa Fe"

Cercada está Santa Fe    con mucho lienzo encerado,
al derredor muchas tiendas    de seda, oro y brocado,
donde están duques y condes,    señores de grande estado,
y otros muchos capitanes    que lleva el rey don Fernando;
todos de valor crecido,    como ya habréis notado

in full armor,   riding a good horse;
he was heading for La Guarda,   that famous castle;
riding out to greet him came   the nobleman Don Rodrigo.
"In God's name I beg you, bishop,   not to cross the ford,
because the Moors are numerous   who have come to La Guarda;
they've killed three of my knights,   which caused me great sorrow:
one was my cousin,   another was my brother,
and the third a page of mine   who was raised in my house.
Let's turn back, my lords,   let's return and bury them;
we'll be doing God a service   and honoring Christians."
At that point in their talk,   Don Diego de Haro arrived:
"Press forward, knights,   for my cattle are being stolen;
if some commoner were behind it,   I'd have prevented it by now,
but there's someone here   who takes pleasure in my misfortunes;
it's not for me to identify him:   he wears a white vestment."
Hearing this, the bishop   spurred his horse.
His horse was nimble   and leaped a fence,
but while climbing a slope,   where he could first see a plain,
he sighted many white shields,   many red burnooses,
and many lance points   gleaming in the field.
He charged into their midst   like an intrepid lion;
out of three companies of Moors   he routed two,
thanks to the loyal aid   he received from his followers;
though some of them died,   they won eternal fame.
They all pushed ahead,   not one hung back;
following his captain,   even the coward is brave.
The Christians won honor,   the Moors lost the field:
ten Moors lost their lives   for every dead Christian;
if some of them escaped,   it was thanks to their horses' hooves.
By their great gallantry   they won all the glory.
And so, after that victory,   as masters of the battlefield
they returned to Jaén   with the honor they had earned.

## 24. "Santa Fe Is Encircled"

Santa Fe is encircled   with much waxed cloth;
all around are many tents   of silk, gold, and brocade,
in which are dukes and counts,   lords of high estate,
and many other captains   brought by King Fernando;
all of full-fledged valor,   as you will have noted,

en la guerra que se ha hecho    contra el granadino estado.
Cuando a las nueve del día    un moro se ha demostrado
encima un caballo negro    de blancas manchas manchado,
cortados ambos hocicos,    porque lo tiene enseñado
el moro que con sus dientes    despedace a los cristianos.
El moro viene vestido    de blanco, azul y encarnado,
y debajo esta librea    traía un muy fuerte jaco,
y una lanza con dos hierros    de acero muy bien templado
y una adarga hecha en Féz    de un ante rico estimado.
Aqueste perro, con befa,    en la cola del caballo,
la sagrada Ave María    llevaba haciendo escarnio.
Llegando junto a las tiendas,    de esta manera ha hablado:
—¿Cuál será aquel caballero    que sea tan esforzado
que quiera hacer conmigo    batalla en aqueste campo?
Salga uno, salgan dos,    salgan tres o salgan cuatro.
El alcaide de los donceles    salga, que es hombre afamado;
salga ese conde de Cabra,    en la guerra experimentado;
salga Gonzalo Férnandez,    que es de Córdoba nombrado;
o, si no, Martín Galindo,    que es valeroso soldado;
salga ese Portocarrero,    señor de Palma nombrado,
o el bravo don Manuel    Ponce de León llamado,
aquel que sacara el guante    que por industria fue echado
donde estaban los leones    y él le sacó muy osado.
Y, si no salen aquestos,    salga el mismo rey Fernando,
que yo le daré a entender    si soy de valor sobrado.
Los caballeros del rey    todos le están escuchando.
Cada uno pretendía    salir con el moro al campo.
Garcilaso estaba allí,    mozo gallardo, esforzado;
licencia le pide al rey    para salir al pagano.
—Garcilaso, sois muy mozo    para emprender este caso;
otros hay en el real    para poder encargarlo.
Garcilaso se despide    muy confuso y enojado,
por no tener la licencia    que al rey había demandado.
Pero muy secretamente    Garcilaso se había armado
y en un caballo morcillo    salido se había al campo.
Nadie le ha conocido    porque sale disfrazado.
Fuese donde estaba el moro    y de esta suerte le ha hablado:
—¡Ahora verás, el moro,    si tiene el rey don Fernando
caballeros valerosos    que salgan contigo al campo!
Yo soy el menor de todos    y vengo por su mandado.
El moro cuando le vio    en poco le había estimado,

in the war being waged    against the state of Granada.
At nine in the morning    a Moor appeared,
riding a black horse    with white spots,
both its lips cut off,    because it was trained
by the Moor to tear apart    Christians with its teeth.
The Moor was dressed    in white, blue, and red,
and beneath that heraldic garb    he wore a very strong mail jacket;
he bore a two-pointed lance    of very well tempered steel
and a shield made in Fez    from a valuable elk hide.
That dog, with contempt,    had tied to his horse's tail
the Holy Virgin Mary    as a sign of mockery.
Arriving near the tents,    he spoke in this manner:
"Who shall that knight be    who is brave enough
to do battle with me    on this field?
Let one come out, let two come out,    let three or four come out!
Let the master of the young knights    come out, that famous man!
Let the Count of Cabra come out,    so experienced in warfare!
Let Gonzalo Fernández come out,    who is called "of Córdoba"!
Or, if not, Martín Galindo,    who is a valorous soldier!
Let Portocarrero come out,    who is called the lord of Palma,
or that wild Don Manuel,    called Ponce de León,
the one who retrieved the glove    that had been thrown intentionally
into the lions' pit,    retrieving it with great daring!
And if they don't come out,    let King Fernando himself come out,
and I'll give him to understand    that I'm of the highest valor!"
All the king's knights    were listening to him.
Each one requested leave    to ride out to the field with the Moor.
Garcilaso was present,    a gallant, brave youth;
he asked the king's permission    to confront the heathen.
"Garcilaso, you're too young    to accept this challenge;
there are others in the camp    who can respond to it."
Garcilaso departed    very embarrassed and angry,
because he hadn't obtained the leave    he had asked of the king.
But in great secrecy    Garcilaso had donned his armor,
and on a ruddy-faced black horse    he rode out to the field.
No one recognized him    because he had hidden his identity.
He rode to where the Moor was,    and addressed him thus:
"Now, Moor, you shall see    whether King Fernando has
knights valiant enough    to ride out to the field with you!
I am the least of them all    and I come at his command."
When the Moor saw him,    he thought little of him

y díjole de esta suerte:    —Yo no estoy acostumbrado
a hacer batalla campal    sino con hombres barbados.
Vuélvete, rapaz —le dice—,    y venga el más estimado.
Garcilaso, con enojo,    puso piernas al caballo;
arremetió para el moro    y un gran encuentro le ha dado.
El moro, que aquesto vio,    revuelve así como un rayo.
Comienza la escaramuza    con un furor muy sobrado.
Garcilaso, aunque era mozo,    mostraba valor sobrado.
Diole al moro una lanzada    por debajo del sobaco;
el moro cayera muerto,    tendido le había en el campo.
Garcilaso con presteza    del caballo se ha apeado.
Cortárale la cabeza    y en el arzón la ha colgado.
Quitó el Ave María    de la cola del caballo.
Hincado de ambas rodillas    con devoción la ha besado,
y en la punta de la lanza    por bandera la ha colgado.
Subió en su caballo luego    y el del moro había tomado.
Cargado de estos despojos    al real se había tornado,
do estaban todos los grandes,    también el rey don Fernando.
Todos tienen a grandeza    aquel hecho señalado;
también el rey y la reina    mucho se han maravillado
en ser Garcilaso mozo    y haber hecho un tan gran caso.
Garcilaso de la Vega    desde allí se ha intitulado,
porque en la Vega hiciera    campo con aquel pagano.

## 25. Romance de don Manuel Ponce de León

—¿Cuál será aquel caballero    de los míos más preciado,
que me traiga la cabeza    de aquel moro señalado
que delante de mis ojos    a cuatro ha lanceado,
pues que las cabezas trae    en el pretal del caballo?
Oídolo ha don Manuel,    que andaba allí paseando,
que de unas viejas heridas    no estaba del todo sano.
Apriesa pide las armas,    y en un punto fue armado,
y por delante el corredor    va arremetiendo el caballo.
Con la gran fuerza que puso,    la sangre le ha reventado,
gran lástima le han las damas    de verle que va tan flaco.
Ruéganle todos que vuelva,    mas él no quiere aceptarlo.
Derecho va para el moro,    que está en la plaza parado.

and addressed him thus:   "I am not accustomed
to do pitched battle   with other than bearded men.
Go back, boy," he said,   "and let the most highly esteemed come!"
In anger Garcilaso   clapped thighs to his horse;
he charged the Moor   and clashed with him violently.
Seeing this, the Moor   turned around like lightning.
The skirmish began   with fury at the highest pitch.
Though Garcilaso was young,   he displayed extreme valor.
He gave the Moor a lance blow   beneath the armpit;
the Moor fell dead;   he had laid him out on the field.
Quickly Garcilaso   alighted from his horse.
He cut off his head   and hung it from his saddletree.
He removed the image of Mary   from the horse's tail.
Sinking to both knees,   he kissed it fervently,
and on the tip of his lance   he hung it as a banner.
At once he mounted his horse   and took the Moor's.
Laden with that booty,   he returned to the camp,
where all the grandees were,   and King Fernando, too.
They all thought his remarkable deed   showed greatness;
the king and queen, too,   were greatly amazed
that Garcilaso, being so young,   had done so great a deed.
Garcilaso de la Vega[10]   he was named thenceforth
because in the Vega he had fought   against that heathen.

## 25. Ballad of Manuel Ponce de León

"Who shall that knight be,   the most esteemed of my men,
who brings me the head   of that remarkable Moor
who, before my eyes,   has lanced four,
and now indeed bears their heads   in his horse's breast strap?"
This was heard by Don Manuel,   who was walking by,
and was not yet fully healed   of some old wounds.
Quickly he asked for armor,   and donned it in a moment,
and toward the marauder   he charged with his horse.
With the great effort he made,   his blood gushed forth,
causing the ladies great pity   to see him so weak.
Everyone begged him to return,   but he refused.
He headed straight for the Moor,   who was waiting on open ground.

---

10. "Of the Vega," the fertile plain outside of the city of Granada.

El moro, desque lo vido, de esta manera ha hablado:
—Bien sé yo, don Manuel, que vienes determinado,
y es la causa conocerme por las nuevas que te han dado;
mas, porque logres tus días, vuélvete y deja el caballo,
que yo soy el moro Muza, ese moro tan nombrado,
soy de los Amnoradíes, de quien el Cid ha temblado.
—Yo te lo agradezco, moro, que de mí tengas cuidado,
que pues las damas me envían, no volveré sin recaudo.
Y sin hablar más razones, entrambos se han apartado,
y a los primeros encuentros el moro deja el caballo,
y puso mano a un alfanje, como valiente soldado.
Fuese para don Manuel, que ya le estaba aguardando,
mas don Manuel, como diestro, la lanza le había terciado,
vara y media queda fuera, que le queda blandeando,
y desque muerto lo vido, apeóse del caballo.
Cortado ha la cabeza, y en la lanza la ha hincado,
y por delante las damas al buen rey la ha presentado.

## 26. Romance de don Manuel de León

Ese conde don Manuel, que de León es nombrado,
hizo un hecho en la corte que jamás será olvidado,
con doña Ana de Mendoza, dama de valor y estado:
y es que, después de comer, andándose paseando
por el palacio del rey, y otras damas a su lado,
y caballeros con ellas que las iban requebrando,
a unos altos miradores por descanso se han parado,
y encima la leonera la doña Ana ha asomado,
y con ella casi todos, cuatro leones mirando,
cuyos rostros y figuras ponían temor y espanto.
Y la dama por probar cuál era más esforzado,
dejóse caer el guante, al parecer, descuidado:
dice que se la ha caído, muy a pesar de su grado.
Con una voz melindrosa de esta suerte ha proposado:
—¿Cuál será aquel caballero de esfuerzo tan señalado,
que saque de entre leones el mi guante tan preciado?
Que yo le doy mi palabra que será mi requebrado;
será entre todos querido, entre todos más amado.

When the Moor saw him, he addressed him as follows:
"Don Manuel, I'm well aware you are resolved to come,
and the reason is that you know me by the news you've heard of me;
but, to prolong your days, go back and leave off riding,
for I am the Moor Muza, that Moor of such renown;
I am of the Almoravids, before whom the Cid trembled."
"I thank you, Moor, for your concern for me,
but since the ladies have sent me, I won't return without collecting a tax."
And, making no more palaver, they both drew apart,
and after the first clashes the Moor left his horse
and laid hands on a scimitar like a valiant soldier.
He charged Don Manuel, who already awaited him,
but skillful Don Manuel struck him obliquely with his lance;[11]
it protruded a yard and a half, quivering there;
and when he saw he was dead, he dismounted.
He cut off his head and impaled it on his lance,
and, in the ladies' view, he made the good king a gift of it.

## 26. Ballad of Manuel de León

That Count Manuel who is called "de León"
did a deed at court that will never be forgotten;
it was for Doña Ana de Mendoza, a lady of worth and rank.
It was this: after dining, as she went walking
in the king's palace, other ladies at her side,
and gentlemen with them paying court to them,
they stopped to relax at some high balconies,
and above the lions' pit Doña Ana looked out,
and almost all the rest with her, observing four lions
whose faces and bodies inspired fear and awe.
And the lady, to find out who was the bravest man,
dropped her glove, seemingly by accident:
she said she had dropped it greatly against her will.
In a simpering voice she made this proposal:
"Who shall that knight be, of such remarkable courage,
who will retrieve from amid the lions the glove I prize so highly?
For I give him my word to make him my sweetheart;
he'll be best loved of all, the most cherished of all."

11. Or, possibly: "drove in his lance one third of its length."

—Oído lo ha don Manuel,    caballero muy honrado,
que de la afrenta de todos    también su parte ha alcanzado.
Sacó la espada de cinta,    revolvió su manto al brazo;
entró dentro la leonera    al parecer demudado.
Los leones se lo miran,    ninguno se ha meneado:
salióse libre y exento    por la puerta do habia entrado.
Volvió la escalera arriba,    el guante en la izquierda mano,
y antes que el guante a la dama    un bofetón le hubo dado,
diciendo y mostrando bien    su esfuerzo y valor sobrado:
—Tomad, tomad, y otro día,    por un guante desastrado
no pornéis en riesgo de honra    a tanto buen fijo-dalgo;
y a quien no le pareciere    bien hecho lo ejecutado,
a ley de buen caballero    salga en campo a demandallo.
La dama le respondiera    sin mostrar rostro turbado:
—No quiero que nadie salga,    basta que tengo probado
que sedes vos, don Manuel,    entre todos más osado;
y si de ello sois servido    a vos quiero por velado:
marido quiero valiente,    que ose castigar lo malo.
En mí el refrán que se canta    se ha cumplido, ejecutado,
que dice: "El que bien te quiere,    ese te habrá castigado."
De ver que a virtud y honra    el bofetón ha aplicado,
y con cuánta mansedumbre    respondió, y cuán delicado,
muy contento y satisfecho    don Manuel se lo ha otorgado:
y allí en presencia de todos,    los dos las manos se han dado.


## 27. Romance de la muerte de Albayaldos

¡Santa Fe, cuán bien pareces    en los campos de Granada!
que en ti están duques y condes,    muchos señores de salva,
en ti estaba el buen Maestre    que dicen de Calatrava,
éste a quien temen los moros,    esos moros de Granada,
y aquese que los corría,    picándolos con su lanza,
desde la Puente de Pinos    hasta la Sierra Nevada,
y después de bien corrida    da la vuelta por Granada.
Hasta las puertas de Elvira    llegó a hincar su lanza;
las puertas eran de pino,    de claro en claro las pasa.
Sacábales los captivos    que estaban en la barbacana,
tómales los bastimentos    que vienen para Granada.
No tienen ningún moro    que a demandárselo salga,
sino fuera un moro viejo    que Penatilar se llama,

This was heard by Don Manuel,    a highly honored knight,
who received his share    of the general insult.
He drew his sword from its belt,    wrapped his cloak around his arm,
and entered the lions' pit,    looking upset.
The lions watched him,    but none moved:
free and unscathed he left    by the door through which he had entered.
He climbed back up the stairs,    the glove in his left hand,
and before giving the lady her glove    he gave her a slap,
saying, as he demonstrated    his extreme courage and valor:
"Take it, take it, and another day    for the sake of a miserable glove
do not set at risk the honor    of so many good noblemen!
And whoever doesn't consider    my action well taken,
like a true knight    let him seek justice of me in the field!"
The lady answered him    with no sign of anger on her face:
"I wish no one to challenge you;    it's enough that I've proved
that you, Don Manuel,    are the most daring of all;
and, if it's all right with you,    I want you as my spouse:
I want a valiant husband    who dares to punish evil.
In my case the well-known proverb    has proved true, has been fulfilled,
which says: 'He who loves you    will punish you.'"
Seeing that she took the slap    as a lesson in virtue and honor,
and that her reply was so gentle    and delicate,
with great contentment and satisfaction    Don Manuel granted her wish,
and there in the presence of all    they gave each other their hand.

## 27. Ballad of the Death of Albayaldos

Santa Fe, how good you look    in the fields of Granada!
For in you there are dukes and counts,    many lords of high rank;
in you there is the good Master    called "of Calatrava,"
he whom the Moors fear,    the Moors of Granada,
the man who raids their land,    piercing them with his lance,
from Puente de Pinos    to the Sierra Nevada;
after a good raid    he returned to Granada.
In the very gates of Elvira    he succeeded in thrusting his lance;
the gates were of pine,    but he pierced them clean through.
He rescued the prisoners    who were in the barbican
and took away the provisions    that were coming to Granada.
They had no Moor    who would ride out and challenge him,
except for one old Moor    named Penatilar,

que salió con dos mil moros,   y volvió huyendo a Granada.
Sabido lo ha Albayaldos   allá allende do estaba,
hiciera armar un navío,   pasara la mar salada.
Sálenselo a recibir   esos moros de Granada,
allá se lo aposentaban   en lo alto de la Alhambra.
Íbaselo a ver el rey,   el rey Alijar de Granada:
—Bien vengades, Albayaldos,   buena sea vuestra llegada.
Si venís a ganar sueldo,   dároslo he de buena gana,
y si venís por mujer,   dárseos ha mora lozana:
de tres hijas que yo tengo,   dárseos ha la más gallarda.
—¡Mahoma te guarde, rey,   Alá sea la tu guarda!
que no vengo a ganar sueldo,   que en mis tierras lo pagaba;
ni vengo a tomar mujer,   porque yo casado estaba;
mas una nueva es venida   de la cual a mí pesaba,
que vos corría la tierra   el Maestre de Calatrava,
y que sin ningún temor   hasta la ciudad llegaba,
y que por la puerta de Elvira   atestaba la su lanza,
y que nadie de vosotros   demandárselo osaba.
A esto vengo yo, el rey,   a esto fue mi llegada,
para prender al Maestre,   y traelle por la barba.
Allí habló luego un moro   que era alguacil de Granada;
—Calles, calles, Albayaldos,   no digas la tal palabra,
que si vieses al Maestre   temblar te hía la barba,
porque es muy buen caballero   y esforzado en la batalla.
Cuando lo oyó Albayaldos,   enojadamente habla:
—Calles, calles, perro moro,   si no darte he una bofetada,
porque yo soy caballero,   y cumpliré mi palabra.
—Si me la das, Albayaldos,   serte ha bien demandada.
El rey desque vio esto   el guante en medio arrojara:
—Calledes vos, alguacil,   no se os debe dar nada,
que Albayaldos es mancebo;   no miró lo que hablaba.
Allí hablara Albayaldos,   al rey de esta suerte habla:
—Dédesme vos dos mil moros,   los que a mí me agradaban,
y a ese fraile capilludo   yo os le traeré por la barba.
Diérale el rey dos mil moros,   lo que él le señalara:
todos los toma mancebos,   casado no le agradaba.
Sabídolo ha el Maestre   allá en Santa Fe do estaba,
salióselos a recibir   por aquella vega llana
con quinientos comendadores,   que entonces más no alcanzaba.
A los primeros encuentros   un comendador a pie anda;
Avendaño habia por nombre,   Avendaño se llamaba.

who sallied out with two thousand Moors    and fled back to Granada.
This was learned by Albayaldos    where he was staying;
he had a ship fitted out    and crossed the salt sea.
The Moors of Granada    came out to welcome him;
they lodged him there    on the heights of the Alhambra.
The king went to see him,    king Alijar of Granada:
"Welcome, Albayaldos,    may your coming be lucky!
If you've come to earn pay,    I'll give it to you gladly;
if you've come for a wife,    I'll give you a sprightly Moorish woman:
of three daughters that I have    I'll give you the most graceful."
"Mohammed keep you, king,    Allah be your guard!
I come not to earn pay,    for in my land I disburse it;
nor do I come to take a wife,    for I am married;
but news has come    that grieved me:
that your land is being raided    by the Master of Calatrava,
and that, showing no fear,    he came right up to the city
and in the gate of Elvira    thrust his lance,
and that none of you    dared to call him out for it.
For this I have come, king,    for this purpose was my arrival,
to capture the Master    and drag him by his beard."
Then a Moor spoke up    who was the constable of Granada:
"Be still, be still, Albayaldos,    don't say such things,
for it you saw the Master,    your beard would tremble,
since he's a very good knight    and courageous in battle."
When Albayaldos heard this,    he said angrily:
"Be still, be still, dog of a Moor,    or else I'll slap you,
for I am a knight    and I'll keep my word."
"If you slap me, Albayaldos,    I'll surely requite you for it."
When the king saw this,    he threw his glove between them:
"Be still, constable,    he has incurred no fault with you,
for Albayaldos is young;    he didn't know what he was saying."
Then Albayaldos spoke up,    addressing the king as follows:
"Give me two thousand Moors,    the ones that please me,
and that cowled friar    I'll drag to you by the beard."
The king gave him two thousand Moors,    the ones he indicated:
he chose none but young men,    he didn't want married men.
The Master learned of this    there at Santa Fe where he was;
he rode out to meet them    on that flat plain
with five hundred commanders of his Order,    all he could then muster.
At the first encounter,    one commander lost his mount;
his name was Avendaño,    Avendaño he was called.

Punchándole anda Albayaldos　con la punta de la lanza,
a grandes voces diciendo,　con su lanza ensangrentada:
—Date, date, capilludo,　a la casa de Granada.
—¡Ni por vos, el moro perro,　ni por la vuestra compaña!
Ellos en aquesto estando,　el Maestre que allegaba,
a grandes voces diciendo:　*¡Santiago!* y *¡Calatrava!*
Álzase en los estribos,　y la lanza le arrojaba;
dióle por el corazón,　salido le había a la espalda.
Como ovejas sin pastor　que andan descaminadas,
ansí andaban los moros　desque Albayaldos faltara,
que de dos mil y quinientos　treinta solos escaparan,
los cuales vuelven huyendo,　y se encierran en Granada.
Bien lo ha visto el rey moro　de las torres donde estaba;
si miedo tenía de antes,　mucho más allí cobrara.

## 28. Romance de Sayavedra

Río Verde, Río Verde,　más negro vas que la tinta.
Entre ti y Sierra Bermeja　murió gran caballería.
Mataron a Ordiales,　Sayavedra huyendo iba;
con el temor de los moros　entre un jaral se metía.
Tres días ha, con sus noches,　que bocado no comía;
aquejábale la sed　y la hambre que tenía.
Por buscar algún remedio　al camino se salía.
Visto lo habían los moros　que andan por la serranía.
Los moros, desque lo vieron,　luego para él se venían.
Unos dicen: —¡Muera, muera!,　otros dicen: —¡Viva, viva!
Tómanle entre todos ellos,　bien acompañado iba.
Allá le van a presentar　al rey de la morería.
Desque el rey moro lo vido,　bien oiréis lo que decía:
—¿Quién es ese caballero　que ha escapado con la vida?
—Sayavedra es, señor,　Sayavedra el de Sevilla;
el que mataba tus moros　y tu gente destruía,
el que hacía cabalgadas　y se encerraba en su manida.
Allí hablara el rey moro,　bien oiréis lo que decía:
—Dígasme tú, Sayavedra,　sí Alá te alargue la vida,
si en tu tierra me tuvieses　¿qué honra tú me harías?
Allí habló Sayavedra,　de esta suerte le decía:
—Yo te lo diré, señor,　nada no te mentiría:
si cristiano te tornases,　grande honra te haría

Albayaldos was pricking him    with the tip of his lance,
shouting loudly,    his lance bloodied:
"Surrender, surrender, man in the cowl,    to the house of Granada!"
"Not to you, dog of a Moor,    or to your followers!"
While they were talking thus,    the Master rode up,
shouting loudly    "Santiago!" and "Calatrava!"
He stood up in his stirrups    and hurled his lance at him;
he struck him in the heart,    and it came out his back.
Like sheep without a shepherd    that go astray,
thus went the Moors    after the loss of Albayaldos,
for out of two thousand five hundred    only thirty escaped,
who returned in flight    and shut themselves up in Granada.
The Moorish king saw this clearly    from the towers where he stood;
if he had felt fear previously,    he felt much more then.

## 28. Ballad of Sayavedra

Río Verde, Río Verde,    you run blacker than ink.
Between you and Sierra Bermeja    many horsemen died.
Ordiales was killed,    Sayavedra fled;
out of fear of the Moors    he hid in the brush.
Three days and three nights    he ate not a morsel;
he suffered from thirst    and the hunger he felt.
To seek some relief    he went out onto the road.
He was seen by the Moors    who roamed the mountains.
When the Moors saw him    they pursued him at once.
Some said: "He shall die!"    Others said: "Let him live!"
He was caught between them    and proceeded in numerous company.
There they made a gift of him    to the king of Moors' land.
When the Moorish king saw him,    you'll hear what he said:
"Who is this knight    that has escaped with his life?"
"It's Sayavedra, sire,    Sayavedra of Seville,
he who killed your Moors    and destroyed your people,
he who made incursions    and then hid away in his lair."
Then the Moorish king spoke,    you'll hear what he said:
"Tell me, Sayavedra    (so may Allah lengthen your days!),
if you had me in your land,    what honor would you pay me?"
Then Sayavedra spoke up,    pronouncing these words:
"I'll tell you, sire,    nor will I lie to you:
if you became a Christian,    I'd pay you great honor,

y si así no lo hicieses,    muy bien te castigaría:
la cabeza de los hombros    luego te la cortaría.
—Calles, calles, Sayavedra,    cese tu melancolía;
tórnate moro si quieres    y verás qué te daría:
darte he villas y castillos    y joyas de gran valía.
Gran pesar ha Sayavedra    de esto que decir oía.
Con una voz rigurosa,    de esta suerte respondía:
—Muera, muera Sayavedra,    la fe no renegaría,
que mientras vida tuviere    la fe yo defendería.
Allí hablara el rey moro    y de esta suerte decía:
—Prendedlo, mis caballeros,    y de él me haced justicia.
Echó mano a su espada,    de todos se defendía;
mas como era uno solo,    allí hizo fin su vida.

## 29. Romance de don Alonso de Aguilar

Estando el rey don Fernando    en conquista de Granada
con valientes capitanes    de la nobleza de España:
armados estaban todos    de ricas y fuertes armas.
El rey los llama en su tienda    un lunes por la mañana.
Desque los tuviera juntos,    de esta manera les habla:
—¿Cuál será aquel caballero    que, por ensalzar su fama,
mostrando su gran esfuerzo    sube a la sierra mañana?
Unos a otros se miran,    el *sí* ninguno le daba,
que la ida es peligrosa,    mucho más es la tornada;
con el temor que tienen    a todos tiembla la barba.
Levantóse don Alonso    que de Aguilar se llamaba.
—Yo subiré allá, buen rey,    desde ahora lo aceptaba;
tal empresa como aquesa    para mí estaba guardada.
Quiero morir o vencer    aquesa gente pagana:
que si Dios me da salud    la injuria será vengada.
Armóse luego ante el rey    de las sus armas preciadas;
saltó sobre un gran caballo,    y su escudo embrazara;
gruesa lanza con dos hierros    en la su mano llevaba.
Valiente va don Alonso,    su esfuerzo gran temor daba;
van con él sus caballeros,    toda su noble compaña.
Entre moros y cristianos    se traba cruel batalla:
los moros, como son muchos,    a los cristianos maltratan.
Huyendo van los cristianos,    huyendo por una playa.
Esfuérzalos don Alonso    diciendo tales palabras:

but if you didn't,    I'd punish you severely:
I'd immediately cut your head    off your shoulders."
"Be still, be still, Sayavedra,    let your melancholy cease;
become a Moor if you wish    and you'll see what I'll give you:
I'll give you towns and castles    and gems of great value."
Sayavedra was deeply grieved    by the words he had heard.
In a stern voice    he replied as follows:
"Let Sayavedra die, die;    I won't renounce my religion,
because as long as I live    I'll defend my faith."
Then the Moorish king spoke,    saying these words:
"Seize him, my knights,    and execute him for me!"
He laid hands to his sword,    he defended himself against all,
but since he was alone there,    his life came to an end.

## 29. Ballad of Alonso de Aguilar

While King Fernando    was conquering Granada
with valiant captains    from the nobility of Spain,
everyone was clad    in costly, strong armor.
The king called them to his tent    one Monday morning.
When they were assembled,    he addressed them thus:
"Who shall that knight be    who, to enhance his fame
and show his great courage,    will ascend the hills tomorrow?"
They looked at one another,    but no one agreed to do it,
for the way there was perilous    and the way back even more so;
they were so afraid    that their beards trembled.
Then there arose Don Alonso,    called Alonso de Aguilar.
"I'll go up there, good king;    I accept as of this moment;
an enterprise like this    was reserved for me alone.
I shall either die or conquer    that heathen folk:
for if God lets me live,    our affront will be avenged."
At once, in front of the king, he donned    his costly armor;
he leaped onto a tall horse    and grasped his shield;
a thick lance with two points    he carried in his hand.
Don Alonso proceeded bravely,    his courage instilling great fear;
with him went his knights,    all his noble company.
Between Moors and Christians    a cruel battle was joined:
since the Moors outnumbered them,    they manhandled the Christians.
The Christians fled,    fled down a riverbank.
Don Alonso encouraged them,    speaking these words:

—¡Vuelta, vuelta, caballeros,   vuelta, vuelta a la batalla!
que aunque ellos eran muchos,   cobarde es el que desmaya.
Acordaos del gran esfuerzo   de la gente castellana.
Mejor es aquí morir   ejercitando las armas,
que no vivir con deshonra   con vida tan aviltada:
que muriendo viviremos,   pues vivirá nuestra fama,
que la vida presto muere,   la honra mucho duraba.
Con estas palabras todos   muy gran esfuerzo tomaban;
murieron como valientes,   ninguno con vida escapa.
Solo queda don Alonso,   el cual, blandiendo su lanza,
se mete entre los moros   con crecida y grande saña;
a muchos quita la vida,   a otros muy mal los llaga.
En torno lo cercan moros   con grita y gran algazara.
Tantos moros tiene muertos,   que sus cuerpos lo amparaban.
Cércanlo de todas partes,   muy malamente lo llagan;
siete lanzadas tenía,   todas el cuerpo le pasan.
Muerto yace don Alonso,   su sangre la tierra baña.
Llorando está, llorando   una captiva cristiana
que cuando niño pequeño   a sus pechos le criara.
Estaba cerca del cuerpo,   arañando la su cara;
tanto llora la captiva,   que de llorar se desmaya,
y después de vuelta en sí   con don Alonso se abraza,
besaba el cuerpo defunto,   en lágrimas lo bañaba,
torcía sus blancas manos,   los ojos al cielo alzaba,
los gritos que estaba dando   junto a los cielos llegaban,
las lástimas que decía   los corazones traspasan:
—¡Don Alonso, don Alonso!   ¡Dios perdone la tu alma!
que te mataron los moros,   los moros del Alpujarra:
no se tiene por buen moro   quien no te daba lanzada.
Lloren todos como yo,   lloren tu muerte temprana,
llórete el rey don Fernando,   tu vida poco lograda,
llore Aguilar y Montilla   tal señor cómo le matan,
lloren todos los cristianos   pérdida tan lastimada;
llore ese Gran Capitán   pérdida tan señalada,
que muerte de tal hermano   razón es, la gima y plaña:
que tu esfuerzo tan crecido   esta muerte te causara.
Dechado tomen los buenos   para tomar noble fama,
pues murió como valiente,   y no en regalos de damas;
murió como caballero,   matando gente pagana.
Y estas palabras diciendo,   otra vez se traspasaba.
Llegó allí un moro viejo,   la barba crecida y cana.

"Back, back, knights,   back, back to the battle!
For, though they are many,   he who loses heart is a coward.
Remember the great courage   of the Castilian people.
It's better to die here   using our weapons
than to live in dishonor   with a life so besmirched:
for in death we shall live,   since our fame shall live,
because life passes quickly   but honor lasts long."
At these words they all   regained great courage;
they died like brave men,   not one escaping alive.
The only one left was Don Alonso,   who, brandishing his lance,
plunged into the Moors   with great, extreme fury;
he took many lives   and wounded others very badly.
The Moors surrounded him   with shouts and loud war cries.
He killed so many Moors   that the heap of bodies protected him.
He was surrounded on all sides   and very badly wounded;
he had seven lance wounds,   all of which pierced his body.
Don Alonso lay dead,   his blood soaking the earth.
Weeping there, weeping, stood   a female Christian captive
who, when he was a small boy,   had nursed him at her breast.
She stood near his body,   scratching her face;
the captive wept so much   that she fainted from her weeping;
after she came to,   she embraced Don Alonso,
kissed his dead body,   bathed him in tears,
wrung her white hands,   and raised her eyes to heaven;
the cries she uttered   reached the skies;
the pity she expressed   was heart-rending:
"Don Alonso, Don Alonso!   God have mercy on your soul!
For you were killed by the Moors,   the Moors of Alpujarra:
the man who failed to spear you   doesn't consider himself a good Moor.
Let everyone weep as I do,   weep your untimely death;
let King Fernando weep for you   and your too-brief life;
let Aguilar and Montilla weep   for the death of such a lord;
let all Christians weep   for such a pitiful loss;
let the Great Captain weep   for such a preeminent loss,
for the death of such a brother   deserves moaning and tears:
for your extreme courage   caused you to die this way.
Let good men take example   to gain a noble reputation,
since he died like a brave man,   and not in the soft company of ladies;
he died like a knight,   slaying heathen folk."
And saying these words,   again she felt great pain.
An old Moor came there,   his beard long and white.

—No quiera Alá, dijo a voces,   a ti más ofensa se haga.
Echó mano a un alfanje,   la cabeza le cortara;
tomóla por los cabellos,   para su rey la llevaba,
diciendo: —Tal caballero   esforzado y de tal fama,
no es justo siendo muerto,   que tal baldón se le haga.
El rey moro que lo vido,   gran pesar de ello cobrara;
el cuerpo manda traer   de allí donde muerto estaba.
Enviólo al rey don Fernando,   y la cabeza cortada;
el rey hubo gran placer   en que muerto le cobraba,
que puesto que allí muriera,   su fama siempre volaba.

He said loudly: "Allah forbid    that you be affronted any longer!"
He laid hands on a scimitar    and cut off his head;
he picked it up by the hair    and brought it to his king,
saying: "A knight like this,    brave and so renowned,
should not, when dead,    be so insulted."
When the Moorish king saw this,    it grieved him greatly;
he ordered that the body be brought    from where it lay dead.
He sent it to King Fernando    along with the severed head;
the king was greatly pleased    to recover his dead body,
for although he died in that place,    his renown soars forever.

# Romances carolingios

## 30. Romance del conde Guarinos

¡Mala la vistes, franceses,    la caza de Roncesvalles!
Don Carlos perdió la honra,    murieron los doce pares,
cativaron a Guarinos    almirante de las mares:
los siete reyes de moros    fueron en su cativar.
Siete veces echan suertes    cuál de ellos lo ha de llevar;
todas siete le cupieron    a Marlotes el infante.
Más lo preciara Marlotes    que Arabia con su ciudad.
Dícele de esta manera,    y empezóle de hablar:
—Por Alá te ruego, Guarinos,    moro te quieras tornar;
de los bienes de este mundo    yo te quiero dar asaz.
Las dos hijas que yo tengo    ambas te las quiero dar,
la una para el vestir,    para vestir y calzar,
la otra para tu mujer,    tu mujer la natural.
Darte he en arras y dote    Arabia con su ciudad;
si más quisieses, Guarinos,    mucho más te quiero dar.
Allí hablara Guarinos,    bien oiréis lo que dirá:
—¡No lo mande Dios del cielo    ni Santa María su Madre,
que deje la fe de Cristo    por la de Mahoma tomar,
que esposica tengo en Francia,    con ella entiendo casar!
Marlotes con gran enojo    en cárceles lo manda echar
con esposas a las manos    porque pierda el pelear;
el agua fasta la cinta    porque pierda el cabalgar;
siete quintales de fierro    desde el hombro al calcañar.
En tres fiestas que hay en el año    le mandaba justiciar;
la una Pascua de Mayo,    la otra por Navidad,
la otra Pascua de Flores,    esa fiesta general.
Vanse días, vienen días,    venido era el de San Juan,
donde cristianos y moros    hacen gran solemnidad.

74

# Ballads of Charlemagne and His Peers

## 30. Ballad of Count Guarinos

It was an evil event for you, Frenchmen,    that pursuit at Roncesvalles!
King Carlos lost his honor,    his twelve peers died,
and Guarinos was captured,    the admiral of the seas:
the seven Moorish kings    took part in his capture.
Seven times they cast lots    to see which one would take him;
all seven times they fell    to Prince Marlotes.
Marlotes valued him more    than Arabia and its capital city.
He spoke to him thus    as he began to address him:
"By Allah I beseech you, Guarinos,    to become a Moor;
of the good things of this world    I shall give you plenty.
The two daughters I have    I will give you, both of them,
one to put on your clothes,    your clothes and shoes,
the other to be your wife,    your lawful wife.
I'll give you as bride gift and dowry    Arabia and its capital;
if you want more, Guarinos,    I'll give you much more."
Then Guarinos spoke up,    you shall hear what he had to say:
"May God in heaven forbid it,    and St. Mary His Mother,
that I should abandon the Christian faith    and accept that of Mohammed,
for I have a betrothed in France    whom I intend to marry!"
In great anger Marlotes    ordered him thrown into jail
with handcuffs on his wrists,    so he'd lose the power to fight,
with water up to his waist,    so he'd lose the skill to ride,
with fifteen hundred pounds of iron    from his shoulders to his heels.
On the three high holidays of the year    he ordered him beaten,
once at Pentecost,    once at Christmas,
and once at Easter,    that universal feast.
Days came, days went,    St. John's Day arrived,
when Christians and Moors    perform great ceremonies.

Los cristianos echan juncia,    y los moros arrayán;
los judíos echan eneas    por la fiesta más honrar.
Marlotes con alegría    un tablado mandó armar,
ni más chico ni más grande,    que al cielo quiere llegar.
Los moros con alegría    empiézanle de tirar:
tira el uno, tira el otro,    no llegan a la mitad.
Marlotes con enconía    un plegón mandara dar,
que los chicos no mamasen,    ni los grandes coman pan,
fasta que aquel tablado    en tierra haya de estar.
Oyó el estruendo Guarinos    en las cárceles do está:
—¡Oh válasme Dios del cielo    y Santa María su Madre!
o casan hija de rey,    o la quieren desposar,
o era venido el día    que me suelen justiciar.
Oídolo ha el carcelero    que cerca se fue a hallar:
—No casan hija de rey,    ni la quieren desposar,
ni es venida la Pascua    que te suelen azotar;
mas era venido un día,    el cual llaman de San Juan,
cuando los que están contentos    con placer comen su pan.
Marlotes de gran placer    un tablado mandó armar;
el altura que tenía    al cielo quiere allegar.
Hanle tirado los moros,    no le pueden derribar;
Marlotes de enojado    un plegón mandara dar,
que ninguno no comiese    fasta habello de derribar.
Allí respondió Guarinos,    bien oiréis qué fue a hablar:
—Si vos me dais mi caballo,    en que solía cabalgar,
y me diésedes mis armas,    las que yo solía armar,
y me diésedes mi lanza,    la que solía llevar,
aquellos tablados altos    yo los entiendo derribar,
y si no los derribase    que me mandasen matar.
El carcelero que esto oyera    comenzóle de hablar:
—¡Siete años había, siete    que estás en este lugar,
que no siento hombre del mundo    que un año pudiese estar,
y aún dices que tienes fuerza    para el tablado derribar!
Mas espera tú, Guarinos,    que yo lo iré a contar
a Marlotes el infante    por ver lo que me dirá.
Ya se parte el carcelero,    ya se parte, ya se va;
como fue cerca del tablado    a Marlotes fue a hablar:
—Unas nuevas vos traía    queráismelas escuchar:
sabé que aquel prisionero    aquesto dicho me ha:
que si le diesen su caballo,    el que solía cabalgar,
y le diesen las sus armas,    que él se solía armar,

The Christians strew sedge;   the Moors, myrtle;
the Jews strew bulrushes   in honor of the holiday.
Cheerfully Marlotes   had scaffolding erected for javelin hurling,
of precisely such a height   that it almost reached the sky.
Cheerfully the Moors   began to hurl;
one hurls, another hurls,   they don't reach even its midpoint.
In rancor Marlotes   had a proclamation made
that infants were not to suckle   nor adults to eat bread
until that scaffolding   was knocked down to the ground.
Guarinos heard the din   in the prison where he was:
"May God in heaven stand by me,   and St. Mary His Mother!
Either they're marrying off a daughter of the king   or she's being betrothed,
or the day has come   when they usually beat me."
This was heard by the jailer,   who was nearby:
"No daughter of the king is being married   or betrothed,
nor has the holiday arrived   when they usually lash you;
but the day has come   that is called St. John's,
when those who are contented   eat their bread gladly.
With great pleasure Marlotes   had scaffolding erected;
it's so high,   it almost reaches the sky.
The Moors have hurled at it   but can't topple it;
Marlotes in his anger   has issued a proclamation
that no one is to eat   until it is toppled."
Then Guarinos replied,   you shall hear what he said:
"If you give me my horse,   the one I used to ride,
and give me my armor,   the suit I used to wear,
and give me my lance,   the one I used to wield,
that lofty scaffolding   I intend to topple,
and if I don't topple it,   let them have me killed."
Hearing this, the jailer   began to address him:
"It's seven years, seven,   that you've been in this place,
where I wouldn't think that anyone   could last a year,
and you still claim to have the strength   to topple the scaffold!
But just you wait, Guarinos,   for I shall go and report this
to Prince Marlotes   to see what he will tell me."
Now the jailer departs,   now he departs, now he leaves;
when he was near the scaffold,   he said to Marlotes:
"I bring you news   which I beg you to listen to:
know that the prisoner   has told me this:
if they give him his horse,   the one he used to ride,
and give him his armor,   the suit he used to wear,

que aquestos tablados altos    él los entiende derribar.
Marlotes de que esto oyera    de allí lo mandó sacar;
por mirar si en caballo    él podría cabalgar,
mandó buscar su caballo,    y mandáraselo dar,
que siete años son pasados    que andaba llevando cal.
Armáronlo de sus armas,    que bien mohosas están.
Marlotes desque lo vido    con reír y con burlar
dice que vaya al tablado    y lo quiera derribar.
Guarinos con grande furia    un encuentro le fue a dar,
que más de la mitad dél    en el suelo fue a echar.
Los moros de que esto vieron    todos le quieren matar;
Guarinos como esforzado    comenzó de pelear
con los moros, que eran tantos,    que el sol querían quitar.
Peleara de tal suerte    que él se hubo de soltar,
y se fuera a su tierra    a Francia la natural:
grandes honras le hicieron    cuando le vieron llegar.

## 31. Romance de doña Alda

En París está doña Alda,    la esposa de don Roldán,
trescientas damas con ella    para la acompañar:
todas visten un vestido,    todas calzan un calzar,
todas comen a una mesa,    todas comían de un pan,
sino era doña Alda    que era la mayoral;
las ciento hilaban oro,    las ciento tejen cendal,
las ciento tañen instrumentos    para doña Alda holgar.
Al son de los instrumentos    doña Alda adormido se ha,
ensoñado había un sueño,    un sueño de gran pesar.
Recordó despavorida    y con un pavor muy grande,
los gritos daba tan grandes    que se oían en la ciudad.
Allí hablaron sus doncellas,    bien oiréis lo que dirán:
—¿Qué es aquesto, mi señora?    ¿quién es el que os hizo mal?
—Un sueño soñé, doncellas,    que me ha dado gran pesar:
que me veía en un monte    en un desierto lugar;
de so los montes muy altos    un azor vide volar,
tras dél viene una aguililla    que lo ahinca muy mal.
El azor, con grande cuita,    metióse so mi brial,
el aguililla, con grande ira,    de allí lo iba a sacar;
con las uñas lo despluma,    con el pico lo deshace.
Allí habló su camarera,    bien oiréis lo que dirá:

this lofty scaffolding    he intends to topple."
When Marlotes heard this,    he ordered him taken out of there;
to see whether he could    sit a horse,
he had his horse fetched    and ordered it given to him;
seven years had gone by    since it had trodden a street.
They dressed him in his armor,    which was very rusty.
When Marlotes saw him,    he laughed and mocked,
telling him to go to the scaffold    and try to knock it down.
With great fury Guarinos    dashed toward it,
so that more than half of it    crashed to the ground.
When the Moors saw this,    they all wanted to kill him;
like the brave man he was, Guarinos    began to fight
with the Moors, who were so numerous    they almost blocked out the sun.
He fought so well    that he managed to get free
and returned to his country,    his homeland France:
they paid him great honor    when they saw him arrive.

## 31. Ballad of Doña Alda

Doña Alda is in Paris,    the betrothed of Don Roldán,
three hundred ladies with her    to keep her company:
all wear the same gowns,    all wear the same shoes,
all eat at one table,    all eat the same food,
except for Doña Alda,    who is of higher rank:
a hundred spin gold,    a hundred weave fine silk,
a hundred play instruments    to entertain Doña Alda.
To the sound of the instruments    Doña Alda has fallen asleep,
she has dreamed a dream,    a very grievous dream.
She awoke in fright    and with very great fear;
her shrieks were so loud    they could be heard in town.
Then her maidens spoke,    you shall hear what they said:
"What's this, my lady?    Who has harmed you?"
"I dreamed a dream, maidens,    that gave me much grief:
I found myself on a mountain    in a wilderness:
from under the very high mountains    I saw a goshawk fly;
behind it came a young eagle,    which attacked it violently.
The hawk, in great distress,    hid beneath my gown;
the eagle, in a great rage,    came to take it from there:
it plucked it with its talons,    it mangled it with its beak."
Then her lady's maid spoke,    you shall hear what she said:

—Aquese sueño, señora,   bien os lo entiendo soltar:
el azor es vuestro esposo   que viene de allén la mar,
el águila sodes vos,   con la cual ha de casar,
y aquel monte es la iglesia   donde os han de velar.
—Si así es, mi camarera,   bien te lo entiendo pagar.
Otro día de mañana   cartas de fuera le traen;
tintas venían por dentro,   de fuera escritas con sangre,
que su Roldán era muerto   en la caza de Roncesvalles.

## 32. Romance del conde Claros de Montalván

Media noche era por filo,   los gallos querían cantar,
conde Claros con amores   no podía reposar:
dando muy grandes sospiros   que el amor le hacía dar,
por amor de Claraniña   no le deja sosegar.
Cuando vino la mañana   que quería alborear,
salto diera de la cama   que parece un gavilán.
Voces da por el palacio,   y empezara de llamar:
—Levantá, mi camarero,   dame vestir y calzar.
Presto estaba el camarero   para habérselo de dar:
diérale calzas de grana,   borceguís de cordobán;
diérale jubón de seda   aforrado en zarzahán;
diérale un manto rico   que no se puede apreciar;
trescientas piedras preciosas   al derredor del collar;
tráele un rico caballo   que en la corte no hay su par,
que la silla con el freno   bien valía una ciudad,
con trescientos cascabeles   al rededor del petral;
los ciento eran de oro,   y los ciento de metal,
y los ciento son de plata   por los sones concordar;
y vase para el palacio   para el palacio real.
A la infanta Claraniña   allí la fuera hallar,
trescientas damas con ella   que la van acompañar.
Tan linda va Claraniña,   que a todos hace penar.
Conde Claros que la vido   luego va descabalgar;
las rodillas por el suelo   le comenzó de hablar:
—Mantenga Dios a tu Alteza.   —Conde Claros, bien vengáis.
Las palabras que prosigue   eran para enamorar:
—Conde Claros, conde Claros,   el señor de Montalván,
¡cómo habéis hermoso cuerpo   para con moros lidiar!
Respondiera el conde Claros,   tal respuesta le fue a dar:

"That dream, my lady,    I can interpret for you clearly:
the hawk is your betrothed,    who's coming from overseas;
the eagle is you,    whom he is to marry;
and that mountain is the church    where you are to be wed."
"If that's the case, my servant,    I shall pay you well for it."
On the following morning    she was brought a letter from afar;
it was red inside,    written with blood on the outside,
saying that her Roldán had died    in the pursuit at Roncesvalles.

## 32. Ballad of Count Claros of Montalván

It was the stroke of midnight,    the cocks were about to crow;
for love, Count Claros    was unable to rest:
heaving mighty sighs    that love made him utter,
his love for Claraniña    gave him no peace.
When morning came    and day was about to break,
he jumped out of bed    swiftly as a sparrow hawk.
He shouted in the palace    and began to call:
"Arise, my valet,    bring me clothes and shoes!"
His valet was soon there    to bring him what he wanted:
he gave him scarlet breeches,    half-boots of Cordovan leather;
he gave him a silk doublet    lined with thin striped silk;
he gave him a costly cloak    whose price can't be calculated;
three hundred precious stones    circled the collar;
he brought him a fine horse    with no equal at the court:
its saddle and bridle    were surely worth a city,
with three hundred jingle bells    on its breast strap,
a hundred of gold,    a hundred of brass,
and a hundred of silver    for perfect harmony.
He went to the palace,    to the king's palace.
Princess Claraniña    he found there,
with her three hundred ladies    keeping her company.
Claraniña looked so lovely    that she made everyone pine.
When Count Claros saw her,    he dismounted at once;
kneeling on the ground,    he began to speak:
"God keep Your Highness!"    "Count Claros, welcome!"
The words she said next    cast a spell of love:
"Count Claros, Count Claros,    lord of Montalván,
how handsome is your body    for battling Moors!"
Count Claros replied,    he made this answer:

—Mi cuerpo tengo, señora,     para con damas holgar:
si yo os tuviese esta noche,     señora, a mi mandar,
otro día en la mañana     con cien moros pelear,
si a todos no los venciese     que me mandase matar.
—Calledes, conde, calledes,     y no os queráis alabar:
el que quiere servir damas     así lo suele hablar,
y al entrar en las batallas     bien se saben excusar.
—Si no lo creéis, señora,     por las obras se verá:
siete años son pasados     que os empecé de amar,
que de noche yo no duermo,     ni de día puedo holgar.
—Siempre os preciastes, conde,     de las damas os burlar;
mas déjame ir a los baños,     a los baños a bañar;
cuando yo sea bañada     estoy a vuestro mandar.
Respondiérale el buen conde,     tal respuesta le fue a dar:
—Bien sabedes vos, señora,     que soy cazador real;
caza que tengo en la mano     nunca la puedo dejar.
Tomárala por la mano,     para un vergel se van;
a la sombra de un aciprés,     debajo de un rosal,
de la cintura arriba     tan dulces besos se dan,
de la cintura abajo     como hombre y mujer se han.
Mas la fortuna adversa     que a placeres da pesar,
por ahí pasó un cazador,     que no debía de pasar,
detrás de una podenca,     que rabia debía matar.
Vido estar al conde Claros     con la infanta a bel holgar.
El conde cuando le vido     empezóle de llamar:
—Ven acá tú, el cazador,     así Dios te guarde de mal:
de todo lo que has visto     tú nos tengas poridad.
Darte he yo mil marcos de oro,     y si más quisieres, más;
casarte he con una doncella     que era mi prima carnal;
darte he en arras y en dote     la villa de Montalván:
de otra parte la infanta     mucho más te puede dar.
El cazador sin ventura     no les quiso escuchar:
vase por los palacios     ado el buen rey está.
—Manténgate Dios, el rey,     y a tu corona real:
una nueva yo te traigo     dolorosa y de pesar,
que no os cumple traer corona     ni en caballo cabalgar.
La corona de la cabeza     bien la podéis vos quitar,
si tal deshonra como ésta     la hubieseis de comportar,
que he hallado la infanta     con Claros de Montalván,
besándola y abrazando     en vuestro huerto real:
de la cintura abajo     como hombre y mujer se han.

"Highness, I have this body    for sporting with ladies:
if I had you tonight    at my command, Highness,
tomorrow morning    I'd fight a hundred Moors;
if I didn't beat them all,    let me be put to death!"
"Be still, count, be still,    and refrain from boasting:
men who wish to court ladies    are wont to say such things,
but when time comes for battle    they always have some excuse."
"If you don't believe me, Highness,    my actions will prove it:
it's been seven years now    since I first fell in love with you;
at night I can't sleep,    by day I have no joy."
"You've always boasted, count,    about your powers of seduction;
but let me go to the bath,    to bathe in the bath;
after I've bathed,    I'll be at your service."
The good count replied,    he made this answer:
"You're well aware, Highness,    that I'm a splendid huntsman;
quarry I hold in my hand    I never let go."
He took her by the hand,    they went to an orchard;
in the shade of a cypress,    beneath a rosebush,
above the belt    they kissed each other sweetly,
below the belt    they did as man and woman do.
But adverse fortune,    which turns pleasures to pain,
caused a hunter to pass by    who had no business there,
but was seeking his spaniel    (may it die of rabies!).
He saw Count Claros there    frolicking with the princess.
When the count saw him,    he began to call:
"Come here, huntsman,    so may God keep you from harm:
all that you've seen,    keep it secret for us.
I'll give you a thousand marks in gold    and more if you like;
I'll wed you to a young lady    who's my own cousin;
as bride gift and dowry I'll give you    the town of Montalván:
on her part the princess    can give you much more."
The accursed hunter    refused to heed them:
he went to the palace,    where the good king was.
"God keep you, king,    and your royal crown!
I bring you news    painful and grievous:
it doesn't behoove you to wear a crown    or ride a horse.
The crown from your head    you may well remove,
if you are to tolerate    a dishonor like this;
for I have found the princess    with Claros of Montalván,
kissing and embracing her    in your royal garden:
from the belt down    they were doing as man and woman do."

El rey con muy grande enojo    al cazador mandó matar,
porque había sido osado    de tales nuevas llevar.
Mandó llamar sus alguaciles    apriesa, no de vagar,
mandó armar quinientos hombres    que le hayan de acompañar,
para que prendan al conde    y le hayan de tomar
y mandó cerrar las puertas,    las puertas de la ciudad.
A las puertas del palacio    allá le fueron a hallar,
preso llevan al buen conde    con mucha seguridad,
unos grillos a los pies,    que bien pesan un quintal;
las esposas a las manos,    que era dolor de mirar;
una cadena a su cuello,    que de hierro era el collar.
Cabálganle en una mula    por más deshonra le dar;
metiéronle en una torre    de muy gran escuridad:
las llaves de la prisión    el rey las quiso llevar,
porque sin licencia suya    nadie le pueda hablar.
Por él rogaban los grandes    cuantos en la corte están,
por él rogaba Oliveros,    por él rogaba Roldán,
y ruegan los doce pares    de Francia la natural;
y las monjas de Sant Ana    con las de la Trinidad
llevaban un crucifijo    para al buen rey rogar.
Con ellas va un arzobispo    y un perlado y cardenal;
mas el rey con grande enojo    a nadie quiso escuchar,
antes de muy enojado    sus grandes mandó llamar.
Cuando ya los tuvo juntos    empezóles de hablar:
—Amigos y hijos míos,    a lo que vos hice llamar,
ya sabéis que el Conde Claros,    el señor de Montalván,
de cómo le he criado    fasta ponello en edad,
y le he guardado su tierra,    que su padre le fue a dar,
el que morir no debiera,    Reinaldos de Montalván,
y por facelle yo más grande,    de lo mío le quise dar;
hícele gobernador    de mi reino natural.
Él por darme galardón,    mirad, en qué fue a tocar,
que quiso forzar la infanta,    hija mía natural.
Hombre que lo tal comete    ¿qué sentencia le han de dar?
Todos dicen a una voz    que lo hayan de degollar,
y así la sentencia dada    el buen rey la fue a firmar.
El arzobispo que esto viera    al buen rey fue a hablar,
pidiéndole por merced    licencia le quiera dar
para ir a ver al conde    y su muerte le denunciar.
—Pláceme, dijo el buen rey,    pláceme de voluntad;
mas con esta condición:    que solo habéis de andar

The king, greatly enraged,   had the hunter killed
because he had been so bold   as to bring such news.
He had his constables summoned   quickly and not slowly,
he ordered five hundred men to arm,   to be his escort,
in order to arrest the count   and seize him,
and he had the gates shut,   the gates of the city.
At the palace gates   they found him;
they took the good count prisoner   under heavy guard:
shackles on his feet   weighing at least two hundred pounds;
handcuffs on his wrists   that were painful to behold;
a chain around his neck   —an iron necklace!
They sat him on a she-mule   to dishonor him further;
they placed him in a tower   where it was very dark:
the keys to his cell   the king insisted on keeping,
so that without his permission   no one could speak with him.
All the grandees in the court   interceded for him,
Oliveros interceded for him,   Roldán interceded for him,
and the twelve peers   of France, the homeland, interceded;
and the nuns of St. Anne   and those of the Trinity
brought a crucifix   to intercede with the good king.
With them came an archbishop   and a prelate and cardinal;
but the king, greatly enraged,   refused to hear anyone out;
instead, in his great fury,   he had his grandees summoned.
When they were assembled,   he began to speak:
"My friends and children,   here is why I summoned you:
you know that Count Claros,   lord of Montalván,
was brought up by me   until he became of age,
and I've maintained his estate,   which his father left him,
he who should never have died,   Reinaldos of Montalván;
and to increase it further,   I gave him property of mine;
I made him governor   of my own realm.
To reward me,   see what a way he found!
He has seduced the princess,   my very own daughter.
A man who commits such a crime,   to what should he be sentenced?"
They all said unanimously   that he should be beheaded;
the sentence thus pronounced,   the good king signed it.
Seeing this, the archbishop   spoke to the good king,
asking him as a favor   to give him permission
to go and see the count   and announce his death to him.
"I agree," said the good king,   "I agree gladly,
but on this condition:   you must go alone

con aqueste pajecico    de quien puedo bien fiar.
Ya se parte el arzobispo    y a las cárceles se va.
Las guardas desque lo vieron    luego le dejan entrar;
con él iba el pajecico    que le va a acompañar.
Cuando vido estar al conde    en su prisión y pesar,
las palabras que le dice    dolor eran de escuchar.
—Pésame de vos, el conde,    cuanto me puede pesar,
que los yerros por amores    dignos son de perdonar.
Por vos he rogado al rey,    nunca me quiso escuchar,
antes ha dado sentencia    que os hayan de degollar.
Yo vos lo dije, sobrino,    que vos dejásedes de amar,
que el que las mujeres ama    atal galardón le dan,
que haya de morir por ellas    y en las cárceles penar.
Respondiera el buen conde    con esfuerzo singular:
—Calledes por Dios, mi tío,    no me queráis enojar;
quien no ama las mujeres    no se puede hombre llamar;
mas la vida que yo tengo    por ellas quiero gastar.
Respondió el pajecico,    tal respuesta le fue a dar:
—Conde, bienaventurado    siempre os deben de llamar,
porque muerte tan honrada    por vos había de pasar;
más envidia he de vos, conde    que mancilla ni pesar:
más querría ser vos, conde,    que el rey que os manda matar,
porque muerte tan honrada    por mí hubiese de pasar.
Llama yerro la fortuna    quien no la sabe gozar,
la priesa del cadahalso    vos, conde, la debéis dar;
si no es dada la sentencia    vos la debéis de firmar.
El conde que esto oyera    tal respuesta le fue a dar:
—Por Dios te ruego, el paje,    en amor de caridad,
que vayas a la princesa    de mi parte a le rogar,
que suplico a su Alteza    que ella me salga a mirar,
que en la hora de mi muerte    yo la pueda contemplar,
que si mis ojos la veen    mi alma no penará.
Ya se parte el pajecico,    ya se parte, ya se va,
llorando de los sus ojos    que quería reventar.
Topara con la princesa,    bien oiréis lo que dirá:
—Agora es tiempo, señora,    que hayáis de remediar,
que a vuestro querido el conde    lo lleven a degollar.
La infanta que esto oyera    en tierra muerta se cae;
damas, dueñas y doncellas    no la pueden retornar,
hasta que llegó su aya    la que la fue a criar.
—¿Qué es aquesto, la infanta?    aquesto, ¿qué puede estar?

with this young page   whom I can trust implicitly."
Now the archbishop departs,   he goes to the dungeons.
When the guards saw him,   they admitted him at once;
with him went the young page   who was to escort him.
When he saw the count   a sorrowful prisoner,
the words he spoke to him   were painful to hear.
"I'm sorry for you, count,   as sorry as I can be,
because crimes committed for love   deserve to be pardoned.
I interceded for you with the king,   but he refused to listen;
instead, he handed down the sentence   that you're to be beheaded.
I told you, nephew,   to leave off loving,
because he who loves women   is rewarded like this:
he must die for their sake   and suffer in a dungeon."
The good count replied   with outstanding courage;
"For the love of God, be still, uncle,   don't enrage me;
the man who doesn't love women   can't call himself a man;
as for me, the life I possess   I wish to give for them."
The young page replied,   he made this answer:
"Count, a lucky man   you should always be called,
because so honorable a death   has fallen to your lot!
I feel more envy for you, count,   than pity or grief:
I'd rather be you, count,   than the king who's having you killed,
so that a death this honorable   might fall to my lot!
Good fortune is called a crime   by those unable to enjoy it;
you, count, should urge them   to take you to the scaffold quickly;
if the sentence weren't pronounced,   you yourself should sign it."
When the count heard this,   he made this answer:
"For the love of God, I beg you, page,   out of Christian charity,
to go to the princess   with a request from me;
I beseech Her Highness   to come as a spectator,
so that at the hour of my death   I can gaze on her,
for if my eyes see her,   my soul won't suffer."
Now the young page departs,   now he departs, now he leaves,
weeping so hard   he almost burst.
He came across the princess,   you shall hear what he said:
"Highness, now is the time   for you to prevent
your lover, the count,   from being taken to be beheaded."
When the princess heard this,   she fell to the ground in a faint;
ladies, women, and maidens   couldn't bring her around
until her governess came,   the one who raised her.
"What's this, princess?   What can this be?"

—¡Ay triste de mí, mezquina,    que no sé qué puede estar!
¡que si al conde me matan    yo me habré desesperar!
—Saliésedes vos, mi hija,    saliésedes a lo quitar.
Ya se parte la infanta,    ya se parte, ya se va:
fuese para el mercado    donde lo han de sacar.
Vido estar el cadahalso    en que lo han de degollar,
damas, dueñas y doncellas    que lo salen a mirar.
Vio venir la gente de armas    que lo traen a matar,
los pregoneros delante    por su yerro publicar.
Con el poder de la gente    ella no podía pasar.
—Apartádvos, gente de armas,    todos me haced lugar,
si no . . . ¡por vida del rey,    a todos mando matar!
La gente que la conoce    luego le hace lugar,
hasta que llegó el conde    y le empezara de hablar:
—Esforzá, esforzá, el buen conde,    y no queráis desmayar,
que aunque yo pierda la vida,    la vuestra se ha de salvar.
El aguacil que esto oyera    comenzó de caminar;
vase para los palacios    adonde el buen rey está.
—Cabalgue la vuestra Alteza,    apriesa, no de vagar,
que salida es la infanta    para el conde nos quitar.
Los unos manda que maten,    y los otros enforcar:
si vuestra Alteza no socorre,    yo no puedo remediar.
El buen rey de que esto oyera    comenzó de caminar,
y fuese para el mercado    ado el conde fue a hallar.
—¿Qué es esto, la infanta?    aquesto, ¿qué puede estar?
¿La sentencia que yo he dado    vos la queréis revocar?
Yo juro por mi corona,    por mi corona real,
que si heredero tuviese    que me hubiese de heredar,
que a vos y al conde Claros    vivos vos haría quemar.
—Que vos me matéis, mi padre,    muy bien me podéis matar,
mas suplico a vuestra Alteza,    que se quiera él acordar
de los servicios pasados    de Reinaldos de Montalván,
que murió en las batallas,    por tu corona ensalzar:
por los servicios del padre    al hijo debes galardonar;
por malquerer de traidores    vos no le debéis matar,
que su muerte será causa    que me hayáis de disfamar.
Mas suplico a vuestra Alteza    que se quiera consejar,
que los reyes con furor    no deben de sentenciar,
porque el conde es de linaje    del reino más principal,
porque él era de los doce    que a tu mesa comen pan.
Sus amigos y parientes    todos te querrían mal,

"Oh, woe is me, I'm so sad,    I don't know what it can be!
For if they kill my count,    I will be in despair!"
"Go out, my daughter,    go out and rescue him!"
Now the princess departs,    now she departs, now she leaves:
she went to the market square,    where he was to be taken.
She saw the scaffold standing    on which he was to be beheaded,
and the ladies, women, and maidens    coming out to watch.
She saw the men-at-arms arrive    taking him to his death,
with criers in front    to proclaim his crime.
There was such a crush of people,    she couldn't get through.
"Step aside, men-at-arms,    everyone make way for me,
or else, by the king's life,    I'll have everyone killed!"
The people, recognizing her,    made way for her at once,
until the count arrived    and she began to address him:
"Courage, courage, good count,    don't lose heart,
for even if I lose my life,    yours will be saved!"
When the constable heard this,    he began to move;
he went to the palace,    where the good king was.
"Mount, Your Highness,    quickly and not slowly,
for the princess has come out    to take the count away from us.
She's ordering that some be killed    and others hanged:
if Your Highness doesn't help,    I can't prevent it."
When the good king heard this,    he started to move,
and went to the market square,    where the count was to be found.
"What's this, princess?    What can this be?
The sentence I handed down    you wish to revoke?
I swear on my crown,    on my royal crown,
that if I had a male heir    who could inherit from me,
you and Count Claros    I would order burned alive!"
"Kill me, my father,    you may well kill me,
but I beseech Your Highness    to deign to remember
the service done you in the past    by Reinaldos de Montalván,
who died in battle    to exalt your crown:
for the father's services    you should reward the son;
you shouldn't kill him    through the spite of treacherous men,
for his death will cause you    to ruin my reputation.
Rather, I beseech Your Highness    to deign to take counsel,
for kings shouldn't hand down    sentences when enraged,
because the count is of the highest    ancestry in the realm,
because he is one of the twelve    who eat bread at your table.
His friends and relatives    would all hold it against you,

revolver te hían guerra,　tus reinos se perderán.
El buen rey que esto oyera　comenzara a demandar:
—Consejo os pido, los míos,　que me queráis consejar.
Luego todos se apartaron　por su consejo tomar.
El consejo que le dieron,　que le haya de perdonar
por quitar males y bregas,　y por la princesa afamar.
Todos firman el perdón,　el buen rey fue a firmar:
también le aconsejaron,　consejo le fueron dar,
pues la infanta quería al conde,　con él haya de casar.
Ya desfierran al buen conde,　ya lo mandan desferrar:
descabalga de una mula,　el arzobispo a desposar.
Él tomóles de las manos,　así los hubo de juntar.
Los enojos y pesares　en placer hubieron de tornar.

## 33. Romance de Gerineldo

—Gerineldo, Gerineldo,　el mi paje más querido,
quisiera hablarte esta noche　en este jardín sombrío.
—Como soy vuestro criado,　señora, os burláis conmigo.
—No me burlo, Gerineldo,　que de verdad te lo digo.
—¿A qué hora, mi señora,　comprir heis lo prometido?
—Entre las doce y la una,　que el rey estará dormido.
Tres vueltas da a su palacio　y otras tantas al castillo;
el calzado se quitó　y del buen rey no es sentido:
y viendo que todos duermen　do posa la infanta ha ido.
La infanta que oyera pasos　de esta manera le dijo:
—¿Quién a mi estancia se atreve?　¿Quién a tanto se ha atrevido?
—No vos turbéis, mi señora,　yo soy vuestro dulce amigo,
que acudo a vuestro mandado　humilde y favorecido.
Enilda le ase la mano　sin más celar su cariño:
cuidando que era su esposo　en el lecho se han metido,
y se hacen dulces halagos　como mujer y marido.
Tantas caricias se hacen　y con tanto fuego vivo,
que al cansancio se rindieron　y al fin quedaron dormidos.
El alba salía apenas　a dar luz al campo amigo,
cuando el rey quiere vestirse,　mas no encuentra sus vestidos:
—Que llamen a Gerineldo,　el mi buen paje querido,
Unos dicen: —No está en casa.　Otros dicen: —No lo he visto.
Salta el buen rey de su lecho　y vistióse de proviso,
receloso de algún mal　que puede haberle venido.

they'd stir up war against you,    you'd lose your kingdom."
When the good king heard this,    he began to ask:
"I ask you for counsel, my men,    please counsel me."
Then they all drew aside    to deliberate.
The advice they gave    was to pardon him
to avoid misfortunes and disputes    and to save the princess's honor.
They all signed the pardon;    the good king signed, too:
they also advised him,    giving him this advice;
since the princess loved the count,    she should marry him.
Now the good count's bonds are loosed,    now they order him unchained:
the archbishop gets off his mule    to wed them.
He took them by the hand,    and thus united them.
Their anger and grief    were converted to pleasure.

## 33. Ballad of Gerineldo

"Gerineldo, Gerineldo,    my dearly beloved page,
I want to talk to you tonight    in this dark garden."
"Since I'm your servant,    lady, you're laughing at me."
"It's no joke, Gerineldo,    I'm speaking to you seriously."
"At what time, my lady,    will you keep your promise?"
"Between twelve and one,    for the king will be asleep."
He makes three circuits of the palace,    and the same number of the castle;
he removed his shoes    and he wasn't heard by the good king:
finding everyone asleep,    he went to where the princess rested.
Hearing steps, the princess    spoke to him as follows:
"Who dares come to my room?    Who has been so bold?"
"Don't be alarmed, my lady,    it's I, your sweet friend,
complying with your summons    humbly, as your favored suitor."
Enilda grasped his hand,    no longer concealing her love:
as if he were her husband,    they went to bed,
and indulged in sweet cajolery    like man and wife.
They caressed each other so,    and with such burning fire,
that they succumbed to fatigue    and finally fell asleep.
Dawn was barely breaking,    giving light to the friendly fields,
when the king wanted to dress    but couldn't find his clothes:
"Have Gerineldo called,    the good page I love."
Some said: "He's not in."    Others: "I haven't seen him."
The good king jumped out of bed    and dressed at once,
fearful of some misfortune    that might have befallen him.

Al cuarto de Enilda entrada,    y en su lecho halla dormidos
a su hija y a su paje    en estrecho abrazo unidos.
Pasmado quedó y parado    el buen rey muy pensativo:
pensándose qué hará    contra los dos atrevidos.
—¿Mataré yo a Gerineldo,    al que cual hijo he querido?
¡Si yo matare la infanta    mi reino tengo perdido!
En tal estrecho el buen rey,    para que fuese testigo,
puso la espada por medio    entre los dos atrevidos.
Hecho esto se retira    del jardín a un bosquecillo.
Enilda al despertarse,    notando que estaba el filo
de la espada entre los dos,    dijo asustada a su amigo:
—Levántate, Gerineldo,    levántate, dueño mío,
que del rey la fiera espada    entre los dos ha dormido.
—¿Adónde iré, mi señora?    ¿Adónde me iré, Dios mío?
¿Quién me librará de muerte,    de muerte que he merecido?
—No te asustes, Gerineldo,    que siempre estaré contigo:
márchate por los jardines    que luego al punto te sigo.
Luego obedece a la infanta,    haciendo cuanto le ha dicho:
pero el rey, que está en acecho,    se le hace encontradizo.
—¿Dónde vas, buen Gerineldo?    ¿Cómo estás tan sin sentido?
—Paseaba estos jardines    para ver si han florecido,
y vi que una fresca rosa,    el calor ha deslucido.
—Mientes, mientes, Gerineldo,    que con Enilda has dormido.
Estando en esto el sultán,    un gran pliego ha recibido:
ábrelo luego, y al punto    todo el color ha perdido.
—Que prendan a Gerineldo,    que no salga del castillo.
En esto la hermosa Enilda    cuidosa llega a aquel sitio.
De lo que pasa informada,    y conociendo el peligro,
sin esperar a que torne    el buen rey enfurecido,
salta las tapias ligera    en pos de su amor querido.
Huyendo se va a Tartaria    con su amante y fiel amigo,
que en un brioso caballo    la atendía en el ejido.
Allí antes de casarse    recibe Enilda el bautismo,
y las joyas que lleva    en dos cajas de oro fino
una vida regalada    a su amante han prometido.

## 34. Primer romance de Gaiferos

Estábase la condesa    en su estrado asentada,
tijericas de oro en mano    su hijo afeitando estaba.

Entering Enilda's room,   he found sleeping in her bed
his daughter and his page   linked in a close embrace.
Astonished and dumbfounded was   the good king, and very pensive,
wondering what to do   to the bold couple.
"Shall I kill Gerineldo,   whom I've loved like a son?
If I kill the princess,   my kingdom is lost!"
In that dilemma the good king,   to leave proof of his presence,
placed his sword between   the two bold lovers.
Doing this, he withdrew   to a little grove in the garden.
When Enilda awoke,   she noticed that the edge
of the sword was between them,   and she said to her lover in alarm:
"Arise, Gerineldo,   arise, my master,
for the king's fierce sword   has slept between us."
"Where shall I go, my lady?   Where shall I go, oh God?
Who will save me from death,   from the death I have deserved?"
"Don't be alarmed, Gerineldo,   for I will always be with you:
walk around the gardens,   and I'll follow you right away."
At once he obeyed the princess,   doing all that she said;
but the king, who lay in wait,   came up to meet him.
"Where are you going, good Gerineldo?   Why are you so stunned?"
"I was strolling in these gardens   to see if the flowers were out,
and I saw that a fresh rose   had been burned up by the heat."
"You lie, you lie, Gerineldo,   for you have slept with Enilda."
Just as the sultan said that,   he received a large folded paper;
he opened it at once, and on the spot   he turned altogether pale.
"Let Gerineldo be arrested,   let him not leave the castle!"
Just then beautiful Enilda   came to that spot, feeling worried.
Informed of what was happening,   and recognizing the danger,
without awaiting the return   of the good king in his rage,
she nimbly leapt over the wall   to follow her dear sweetheart.
In flight she went to Tartary   with her lover and faithful friend,
who, riding a spirited steed,   was awaiting her on the common.
There, before being married,   Enilda was baptized,
and the jewels she brought along   in two caskets of pure gold
assured her lover   of a life of comfort.

## 34. First Ballad of Gaiferos

The countess was   seated in her drawing room;
golden scissors in her hand,   she was trimming her son's hair.

Palabras le está diciendo,    palabras de antigüedad,
las palabras eran tales    que al niño hacen llorar:
—Dios te dé barbas en rostro    y en el cuerpo fuerza grande;
dete Dios ventura en armas    como al paladín Roldán,
porque vengases, mi hijo,    la muerte de vuestro padre:
matáronlo a traición    por casar con vuestra madre;
ricas bodas me hicieron    las cuales Dios no ha parte,
ricos paños me cortaron,    la reina no los ha tales.
Maguera pequeño el niño    bien entendido lo ha;
allí respondió Gaiferos,    bien oiréis lo que dirá:
—Así lo ruego a Dios del cielo    y a Santa María madre.
Oído lo había el conde    en los palacios do está.
—Calléis, calléis, la condesa,    boca mala sin verdad,
que yo no matara al conde,    ni lo hiciera matar,
mas tus palabras, condesa,    el niño las pagará.
Mandó llamar escuderos,    criados son de su padre,
para que lleven al niño,    que lo lleven a matar;
la muerte que les dijera    mancilla es de la escuchar:
—Córtenle el pie del estribo,    la mano del gavilán,
sáquenle ambos los ojos,    por más seguro andar,
y el dedo y el corazón    traédmelo por señal.
Ya lo llevan a Gaiferos,    ya lo llevan a matar,
fablaban los escuderos    con mancilla que de él han:
—¡Oh, válasme Dios del cielo    y Santa María su madre!
si este niño matamos,    ¿qué galardón nos darán?
Ellos en aquesto estando,    no sabiendo qué farán,
vieron venir una perrica,    la cual era de la madre;
allí fabló uno de ellos,    bien oiréis lo que dirá:
—Matemos esta perrica    por nuestra seguridad,
saquémosle el corazón    y llevémoslo al Galván,
cortémosle el dedo chico,    por llevar mejor señal.
Ya toman a Gaiferos    para el dedo le cortar.
—Venid acá, vos, Gaiferos,    y querednos escuchar:
vos idos de aquesta tierra,    que no parezcáis aquí más.
Ya le daban entre señas    el camino que fará:
Iros heis de tierra en tierra    a do vuestro tío está.
Gaiferos, desconsolado,    para un monte se va;

She was speaking to him    words of antiquity;[12]
the words were such    that they made the boy cry:
"May God give you a beard    and great bodily strength!
May God give you good fortune in battle    like the paladin Roldán's,
so that, my son, you can avenge    your father's death!
He was killed treacherously    because he wed your mother;
I was given a costly wedding    in which God had no share;[13]
rich fabrics were tailored for me,    such as the queen doesn't own."
Though young, the boy    has understood it all;
then Gaiferos replied,    you shall hear what he said:
"I ask the same of God in heaven    and His Mother, St. Mary."
This was heard by the count    in the palace where he was.
"Be still, be still, countess,    truthless slanderer,
for I didn't kill the count    or have him killed;
but your words, countess,    the boy shall pay for."
He had squires summoned,    who were servants of his father,
to take the boy away,    take him away and kill him;
the death he ordered for him    is pitiful to hear:
"Cut off his stirrup foot[14]    and his hawk-bearing hand,[15]
put out both his eyes    to make more sure of him,
and bring me as evidence    a finger and his heart."
Now they take Gaiferos away,    take him away to kill him;
the squires said    in their compassion for him:
"Oh, may God in heaven stand by me,    and His Mother, St. Mary!
If we kill this boy,    what reward will we be given?"
While they were saying this,    unsure what to do,
they saw a little bitch coming    that belonged to his mother;
then one of them spoke up,    you shall hear what he said:
"Let's kill this little dog    for our safety;
let's take out its heart    and bring it to Galván;
let's cut off his little finger    to bring better proof."
Now they take Gaiferos    to cut off his finger.
"Come here, Gaiferos,    and please listen to us:
depart from this land    and never show your face here again!"
Then they pointed out to him    the path he was to take:
"You shall go from land to land    until you reach your uncle's home."
Gaiferos, despondent,    entered a forest;

---

12. *Antigüedad* is considered to be an error in the source for *gravedad* ("serious-ness"). Another version of the ballad has: *gran pesar* ("great grievousness"). 13. A conjecture; the phrase may merely connote the extreme costliness of the wedding. 14. The left. 15. The right.

los escuderos se volvieron    para do estaba Galván,
danle dedo y corazón    y dicen que muerto lo han.
La condesa que esto oyera    empezara a gritos dar,
lloraba de sus ojos    que querría reventar.
Dejemos a la condesa    que muy grande llanto hace,
y digamos de Gaiferos    y del camino que hace,
que de día ni de noche    no hace sino caminar
hasta que llegó a la tierra    adonde su tío estaba.
Dícele de esta manera    y empezóle de fablar:
—Manténgaos Dios, el mi tío,    —Mi sobrino, bien vengáis,
¿qué buena venida es ésta?    vos me la queráis contar.
—La venida que yo vengo    triste es y con pesar
que Galván, con grande enojo,    mandado me había matar;
mas lo que os ruego, mi tío,    y lo que os vengo a rogar,
que vamos a vengar la muerte    de aquel buen conde, mi padre;
matáronle a traición    por casar con la mi madre.
—Soseguéis, el mi sobrino,    vos queráis asosegar,
que la muerte de mi hermano    bien la iremos a vengar.
Y ellos así estuvieron    dos años, y aún más,
hasta que dijo Gaiferos    y empezara de fablar:

## 35. Síguese el segundo romance de Gaiferos

—Vámonos, dijo, mi tío,    en París, esa ciudad,
en figura de romeros,    no nos conozca Galván,
que si Galván nos conoce    mandarnos hía matar.
Encima de ropas de seda    vistamos la de sayal,
llevemos nuestras espadas,    por más seguros andar,
llevemos sendos bordones,    por la gente asegurar.
Ya se parten los romeros,    ya se parten, ya se van,
de noche por los caminos,    de día por los jarales.
Andando por sus jornadas    a París llegado han;
las puertas hallan cerradas,    no hallan por dónde entrar.
Siete vueltas la rodean    por ver si podrán entrar,
y al cabo de las ocho,    un postigo van a fallar.
Ellos que se vieron dentro    empiezan a demandar:
no preguntan por mesón,    ni menos por hospital,
preguntan por los palacios    donde la condesa está;

the squires returned    to where Galván was;
they gave him the finger and the heart    and said they had killed him.
When the countess heard this,    she started to scream,
weeping so hard    she nearly burst.
Let us leave the countess    making this great lament,
and let us tell of Gaiferos    and his journey;
for by day and night    he never ceased to travel
until he reached the land    where his uncle was.
Speaking these words,    he began to address him:
"God keep you, my uncle!"    "My nephew, welcome!
What good wind brings you here?    Please tell me about it."
"My coming    is a sad and grievous one,
for Galván, in a great rage,    ordered me killed;
but what I ask of you, uncle,    what I have come to ask of you,
is that we go and avenge the death    of the good count, my father;
he was killed treacherously    because he wed my mother."
"Calm down, my nephew,    please be calm,
for the death of my brother    we will surely avenge."
And they remained that way    for two years, and even more,
until Gaiferos spoke    and began to say:[16]

## 35. [There Follows the] Second Ballad of Gaiferos

"Let us go, uncle," he said,    "to the city of Paris
in the guise of hermits,    so Galván won't recognize us,
for if Galván recognizes us,    he'll have us killed.
On top of our silken robes    let's wear one of sackcloth;
let's take our swords    to be more safe,
let's each carry a pilgrim's staff    to reassure the people."
Now the pilgrims depart,    now they depart, now they go,
on the roads by night,    in the brush by day.
Completing their journey,    they reached Paris;
they found the gates shut    and found no way in.
They circled the city seven times    looking for a way in;
at the end of the eighth    they found a small gateway.
Once they were inside,    they began to ask:
they didn't ask for an inn,    or a hospice, either,
they asked for the palace    where the countess dwelt;

---

16. The following poem is a direct continuation of this one.

a las puertas del palacio　　allí lo van a demandar
y allí estaban los escuderos,　　empezáronles a hablar,
vieron estar la condesa　y empezaron de hablar:
—Dios te salve, la condesa.　　—Los romeros, bien vengáis.
—Mandédesnos dar limosna　　por honor de caridad.
—Con Dios vades, los romeros,　　que no os puedo nada dar,
que el conde me había mandado　　a romeros no albergar.
—Desnos limosna, señora,　que el conde no lo sabrá,
así la den a Gaiferos　　en la tierra donde está.
Así como oyó Gaiferos,　　la condesa suspiró;
mandábales dar del vino,　　mandábales dar del pan.
Ellos en aquesto estando,　　el conde llegado ha:
—¿Qué es aquesto, la condesa?　　aquesto, ¿qué puede estar?
¿no os tenía yo mandado　　a romeros no albergar?
Y alzara su mano　puñada le fuera a dar
que sus dientes menudicos　　en tierra los fuera a echar.
Allí hablaron los romeros　y empiezan de hablar:
—¡Por hacer bien la condesa　　cierto no merece mal!
—Calledes vos, los romeros,　　no hayades vuestra parte.
Alzó Gaiferos su espada　　un golpe le fue a dar
que la cabeza de sus hombros　　en tierra la fue a echar.
Allí habló la condesa　llorando con gran pesar:
—¿Quién érades, los romeros,　　que tal cosa vais hacer?
Allí respondió el romero,　　tal respuesta le fuera dar:
—Yo soy Gaiferos, señora,　　vuestro hijo natural.
—Aquesto no puede ser,　　ni era cosa verdad,
que el dedo y el corazón　　yo lo tengo por señale.
—El corazón que vos tenéis　　en persona no fue a estare,
el dedo bien es aqueste　que en esta mano me faltare.
La condesa que esto oyera　　empezóle de abrazare,
la tristeza que ella tiene　　en placer se fue a tornare.

## 36. Romance de don Gaiferos, que trata de cómo sacó a su esposa, que estaba en tierra de moros

Asentado está Gaiferos　　en el palacio real,
asentado al tablero　para las tablas jugar;
los dados tiene en la mano,　　que los quería arrojar,
cuando entró por la sala　don Carlos el emperante.
Desque allí jugar le vido,　　empezóle de mirar;

at the palace gates   they made their request;
there the squires stood,   they began to address them;
they caught sight of the countess   and began to speak to her:
"God save you, countess!"   "Pilgrims, welcome!"
"Have us given alms   in Christian charity."
"Go with God, pilgrims,   for I can give you nothing,
since the count has ordered me   not to entertain pilgrims."
"Give us alms, my lady,   for the count won't find out;
may people do the same for Gaiferos   in the land where he is!"
As soon as she heard "Gaiferos,"   the countess sighed;
she had them given wine,   she had them given bread.
At that moment   the count arrived:
"What's this, countess?   What can this be?
Didn't I order you   not to entertain pilgrims?"
And, raising his hand,   he gave her such a punch
that her tiny teeth   were scattered on the ground.
Then the pilgrims spoke up   and began to say:
"For doing good, the countess   surely doesn't deserve harm!"
"Be still, you pilgrims,   don't interfere!"
Gaiferos raised his sword   and struck him such a blow
that his head left his shoulders   and landed on the ground.
Then the countess spoke,   weeping in great sorrow:
"Who are you, pilgrims,   that you do such a thing?"
Then the pilgrim replied,   he made this answer:
"I am Gaiferos, lady,   your own son."
"That cannot be,   nor is it the truth,
for his finger and heart   I have kept as a token."
"The heart you have   was never in a human being,
and the finger is this one,   missing from this hand."
When the countess heard this,   she began to embrace him;
the sadness she had felt   was converted to gladness.

## 36. Ballad of Gaiferos: How He Rescued His Wife from Moorish Captivity

Gaiferos is seated   in the royal palace,
seated at the draughts board   to play draughts;
he has the dice in his hand,   and is about to toss them,
when Emperor Carlos   enters the great hall.
When he saw him gaming there,   he began to stare at him;

hablándole está hablando    palabras de gran pesar:
—Si tan bueno fueseis, Gaiferos,    para las armas tomar
como sois para los dados    y para las tablas jugar,
vuestra esposa tienen moros,    iríades la a buscar.
Pésame a mi por ello    porque es mi hija carnal,
de muchos fue demandada    y a nadie quiso tomar;
pues con vos casó por amores,    amores le han de sacar.
Gaiferos desque esto vio,    movido de gran pesar,
levantóse del tablero    no queriendo más jugar.
Voces da por el palacio,    que al cielo quieren llegar,
preguntando va preguntando    por su primo don Roldán;
halláralo en el patín,    que quería cabalgar
con algunos caballeros    de los de los doce pares.
Gaiferos desque lo vido    empezóle de hablar:
—Por Dios os ruego, mi primo,    por Dios os quiero rogar,
vuestras armas y caballo    vos me las queráis prestar,
que mi tío el emperador    tan mal me quiso tratar
diciendo que soy para juego    y no para armas tomar.
Bien sabéis vos, el mi primo,    bien sabéis vos la verdad,
si busqué yo a mi esposa    en morisma y cristiandad,
que tres años la busqué    y nunca la pude hallar.
Agora sé que está en Sansueña,    en Sansueña esa ciudad,
sabéis que estoy sin caballo    y armas otro que tal,
que las llevó Montesinos    que se es ido a festejar
allá a los reinos de Hungría    para torneos armar;
pues sin armas y caballo    mal la podré yo sacar.
Por Dios os ruego mi primo    las vuestras me queráis dar.
Don Roldán que aquesto oyera,    tal respuesta le fue a dar:
—Calledes, primo Gaiferos,    no queráis hablar atal;
siete años ha que vuestra esposa    está en captividad;
siempre os he visto en armas    y caballo otro que tal;
agora que no las tenéis,    la queréis ir a buscar.
Sacramento tengo hecho,    allá en San Juan de Letrán,
a ninguno prestar mis armas    no las quiera mal vezar.
Gaiferos cuando esto oyó,    la espada fuera a sacar;
con una voz muy sañosa,    empezara de hablar:
—Bien parece, señor primo,    que siempre me queréis mal;
mas quien a mí ha injuriado,    no lo vais vos a vengar,
que si vos mi primo no fuésedes    con vos querría pelear.
Los grandes que allí se hallan    entre los dos puesto se han.
Don Roldán que así lo vido,    empezóle de hablar:

then he addressed to him    most grievous words:
"Gaiferos, if you were as good    at wielding weapons
as you are with dice    and games of draughts,
you'd go and find your wife,    who's being held by Moors.
I am grieved about it    because she's my own daughter;
many men asked for her hand    and she refused them all;
since she married you for love,    your love must rescue her."
When Gaiferos saw this,    he was stirred with great grief;
he arose from the board,    wishing to play no longer.
He raises a cry in the palace    that nearly reaches the sky;
he goes about asking    for his cousin Don Roldán;
he found him in the patio    about to ride off
with several knights    belonging to the twelve peers.
When Gaiferos saw him,    he began to address him:
"For the love of God, I ask you, cousin,    I ask you for God's sake,
please lend me    your armor and your mount,
for my uncle the emperor    has reviled me so,
saying I'm good for games    but not for wielding weapons!
You know well, cousin,    you know the truth well,
whether I sought my wife    in Moorish and Christian lands,
for I sought her three years    but could never find her.
Now I know she's in Sansueña,    the city of Sansueña;
you know I have no horse,    or armor, either,
for mine were taken by Montesinos,    who has gone to the festivities
there in the kingdom of Hungary    to take part in tournaments;
now, without armor and a mount    I can hardly rescue her.
For God's love, I beg you, cousin,    please give me yours."
When Don Roldán heard this,    he made this answer:
"Be still, cousin Gaiferos,    don't say such things;
it's seven years that your wife    has been in captivity;
I've always seen you with armor    and a horse as well;
now that you don't have them,    you want to go looking for her.
I've sworn an oath    there in St. John Lateran,
to lend no one my equipment,    so it won't be broken in improperly."
When Gaiferos heard this,    he drew his sword;
in a very angry tone    he began to speak:
"It seems to me, my lord cousin,    you're always against me;
but whoever has insulted me,    it won't be you who avenges me,
for if you weren't my cousin,    I'd gladly fight you!"
The grandees who were present    stepped between those two.
As soon as Don Roldán saw this,    he began to speak:

—Bien mostráis vos, don Gaiferos,    que sois de poca edad;
bien oistes un exemplo,    que oistes ser verdad:
que aquél que bien te quisiere    aquél te ha de castigar.
Si fuérades mal caballero,    no os dijera yo lo tal;
mas porque sé que sois bueno,    por esto os quiero castigar,
que mis armas y caballo    a vos no se han de negar
y si queréis compañía    yo os quiero acompañar.
—Mercedes, dijo Gaiferos,    de la buena voluntad;
solo me quiero ir, solo,    para habella de sacar.
Don Roldán mandara luego    sus armas aparejar;
él mismo encubierta el caballo    por mejor le encubertar;
él mesmo le pone las armas    y le ayuda a cabalgar.
Luego cabalgó Gaiferos    con enojo y gran pesar;
a don Roldán le pesaba    de que solo lo vee andar.
Desque ya él se salía    de aquel palacio sin par
con una voz amorosa    le llamaba don Roldán:
—Esperad, primo Gaiferos,    pues solo queréis andar;
dejédesme vuestra espada,    la mía queráis tomar,
y aunque vengan dos mil moros    nunca les volváis la faz;
al caballo dad la rienda    y haga su voluntad,
que si él viere la suya,    bien vos sabrá ayudar
y si vee demasía    de ella vos sabrá sacar.
Ya le da la su espada,    toma la de don Roldán;
da de espuelas al caballo    sálese de la ciudad.
Don Beltrán que ir lo vido,    empezóle de hablar:
—Tornad acá, don Gaiferos,    a vuestra madre a hablar;
tomará con vos consuelo,    que muy tristes llantos hace;
daros hía caballeros,    los que hayáis necesidad.
—Consoladla vos, mi tío,    vos la queráis consolar,
que no volveré en Francia    sin Melisendra tornar.
Don Beltrán que lo oyera    tan enojoso hablar
vuelve riendas al caballo    y entróse en la ciudad.
Gaiferos a tierra de moros    empieza de caminar;
andando por sus jornadas    a Sansueña fue a llegar.
Viernes era aquel día    y de gran solemnidad;
el rey está en la mezquita    para el zalá rezar;
cuando Gaiferos entrara    allá dentro en la ciudad
miraba si viese alguno    a quien poder demandar.
Vio un captivo cristiano    por los adarves andar;
desque lo vio Gaiferos,    empezóle de hablar:
—Dios te salve, el cristiano,    y te torne en libertad,

"You show clearly, Don Gaiferos,   how immature you are;
you must have heard the proverb,   and heard that it was true,
that the man who really likes you   is duty-bound to correct you.
If you were a bad knight,   I wouldn't have said that to you,
but because I know you're good,   that's why I want to correct you;
for my armor and steed   will not be denied you,
and if you want company,   I'll be glad to go with you."
"Thank you," said Gaiferos,   "for your good will;
I want to go alone, alone,   to try and rescue her."
At once Don Roldán ordered   his armor made ready;
he himself draped the horse   so it would be done the best way;
he himself clad him in the armor   and helped him mount.
At once Gaiferos rode off   in vexation and great grief;
Don Roldán was sorry   to see him depart alone.
When he was leaving   that matchless palace,
with an affectionate voice   Don Roldán called to him:
"Wait, cousin Gaiferos!   Since you wish to go alone,
leave your sword with me   and please take mine,
and, even if two thousand Moors come,   never turn your face from them;
give your horse free rein   and do as he wishes,
for if he sees an opportunity,   he'll be able to help you,
and if he sees superior numbers,   he'll save you from them."
Now he gives him his sword   and takes Don Roldán's;
he spurs his horse   and leaves the city.
When Don Beltrán saw him go,   he began to address him:
"Come back here, Don Gaiferos,   and speak with your mother;
she'll take comfort in your presence,   for she's weeping bitterly;
she'll give you knights,   as many as you need."
"Console her yourself, uncle,   please console her,
for I shall not return to France   unless I bring back Melisendra."
When Don Beltrán heard him   speak so angrily,
he turned his horse around   and entered the city.
Gaiferos began to ride   to the land of the Moors;
continuing his journey,   he arrived at Sansueña.
That day was a Friday,   a very holy day;
the king was in the mosque   attending the prayer service;
when Gaiferos entered   the city there,
he looked for someone   to whom he could pose questions.
He saw a Christian captive   walking on the parapet of the wall;
when Gaiferos saw him,   he began to address him:
"God save you, Christian,   and restore your freedom!

nuevas que pedirte quiero    no me las quieras negar:
tú que andas con los moros    si les oíste hablar
si hay alguna cristiana,    que sea de alto lugar.
El cautivo que lo oyera    empezara de hablar:
—Tanto tengo de mis males,    que de otros no puedo curar,
que todo el día los caballos    del rey me mandan curar
y de noche en fondacija    me hacen aprisionar.
Bien sé que hay muchas captivas    cristianas y de linaje,
especialmente hay una    que es de Francia natural:
el rey Almanzor la trata    como a su hija carnal;
sé que muchos reyes moros    con ella quieren casar.
Verla heis en las ventanas    del gran palacio real.
Derecho se va Gaiferos    do los palacios están;
desque estuvo cerca de ellos,    comenzólos de mirar;
vido estar a Melisendra    en una ventana grande;
Melisendra que lo vido    empezara de llorar,
no porque le conosciese    en el gesto y cabalgar,
mas de verlo en armas blancas    de Francia se fue a acordar.
Con una voz muy llorosa    le empezara de llamar:
—Ruego os por Dios, caballero,    que a mí os queráis allegar
y si sois cristiano o moro    no me lo queráis negar.
Daros he unas encomiendas,    ¡bien pagadas os serán!:
caballero, si a Francia ides,    por Gaiferos preguntad;
decidle que su esposica    se le envía a encomendar,
¡que ya me parece tiempo    que la debía buscar!,
que no lo deje por miedo    de con moros pelear,
que si presto no me sacan    mora me quiero tornar.
Casar me han con un rey moro,    que está allende la mar;
de siete reyes de moros    reina me coronarán.
Según los ruegos que me hacen,    mora me harán tornar;
mas amores de Gaiferos    no los puedo olvidar.
Gaiferos desque esto oyera    tal respuesta le fue a dar:
—No lloréis, la mi señora,    no queráis así llorar,
porque estas encomiendas    vos mesma la podéis dar,
porque a mí, allá en Francia,    Gaiferos me suelen llamar.
Yo soy el infante Gaiferos,    primo soy de don Roldán;
amores de Melisendra    son los que acá me traen.
Melisendra que lo oyó    conocióle en el hablar;
quitóse de la ventana,    la escalera fue a tomar;
salióse para la plaza    donde le vido estar.
Gaiferos cuando la vido,    presto la fue a tomar;

The news I wish to ask you    please don't deny me:
you who consort with the Moors,    have you heard them say
whether there's a Christian woman here    of high rank?"
When the captive heard this,    he began to speak:
"I have so many troubles of my own,    I can't worry about other people's,
for every day they make me    tend to the king's horses
and at night they lock me up    in the caravanserai.
I know there are many female captives    who are Christian and well-born;
there's one in particular    who's a native of France:
King Almanzor treats her    like his own daughter;
I know that many Moorish kings    desire to marry her.
You'll see her at the windows    of the big royal palace."
Gaiferos headed straight    to where the palace was located;
when he was near it,    he began to observe it;
he saw Melisendra standing    at a large window;
when Melisendra saw him,    she began to weep,
not because she recognized him    by his mien and manner of riding,
but, seeing him in white armor,    she remembered France.
In a very tearful tone    she began to call to him:
"For the love of God, knight, I beg you    to approach me,
and, whether Christian or Moor,    don't refuse me this!
I shall give you a message    and you'll be well paid for it!
Knight, if you go to France,    ask for Gaiferos;
tell him that his wife    sends him her regards,
for it seems to me high time    that he ought to seek her!
He is not to avoid it out of fear    of battling Moors,
for if I'm not rescued soon,    I must become a Moor.
They'll make me wed a Moorish king    who lives across the sea;
of seven Moorish kings    they'll crown me queen.
To judge by the requests made of me,    they'll convert me to a Moor;
but my love for Gaiferos    I cannot forget."
When Gaiferos heard this,    he made this answer:
"Don't weep, my lady,    please don't weep so,
because this message    you can deliver in person,
since back in France I    am named Gaiferos.
I am Prince Gaiferos,    cousin to Don Roldán;
my love for Melisendra    is what brings me here."
When Melisendra heard this,    she knew him by his speech;
she left the window    and took the stairs;
she went out onto the square    where she saw him standing.
When Gaiferos saw her,    he quickly grasped her;

abrazóla con sus brazos    para haberla de besar.
Allí estaba un perro moro    por las cristianas guardar;
las voces daba tan grandes,    que al cielo quieren llegar.
Al gran alarido del moro,    mandan cerrar la ciudad;
siete veces la rodea,    no halla por do pasar.
Presto sale el rey moro    de la mezquita rezar;
veréis tocar las trompetas,    apriesa y no de vagar;
veréis armar caballeros    y en caballos cabalgar;
tantos se armaron de moros    que era cosa de mirar.
Melisendra que lo vido    empezara de hablar:
—Esforzadvos, don Gaiferos,    no querades desmayar,
que los buenos caballeros    son para necesidad.
Si desta escapáis, Gaiferos,    harto tendréis que contar;
¡si fuese este caballo    como el de don Roldán,
que apretándole las cinchas    y aflojándole el pretal
de muchos moros cercado    se solía él librar!
Gaiferos desque esto oyera    fuérase luego a apear;
apretárale las cinchas    y aflojárale el pretal;
sin poner pie en el estribo,    en él fuera a cabalgar,
y a Melisendra a las ancas    presto la fuera a tomar:
el cuerpo le da por la cinta    porque le pueda abrazar.
En esto venían los moros    de priesa y no de vagar;
las grandes voces que daban,    al caballo hacían saltar;
cuando fue cerca los moros,    la rienda le fue a soltar;
el caballo era ligero,    pasólos de par en par;
siete batallas de moros    todos en zaga le van;
volviérase a Melisendra,    empezóle de hablar:
—No os enojéis, mi señora,    fuerza os será apear
y, en esta gran espesura,    podéis, señora, aguardar,
que los moros son tan cerca    de fuerza nos han de alcanzar.
Vos, señora, no tenéis armas    para haber de pelear,
yo, pues que las traigo buenas,    quiérolas bien emplear.
Apeóse Melisendra    no cesando de llorar;
las rodillas por el suelo,    a Dios comenzó a rogar
que guardase a Gaiferos    y le quisiese ayudar.
Gaiferos vuelve a los moros    con ánimo singular
encima del buen caballo,    que en el mundo no hay su par;
el cual va con tal furor    que la tierra hace temblar.
Do vido la más morisma,    en ella se fue a entrar;
si bien pelea Gaiferos,    el caballo mucho más;
tantos mata de los moros    que no hay cuento ni par.

he put his arms around her   in order to kiss her.
A dog of a Moor was there   to guard the Christian women;
he shouted so loudly,   his cries nearly reached the sky.
Hearing the Moor's loud yells,   they ordered the city gates closed;
he rode around the walls seven times   but found no way out.
Rapidly the Moorish king came out   of the mosque where he prayed;
then you'd have seen trumpets blowing   quickly, and not slowly;
you'd have seen knights don armor   and mount horses;
so many Moors armed themselves,   it was a marvel to see.
When Melisendra saw this,   she began to speak:
"Courage, Don Gaiferos!   Don't lose heart,
for knights show their worth   in the hour of need.
If you escape this danger, Gaiferos,   you'll have plenty to tell about;
if only this horse were   like Don Roldán's!
For, by tightening the girths   and slacking the breast strap,
when surrounded by many Moors   he used to get away!"
When Gaiferos heard this,   he dismounted at once;
he tightened the girths   and slackened the breast strap;
without setting foot in the stirrup   he mounted the horse
and quickly pulled up Melisendra,   seating her behind him:
he offered her his waist   so she could put her arms around it.
At that moment the Moors arrived   quickly, and not slowly;
the loud shouts they gave   made the horse buck;
when the Moors were close,   he gave the horse free rein;
the horse was nimble   and passed right through their midst;
seven companies of Moors   all pursued him;
he turned to look at Melisendra   and began to address her:
"May it not vex you, lady,   but you'll have to dismount
and in this large thicket   you can wait, lady,
for the Moors are so close   they have to catch up with us.
You, lady, have no weapons   to fight with;
I, since I bear good ones,   will make good use of them."
Melisendra dismounted,   weeping constantly;
her knees on the ground,   she began praying to God
to keep Gaiferos safe   and deign to assist him.
Gaiferos turned toward the Moors   with marvelous courage,
riding his good steed,   which had no equal in the world;
it ran with such fury   that it shook the earth.
Wherever it saw most Moors   it plunged into their midst;
if Gaiferos fought well,   the horse did even more so;
it killed so many Moors   that there was no counting them.

El rey Almanzor que esto vido,    empezara de hablar:
—Oh, válasme tú, Mahoma,    aquesto ¿qué puede estar?
Tal fuerza de caballero    en pocos se puede hallar:
o este es el encantado,    ese paladín Roldán
o él es el esforzado    Reinaldos de Montalván
o es Urgel de las mazas,    esforzado y singular;
no hay ninguno de los doce    que bastase hacer tal.
Gaiferos que esto oyó,    tal respuesta le fue a dar:
—Calles, calles, el rey moro,    calles, no digas atal,
que muchos había en Francia    que tanto como esos valen.
No soy yo ninguno d'ellos,    mas yo me quiero nombrar:
yo soy el infante Gaiferos,    primo soy de don Roldán.
El rey Almanzor que lo oyera    con esfuerzo así hablar,
con los más moros que pudo    se metió en la ciudad.
Solo quedaba Gaiferos,    no halla con quien pelear;
volvió riendas al caballo,    va a Melisendra a buscar.
Melisendra que lo vido    a recebirse lo sale;
desque vio las armas blancas    tintas en color de sangre,
con voz triste y muy llorosa    le empieza de interrogar:
—Por Dios os ruego, Gaiferos,    por Dios os quiero rogar,
si traéis alguna herida,    queráismela vos mostrar,
que los moros eran muchos,    quizá os han hecho mal.
—Calledes, dijo Gaiferos,    infanta, no digáis tal,
por más que fueran los moros    no me podían hacer mal,
que estas armas y caballo    son de mi primo Roldán:
caballero que las lleva,    no le pueden hacer mal.
Cabalgad presto, señora,    que no es tiempo de aguardar;
antes que los moros tornen    los puertos se han de pasar.
Ya cabalga Melisendra    en el caballo alazán;
razonando van de amores,    de amores que no de ál;
ni de los moros han miedo,    ni d'ellos sentían parte;
con el placer de los dos,    el descanso era muy grande.
De noche van por camino,    de día por los jarales,
comiendo las hierbas verdes,    bebiendo el agua que hallen,
hasta que entraron en Francia    en tierra de Cristiandad.
Si hasta allí alegres vienen,    mucho más de allí adelante.
A la entrada de un monte,    a la salida de un valle,
caballero de armas blancas    de lejos veen asomar;
Gaiferos desque lo vido,    vuelto se le ha la sangre.
Diciendo está a su señora:    —Este es mayor pesar,
que aquél caballero que asoma    gran esfuerzo es el que trae.

When King Almanzor saw this,    he began to speak:
"Oh, stand by me, Mohammed!    What can this be?
Such power in a knight    is found in very few:
this man is either the charmed one,    the paladin Roldán,
or else the courageous    Reinaldos of Montalván,
or Urgel of the maces,    courageous and outstanding;
there's none among the twelve    capable of doing this."
When Gaiferos heard this,    he made this answer:
"Be still, be still, Moorish king,    be still, don't say that,
for there are many in France    as worthy as they.
I am none of those,    but I'll tell you my name:
I am Prince Gaiferos,    cousin to Don Roldán."
When King Almanzor heard him    speak so bravely,
with all the Moors he could    he shut himself in the city.
Gaiferos was left alone    with no one to fight;
he turned his horse around    and went to fetch Melisendra.
When Melisendra saw him,    she went out to greet him;
when she saw his white armor    reddened with blood,
in a sad, very tearful tone    she began to question him:
"For the love of God, Gaiferos, I beg you,    I beg you for God's sake,
if you have any wound,    please let me see it,
for the Moors were numerous,    perhaps they've hurt you."
"Be still," said Gaiferos,    "princess, don't say such things;
however numerous the Moors,    they were unable to hurt me,
for this armor and this steed    are those of my cousin Roldán:
the knight who possesses them    can't be injured.
Mount quickly, lady,    this is no time to tarry;
before the Moors return    we must cross the mountain passes."
Now Melisendra rides    on the chestnut stallion;
they speak of love as they go,    love and nothing else;
they have no fear of the Moors,    they forget all about them;
with the pleasure that both felt,    their peace was very great.
At night they follow the roads,    by day they ride through the brush,
eating the green herbs,    drinking whatever water they find,
until they entered France    and Christian soil.
If they were happy up to then,    they were much more so from then on.
As they began ascending a hill    upon leaving a valley,
a knight in white armor    they see appearing in the distance;
when Gaiferos saw him,    he felt a violent emotion.
He said to his lady:    "This is a greater grief,
for the knight we see there    is one of great might.

Si es cristiano o moro,    fuerza será pelear.
Apeáos, mi señora,    y venidme a la par.
De la mano la traía,    no cesando de llorar.
Desque el uno cerca el otro,    empiézanse a parejar
las lanzas y los escudos    en son de bien pelear.
Los caballos ya de cerca    empiezan de relinchar;
el relincho del caballo    Gaiferos conoscido ha;
con una voz muy alegre    empezara de hablar
a su esposa Melisendra,    que le venía a la par:
—Perded cuidado, señora,    y tornad a cabalgar,
que el caballo que allí viene    mío es en la verdad;
yo le di mucha cebada    y más le entiendo de dar;
las armas según que veo    mías son otro que tal
y aquél es Montesinos    que me viene a buscar,
que cuando yo me partí    no estaba en la ciudad.
Plugo mucho a Melisendra    que aquello fuese verdad;
ya que se van acercando,    cuasi junto a la par
con voz alta y muy crescida    empiézanse a interrogar.
Conóscense los dos primos    entonces en el hablar.
Apeáronse a gran priesa,    muy grandes fiestas se hacen.
Desque hubieron hablado,    tornaron a cabalgar;
razonando van de amores,    de otro no quieren hablar;
andando por sus jornadas    entran en la Cristiandad;
cuantos caballeros hallan,    los iban a acompañar
y dueñas a Melisendra,    doncellas otro que tal.
Andando por sus jornadas,    a París llegado han;
desque lo supo el emperador,    a recebirse los sale,
con él sale Oliveros,    con él sale don Roldán
con el infante Guarinos,    almirante de la mar;
con él salió don Bermúdez    y el buen viejo don Beltrán;
con él muchos de los Doce    que a su mesa comen pan
y con él iba doña Alda,    la esposa de don Roldán;
con él iba Juliana,    hija del rey Julián,
dueñas, damas, y doncellas    las más altas de linaje.
El emperador los abraza,    no cesando de llorar;
palabras que les decía,    dolor era de escuchar.
Los Doce a don Gaiferos    gran acatamiento le hacen;
teníanlo por esforzado,    mucho más de allí adelante,
pues que sacó a su esposa    de tan gran captividad;
las fiestas que le hacían    no tienen cuento ni par.

Whether he's Christian or Moor,    I'll need to fight him.
Dismount, lady,    and keep beside me."
He took her by the hand    as she wept constantly.
When the two knights were close,    they began to ready
their lances and shields    in the manner of able warriors.
Their horses, now close,    began to neigh;
the neighing of the horse    was recognized by Gaiferos;
in a very cheerful tone    he began to speak
to his wife Melisendra,    who was walking beside him:
"Lose all fear, lady,    and mount again,
for the horse coming there    is verily mine;
I've fed him much barley    and intend to give him more;
as I see, the armor    is mine as well,
and this is Montesinos    coming to find me,
for when I departed    he wasn't in town."
Melisendra was greatly pleased    that such was the case;
now that they had drawn near    and were almost side by side,
in loud, very full tones    they began to question each other.
The two cousins recognized each other    by their voices then.
They dismounted rapidly    and greeted each other effusively.
After a conversation    they mounted once more;
their talk was of love,    they wanted no other subject;
proceeding on their way,    they entered on Christian soil;
all the knights they came across    accompanied them,
and ladies escorted Melisendra,    maidens as well.
Proceeding on their way,    they reached Paris;
when the emperor learned of this,    he went out to greet them;
with him went Oliveros,    with him went Don Roldán
along with Prince Guarinos,    admiral of the sea;
with him went Don Bermúdez    and the good old man Don Beltrán;
with him went many of the twelve    who eat bread at his table,
and with him went Doña Alda,    betrothed of Don Roldán;
with him went Juliana,    daughter of King Julián,
women, ladies, and maidens    of the loftiest ancestry.
The emperor embraced them,    weeping constantly;
the words he spoke to them    were sorrowful to hear.
The twelve paid great respect    to Don Gaiferos;
they considered him brave,    much more than previously,
since he had rescued his wife    from such close captivity;
the celebrations they held for him    were beyond counting.

## 37. Romance del marqués de Mantua

De Mantua salió el marqués     Danés Urgel el leal:
allá va a buscar la caza     a las orillas del mar.
Con él van sus cazadores     con aves para volar;
con él van los sus monteros     con perros para cazar;
con él van sus caballeros     para haberlo de guardar.
Por la ribera del Pou     la caza buscando van.
El tiempo era caluroso,     víspera era de San Juan.
Métense en una arboleda     para refresco tomar;
al derredor de una fuente     a todos mandó asentar.
Viandas aparejadas     traen, procuran yantar.
Desque hubieron yantado     comenzaron de hablar
solamente de la caza     cómo se ha de ordenar.
Al pie están de una breña     que junto a la fuente está.
Oyeron un gran ruido     entre las ramas sonar:
todos estuvieron quedos     por ver qué cosa será;
por las más espesas matas     veen un ciervo asomar;
de sed venía fatigado,     al agua se iba a lanzar;
los monteros a gran priesa     los perros van a soltar:
sueltan lebreles, sabuesos     para le haber de tomar.
El ciervo que los sintió     al monte se vuelve a entrar:
caballeros y monteros     comienzan de cabalgar;
siguiéndole iban el rastro     con gana de le alcanzar:
cada uno va corriendo     sin uno a otro esperar.
El que traía buen caballo     corría más por le atajar:
apártanse unos de otros     sin al marqués aguardar.
El ciervo era muy ligero,     mucho se fue adelantar;
al ladrido de los perros     los más siguiéndole van.
El monte era muy espeso,     todos perdidos se han.
El sol se quería poner,     la noche quería cerrar,
cuando el buen marqués de Mantua     solo se fuera a fallar
en un bosque tan espeso     que no podía caminar.
Andando a un cabo y a otro,     mucho alejado se ha;
tantas vueltas iba dando     que no sabe donde está.
La noche era muy escura,     comenzó recio a tronar;
el cielo estaba nublado,     no cesa de relampaguear.
El marqués que así se vido     su bocina fue a tomar,
a sus monteros llamando:     tres veces la fue a tocar.
Los monteros eran lejos,     por demás era el sonar,

## 37. Ballad of the Marquess of Mantua

From Mantua the marquess departed,   the loyal Urgel the Dane;
he was going out hunting   there by the seashore.
With him went his fowlers   with falcons for hawking;
with him went his huntsmen   with hounds for tracking;
with him went his knights   to guard him.
By the banks of the Pou   they sought game.
The weather was hot,   it was the eve of St. John's Day.
They entered a grove   to cool off;
around a spring   he bade them all be seated.
Cooked food   they bring out, and they set about lunching.
After lunch   they begin to speak
solely about the hunt   and how to plan it.
They were at the foot of some scrubland   beside the spring.
They heard a loud noise   amid the branches:
they all kept still   to see what it was;
through the densest bushes   they see a stag appear;
it was weary with thirst   and wanted to jump into the water;
very rapidly the huntsmen   released the dogs:
they unleashed greyhounds and bloodhounds   to catch it.
The stag, sensing them,   plunged into the woods again:
knights and huntsmen   began to ride;
they followed the track,   eager to catch up with him:
each one dashed off   without awaiting his companions.
Those with good horses   rode faster to cut him off:
they separated from one another   without awaiting the marquess.
The stag was very nimble,   and got far ahead of them;
to the barking of the hounds,   most of them followed him.
The woods were very dense,   they all lost their way.
The sun was about to set,   night was about to fall,
when the good Marquess of Mantua   found himself alone
in a forest so dense   he was unable to walk.
Going in this direction and that,   he wandered far away;
he turned in so many circles,   he didn't know where he was.
The night was very dark,   it began to thunder violently;
the sky was cloudy,   the lightning never stopped.
When the marquess found himself in that trouble,   he took his horn
and called his huntsmen:   he blew it three times.
The huntsmen were far away   and there was too much din;

el caballo iba cansado    de por las breñas saltar;
a cada paso caía,    no se podía menear.
El marqués muy enojado    la rienda le fue a soltar;
por do el caballo quería    lo dejaba caminar.
El caballo era de casta,    esfuerzo fuera a tomar.
Diez millas ha caminado    sin un momento parar;
no va camino derecho    mas por do podía andar.
Caminando todavía    un camino va a topar;
siguiendo por el camino    va a dar en un pinar:
por él anduvo una pieza    sin poder dél se apartar.
Pensó reposar allí    o adelante pasar;
mas por buscar a los suyos    adelante quiere andar.
Del pinar salió muy presto,    por un valle fuera a entrar,
cuando oyó dar un gran grito    temeroso y de pesar,
sin saber que de hombre fuese,    o qué pudiese estar:
solo gran dolor mostraba,    otro no pudo notar,
de que se turbó el marqués,    todo espeluzado se ha,
mas aunque viejo de días    empiézase de esforzar.
Por su camino adelante    empieza de caminar:
a pie va que no a caballo;    el caballo va a dejar,
porque estaba muy cansado,    y no podía bien andar;
en un prado que allí estaba    allí lo fuera a dejar.
Cuando llegó a un río,    en medio de un arenal
un caballo vido muerto,    comenzóle de mirar.
Armado estaba de guerra    a guisa de pelear;
los brazos tenia cortados,    las piernas otro que tal;
un poco más adelante    una voz sintió hablar:
—¡Oh Santa María Señora,    no me quieras olvidar!
¡A ti encomiendo mi alma,    plégate de la guardar!
En este trago de muerte    esfuerzo me quieras dar;
pues a los tristes consuelas    quieras a mí consolar;
y tu muy precioso Hijo    por mí te plega rogar
que perdone mis pecados,    mi alma quiera salvar.
Cuando aquesto oyó el marqués    luego se fuera a apartar;
revolvióse el manto al brazo,    la espada fuera a sacar:
apartado del camino    por el monte fuera a entrar;
hacia do sintió la voz    empieza de caminar.
Las ramas iba cortando    para la vuelta acertar;
a todas partes miraba    por ver qué cosa será;
el camino por do iba    cubierto de sangre está.
Vínole grande congoja,    todo se fue a demudar,

his horse was weary    from leaping through the shrubbery;
it stumbled at every step    and couldn't budge.
In great vexation the marquess    gave it free rein;
wherever the horse wished    he allowed it to go.
The horse was a thoroughbred,    it summoned up strength.
It went ten miles    without ever stopping;
it didn't go in a beeline    but wherever it was able.
Still riding,    he came across a road;
following the road,    he came to a stand of pine:
he proceeded through it some distance,    never able to get out of it.
He wondered whether to rest there    or keep on going;
but in order to seek his men    he determined to push forward.
Very soon he left the pine grove    and entered a valley,
when he heard a loud cry,    frightful and grievous,
not knowing if it was human,    or what it might be:
it merely tokened great sorrow,    he couldn't discern any more,
so that the marquess became upset    and was all a-tremble;
but, though he was old,    he began to take heart.
He began to go    forward on his path,
on foot, not on horse;    he left his horse,
because it was very weary    and couldn't walk well;
in a meadow there    he left it.
When he reached a river    amid an expanse of sand,
he saw a dead horse    and began to observe it.
It had warlike trappings    as if for combat;
its forelegs were cut off    and its hind legs as well;
a little farther along    he heard a voice say:
"O Lady St. Mary,    don't forget me!
To you I commend my soul,    please keep it!
In this sad moment of death    please give me courage.
Since you comfort the sad,    please comfort me;
and your very precious Son,    please ask Him for me
to forgive my sins    and save my soul."
When the marquess heard this,    he moved aside at once;
he wrapped his cloak around his arm    and drew his sword:
leaving the path on one side,    he entered the forest;
he began to walk    to the place the voice was coming from.
He cut off branches    so he could find his way back;
he looked on all sides    to see what it could be;
the path he was following    was covered with blood.
Great sorrow came over him,    he turned altogether pale,

que el espíritu le daba     sobresalto de pesar.
De donde la voz oyera     muy cerca fuera a llegar:
al pie de unos altos robles     vido un caballero estar,
armado de todas armas     sin estoque ni puñal.
Tendido estaba en el suelo,     no cesa de se quejar;
las lástimas que decía     al marqués hacen llorar:
por entender lo que dice     acordó de se acercar.
Atento estaba escuchando     sin bullir ni menearse:
lo que decía el caballero     razón es de lo contar.
—¿Dónde estás, señora mía,     que no te pena mi mal?
De mis pequeñas heridas     compasión solías tomar,
¡agora de las mortales     no tienes ningún pesar!
No te doy culpa, señora,     que descanso en el hablar:
mi dolor que es muy sobrado     me hace desatinar.
Tú no sabes de mi mal     ni de mi angustia mortal;
yo te pedí la licencia     para mi muerte buscar.
Pues yo la hallé, señora,     a nadie debo culpar,
cuanto más a ti, mi bien,     que no me la querías dar;
mas cuando más no podiste     bien sentí tu gran pesar
en la fe de tu querer,     según te vi demostrar.
¡Esposa mía y señora!     no cures de me esperar;
fasta el día del juicio     no nos podemos juntar.
Si viviendo me quisiste,     al morir lo has de mostrar,
no en hacer grandes extremos,     mas por el alma rogar.
¡Oh mi primo Montesinos!     ¡Infante don Merián!
¡Deshecha es la compañía     en que solíamos andar!
¡Ya no esperéis más de verme,     no os cumple más de buscar,
que en balde trabajaréis     pues no me podréis hallar!
¡Oh esforzado don Reinaldos!     ¡Oh buen paladín Roldán!
¡Oh valiente don Urgel!     ¡Oh don Ricardo Normante!
¡Oh marqués don Oliveros!     ¡Oh Durandarte el galán!
¡Oh archiduque don Estolfo!     ¡Oh gran duque de Milán!
¿Dónde sois todos vosotros?     ¿No venís a me ayudar?
¡Oh emperador Carlo Magno,     mi buen señor natural,
si supieses tú mi muerte     cómo la harías vengar!
Aunque me mató tu hijo,     justicia querrías guardar,
pues me mató a traición     viniéndole acompañar.
¡Oh príncipe don Carloto!     ¿qué ira tan desigual
te movió sobre tal caso     a quererme así matar,
rogándome que viniese     contigo por te guardar?
¡Oh desventurado yo,     cómo venía sin cuidar

for his spirit was giving him    a grievous fright.
He was nearly at the spot    from which the voice had come:
at the foot of some tall oaks    he saw a knight lying,
wearing full armor    but with no rapier or dagger.
He was stretched out on the ground,    lamenting ceaselessly;
the pitiful things he said    made the marquess weep:
to make out what he was saying,    he resolved to draw near.
He listened attentively    without stirring or moving:
what the knight was saying    it is fitting to report.
"Where are you, my lady,    that my misfortune doesn't grieve you?
On my minor wounds    you used to take pity,
now for my mortal ones    you have no concern!
I don't blame you, lady,    I'm soothing my grief by talking:
my pain, which is so extreme,    makes me speak foolishness.
You don't know of my misfortune    or of my mortal anguish;
I asked you for permission    to seek my death.
Since I've found it, lady,    I ought to blame no one,
least of all you, my darling,    who didn't want to give it to me;
but when you could do no more,    I felt your deep grief
in the loyalty of your love,    which I saw you prove.
My wife and lady!    Don't trouble to await me;
until Judgment Day    we cannot meet again.
If you loved me while I lived,    you must show it at my death,
not by excessive mourning    but by praying for my soul.
Oh, my cousin Montesinos!    Prince Merián!
Dissolved is the fellowship    of which we used to be a part!
Never expect to see me again,    it behooves you to seek no more,
for you will labor in vain,    since you cannot find me!
Oh, brave Don Reinaldos!    Oh, good paladin Roldán!
Oh, valiant Don Urgel!    Oh, Don Ricardo Normante!
Oh, Marquess Oliveros!    Oh, personable Durandarte!
Oh, Archduke Estolfo!    Oh, Grand Duke of Milan!
Where are you all?    You don't come to help me?
Oh, Emperor Charlemagne,    my good liege lord,
if you knew of my death,    how surely you'd see it avenged!
Though it's your son who killed me,    you'd uphold justice,
since he killed me treacherously    when I came to accompany him.
Oh, Prince Carloto!    What unnatural wrath
led you on such an occasion    to want to kill me like this,
after asking me to come    along with you to protect you?
Oh, luckless me,    coming with no suspicion

que tan alto caballero    pudiese hacer tal maldad!
Pensando venir a caza,    mi muerte vine a cazar.
No me pesa del morir    pues es cosa natural,
¡mas por morir como muero    sin merecer ningun mal,
y en tal parte donde nunca    la mi muerte se sabrá!
¡Oh alto Dios poderoso,    justiciero y de verdad,
sobre mi muerte inocente    justicia quieras mostrar!
¡De esta ánima pecadora    quieras haber piedad!
¡Oh triste reina mi madre,    Dios te quiera consolar,
que ya es quebrado el espejo    en que te solías mirar!
Siempre de mí recelaste    recibir algún pesar,
¡agora de aquí adelante    no te cumple recelar!
En las justas y torneos    consejo me solías dar,
¡agora triste en la muerte    aún no me puedes hablar!
¡Oh noble marqués de Mantua,    mi señor tío carnal!
¿dónde estáis que no oís    mi doloroso quejar?
¡Que nueva tan dolorosa    vos será de gran pesar,
cuando de mí no supieredes    ni me pudieredes hallar!
Hecístesme heredero    por vuestro estado heredar,
¡mas vos lo habréis de ser mío    aunque sois de más edad!
¡Oh mundo desventurado,    nadie debe en ti fiar;
al que mas subido tienes    mayor caída haces dar!
Estas palabras diciendo,    no cesa de sospirar
sospiros muy dolorosos    para el corazón quebrar.
Turbado estaba el marqués,    no pudo más escuchar:
el corazón se le aprieta,    la sangre vuelta se le ha.
A los pies del caballero    junto se fue a llegar;
con la voz muy alterada    empezóle de hablar:
—¿Qué mal tenéis, caballero?    Querádesmelo contar.
¿Tenéis heridas de muerte,    o tenéis otro algún mal?
Cuando lo oyó el caballero    la cabeza probó alzar:
pensó que era su escudero,    tal respuesta le fue a dar:
—¿Qué dices, amigo mío?    ¿Traes con quién me confesar?
Que ya el alma se me sale;    la vida quiero acabar:
del cuerpo no tengo pena,    que el alma querría salvar.
Luego le entendió el marqués    por otro le fuera a tomar:
respondióle muy turbado,    que apenas pudo hablar:
—Yo no soy vuestro criado,    nunca comí vuestro pan,
antes soy un caballero    que por aquí acerté a pasar:
vuestras voces dolorosas    aquí me han hecho llegar
a saber qué mal tenéis,    o de qué es vuestro penar.

that so lofty a knight   could commit such a crime!
Imagining I was going hunting,   I bagged my own death.
I don't grieve about dying,   since it's in the course of nature,
but because I'm dying this way,   undeserving of harm,
and in a place where my death   will never be heard of!
O great and mighty God,   lover of justice and truth,
for my innocent death   please exact justice!
On this sinful soul   please have mercy!
Oh, sad queen, my mother,   may God comfort you,
for now the mirror is broken   in which you once saw yourself reflected!
You always feared   to have grief on my account;
from this day forward   you need no longer fear!
In jousts and tourneys   you used to give me advice;
now, alas, that I die   you can't even speak to me!
Oh, noble Marquess of Mantua,   my lord and uncle by blood,
where are you that you don't hear   my sorrowful lament?
What sorrowful news   it will be to you, and grievous,
when you hear nothing about me   and can't find me!
You made me your heir   to inherit your property,
but you'll have to be mine   even though you're older!
Oh, wretched world,   no one should trust you;
the man who rises highest in you,   you give him the greatest fall!"
Saying these words,   he ceaselessly utters
very sorrowful sighs   that are heartbreaking.
The marquess was upset,   he couldn't go on listening:
his heart was tightening,   his blood was racing.
At the knight's feet   he came up close;
in a very shaken voice   he began to address him:
"What's wrong with you, knight?   Please tell me.
Are you mortally wounded,   or are you in other distress?"
When the knight heard him,   he tried to raise his head:
he thought it was his squire,   and made this answer:
"What did you say, my friend?   Have you brought a priest for me?
For my soul is now departing;   I want to end my life properly:
I'm no longer worried about my body,   I want to save my soul."
At once the marquess realized   he had mistaken him for someone else:
he replied in great agitation,   barely able to speak:
"I'm not your servant,   I never ate your bread;
rather, I'm a knight   who happened to pass this way:
your sorrowful cries   made me come here
to find out what was wrong with you   or what your grief was about.

Pues que caballero sois,    querades vos esforzar,
que para esto es este mundo,    para bien y mal pasar.
Decidme, señor, quién sois    y de qué es vuestro mal,
que si remediarse puede    yo os prometo de ayudar:
no dudéis, buen caballero,    de decirme la verdad.
Tornara en sí Valdovinos,    respuesta le fuera a dar:
—Muchas mercedes, señor,    por la buena voluntad;
mi mal es crudo y de muerte,    no se puede remediar.
Veinte y dos feridas tengo    que cada una es mortal;
el mayor dolor que siento,    es morir en tal lugar,
do no se sabrá mi muerte    para poderse vengar,
porque me han muerto a traición    sin merescer ningun mal.
A lo que habéis preguntado    por mi fe os digo verdad,
que a mí dicen Valdovinos,    que el Franco solían llamar;
hijo soy del rey de Dacia,    hijo soy suyo carnal,
uno de los doce pares    que a la mesa comen pan.
La reina doña Ermeline    es mi madre natural,
el noble marqués de Mantua    era mi tío carnal,
hermano era de mi padre    sin en nada discrepar;
la linda infanta Sevilla    es mi esposa sin dudar:
hame ferido Carloto,    su hijo del emperante,
porque él requirió de amores    a mi esposa con maldad:
porque no le dió su amor    él en mí se fue a vengar,
pensando que por mi muerte    con ella había de casar.
Hame muerto a traición    viniendo yo a le guardar,
porque él me rogó en París    le viniese acompañar
a dar fin a una aventura    en que se quería probar.
Quien quier que seáis, caballero,    la nueva os plega llevar
de mi desastrada muerte    a París, esa ciudad,
y si hacia París no fuerdes    a Mantua le iréis a dar,
que el trabajo que ende habréis    muy bien vos lo pagarán,
y si no quisierdes paga    bien se vos agradecerá.
Cuando aquesto oyó el marqués    la habla perdido ha,
en el suelo dio consigo,    la espada fue arrojar,
las barbas de la su cara    empezólas de arrancar,
los sus cabellos muy canos    comiénzalos de mesar.
A cabo de una gran pieza    en pie se fue a levantar;
allegóse al caballero    por las armas le quitar.
Desque le quitó el almete    comenzóle de mirar:
estaba bañado en sangre,    con la color muy mortal;
estaba desfigurado,    no lo podía figurar,

Since you're a knight,    please take heart,
for this is the way of the world,    to undergo good and bad.
Sir, tell me who you are    and what your trouble is,
for if there's any remedy,    I promise to help you;
don't hesitate, good knight,    to tell me the truth."
Valdovinos regained his composure    and made this answer:
"Many thanks, sir,    for your good will;
my distress is cruel and fatal,    it can't be remedied.
I bear twenty-two wounds    of which each one is mortal;
the greatest grief I feel    is to die in such a place,
where no one will learn of my death    and be able to avenge me,
because I was killed treacherously,    undeserving of harm.
To what you asked    I say truthfully, by my faith,
that I'm named Valdovinos,    often called 'the candid';
I'm son to the king of Dacia,    I'm his legitimate son,
one of the twelve peers    who dine at the emperor's table.
Queen Ermeline    is my true mother,
the noble Marquess of Mantua    is my own uncle,
my father's brother    and in no way different from him;
the lovely Princess Sevilla    is my wife beyond a doubt:
I was wounded by Carloto,    the emperor's son,
because he courted    my wife evilly:
because she didn't give him her love,    he took revenge on me,
thinking that by my death    he'd be able to marry her.
He killed me treacherously    when I came to protect him,
after asking me in Paris    to accompany him,
to accomplish an adventure    in which he wished to test himself.
Whoever you are, knight,    please take the news
of my ill-starred death    to the city of Paris,
and if you're not going to Paris,    take it to Mantua,
and the trouble it will cause you    will be very well repaid;
if you do not wish for pay,    they'll thank you for it handsomely."
When the marquess heard this,    he lost the power to speak;
he fell to the ground,    he threw away his sword,
the beard on his chin    he began to pull out,
his very white hair    he began to tear.
After a long while    he got back on his feet;
he approached the knight    to remove his armor.
After removing his helmet,    he began to observe him:
he was soaked with blood,    he was deathly pale;
he was so disfigured    he was unrecognizable;

ni le podía conoscer    en el gesto ni el hablar;
dudando estaba, dudando    si era mentira o verdad.
Con un paño que traía    la cara le fue a limpiar:
desque la hubo limpiado    luego conocido lo ha.
En la boca lo besaba    no cesando de llorar,
las palabras que decía    dolor es de las contar.
—¡Oh sobrino Valdovinos,    mi buen sobrino carnal!
¿Quién vos trató de tal suerte?    ¿Quién vos trajo a tal lugar?
¿Quién es el que a vos mató    que a mí vivo fue a dejar?
¡Mas valiera la mi muerte    que la vuestra en tal edad!
¿No me conocéis, sobrino?    ¡Por Dios me queráis hablar!
Yo soy el triste marqués    que tío solíades llamar,
yo soy el marqués de Mantua    que debo de reventar
llorando la vuestra muerte    por con vida no quedar.
¡Oh desventurado viejo!    ¿Quién me podrá conortar?
que pérdida tan crecida    más dolor es consolar.
Yo la muerte de mis hijos    con vos podría olvidar.
Agora, mi buen señor,    de nuevo habré de llorar.
A vos tenía por sobrino    para mi estado heredar,
agora por mi ventura    yo vos habré de enterrar.
Sobrino, de aquí adelante    yo no quiero vivir más:
ven, muerte, cuando quisieres,    no te quieras detardar;
¡mas al que menos te teme    le huyes por más penar!
¿Quién le llevará las nuevas    amargas de gran pesar
a la triste madre vuestra?    ¿Quién la podrá consolar?
Siempre lo oí decir,    agora veo ser verdad,
que quien larga vida vive    mucho mal ha de pasar:
por un placer muy pequeño    pesares ha de gustar.
De estas palabras y otras    no cesaba de hablar
llorando de los sus ojos    sin poderse conortar.
Esforzóse Valdovinos    con el angustia mortal;
desque conoció a su tío    alivio fuera a tomar:
tomóle entrambas las manos,    muy recio le fue apretar:
disimulando su pena    comenzó al marqués hablar:
—No lloredes, señor tío,    por Dios no queráis llorar,
que me dais doblada pena    y al alma hacéis penar;
mas lo que vos encomiendo    es por mí queráis rogar,
y no me desamparéis    en este esquivo lugar;
fasta que yo haya espirado,    no me querades dejar.
Encomiéndoos a mi madre,    vos la queráis consolar,
que bien creo que mi muerte    su vida habrá de acabar;

he couldn't tell him    by his face or his voice;
he stood there wondering    whether it was true or a lie.
With a cloth that he had    he cleaned his face:
after cleaning it,    he recognized him at once.
He kissed him on the lips,    weeping constantly;
the words that he spoke    are sorrowful to relate:
"Oh, nephew Valdovinos,    my very own good nephew!
Who treated you this way?    Who brought you to this place?
Who is it that killed you    and left me still alive?
Better that I had died    than you at your age!
Don't you know me, nephew?    By God, please speak to me!
I am the unhappy marquess    you used to call your uncle,
I am the Marquess of Mantua,    who will probably perish
bewailing your death,    and will be left lifeless.
Oh, miserable old man!    Who'll be able to console me?
For consolation is a greater sorrow    when the loss is so crushing.
With you alive I could have forgotten    the death of my sons.
Now, good lord,    I'll have to weep again.
I had you for a nephew    to inherit my property;
now, to my misfortune,    I'll have to bury you.
Nephew, from this day forth    I no longer wish to live:
come, death, whenever you please,    don't delay;
but the man who fears you least    you shun to grieve him more!
Who will bear the news,    bitter and most grievous,
to your sad mother?    Who'll be able to comfort her?
I've always heard it said,    and now I see it's true,
that whoever lives a long life    must undergo much sorrow:
for one very small pleasure    he must taste troubles."
These words and others    he didn't cease to speak,
with tears in his eyes,    unable to be comforted.
Valdovinos struggled    with his mortal anguish;
when he recognized his uncle,    he felt some relief:
he took both his hands    and squeezed them very hard;
concealing his grief,    he began to say to the marquess:
"Don't weep, lord uncle,    for God's sake don't weep,
for you give me double sorrow    and make my soul suffer;
but what I urge you to do    is to pray for me
and not leave me alone    in this inhospitable place;
until I have expired    please don't desert me.
I entrust my mother to you,    please comfort her,
for I surely believe my death    will cause her life to end;

encomiéndoos a mi esposa,    por ella queráis mirar;
el mayor dolor que siento    es no la poder hablar.
Ellos estando en aquesto    su escudero fue a llegar:
un ermitaño traía    que en el bosque fue a hallar,
hombre de muy santa vida    de orden sacerdotal.
Cuando llegó el ermitaño    el alba quería quebrar.
Esforzando a Valdovinos    comenzóle amonestar
que olvidase aqueste mundo    y de Dios se quiera acordar.
Aparte se fue el marqués    por dalles mejor lugar;
el escudero a otra parte    también se fuera apartar:
el marqués de quebrantado    gran sueño le fue a tomar.
Confesóse Valdovinos    a toda su voluntad.
Estando en su confesión,    ya que quería acabar,
las angustias de la muerte    comienzan de le aquejar:
con el dolor que sentía    una gran voz fuera a dar:
llama a su tío el marqués,    comenzó así de hablar:
—Adiós, adiós, mi buen tío,    adiós vos queráis quedar,
que yo me voy de este mundo    para la mi cuenta dar:
lo que vos ruego y encomiendo    no lo queráis olvidar:
dadme vuestra bendición,    la mano para besar.
Luego perdiera el sentido,    luego perdiera el hablar,
los dientes se le cerraron,    los ojos vuelto se le han.
Recordó luego el marqués,    a él se fuera a llegar,
muchas veces lo bendice    no cesando de llorar.
Absolvióle el ermitaño;    por él comienza a rezar.
A cabo de poco rato    Valdovinos fue a espirar.
El marqués de verlo así    amortecido se ha,
consuélalo el ermitaño,    muchos ejemplos le da:
el marqués como discreto    acuerdo fuera a tomar,
pues remediar no se puede,    a haberse de conortar.
Lo que hacía el escudero    lástima era de mirar;
rescuñaba la su cara,    sus ropas rasgado ha,
sus barbas y sus cabellos    por tierra los va a lanzar.
A cabo de una gran pieza,    que ambos cansados están,
el marqués al ermitaño    comienza de preguntar:
—Pídoos por Dios, padre honrado,    respuesta me queráis dar:
¿dónde estamos, o en qué reino,    en qué señorío o lugar?
¿Cómo se llama esta tierra?    ¿Cúya es, y a qué mandar?
El ermitaño responde:    —Pláceme de voluntad:
debéis de saber, señor,    que esta es tierra sin poblar:
otro tiempo fue poblada,    despoblóse por gran mal,

I entrust my wife to you,    please look after her;
the greatest pain I feel    is not being able to speak to her."
At that point in their talk    his squire arrived;
he brought along a hermit    he had found in the woods,
a man of very holy living    and an ordained priest.
When the hermit arrived,    dawn was about to break.
Encouraging Valdovinos,    he began to admonish him
to forget this world    and set his thoughts on God.
The marquess drew aside    to give them more privacy;
in another direction the squire    also drew aside;
the marquess was so exhausted,    he fell into deep sleep.
Valdovinos made confession    as fully as he wished.
While still confessing,    and already about to finish,
the throes of death    began to assail him;
at the pain he felt    he uttered a loud cry;
he called his uncle, the marquess,    and started speaking thus:
"Farewell, farewell, good uncle,    may you remain with God!
for I am leaving this world    to make my reckoning;
what I beseech and urge you to do,    please don't forget it;
give me your blessing,    your hand to kiss."
Then he lost consciousness,    then he lost the power to speak;
he clenched his teeth    and his eyes turned up.
At once the marquess awoke    and approached him;
he blessed him again and again,    never ceasing to weep.
The hermit gave him absolution    and began to pray for him.
After a little while    Valdovinos breathed his last.
The marquess, seeing him dead,    fell in a faint;
the hermit consoled him,    giving him many pious examples;
like the wise man that he was,    the marquess resolved
that since it couldn't be helped,    he had to take comfort.
What the squire was doing    was pitiful to behold;
he scratched his face,    he tore his clothes,
his beard and hair    he flung to the ground.
After a long while,    when they were both tired,
the marquess began    to question the hermit:
"Fod God's love, I ask you, honorable father,    to reply:
Where are we, in what realm,    in what domain or place?
What's the name of this land?    Whose is it, under whose control?"
The hermit replied:    "I'll tell you very gladly:
you should know, sir,    that this is uninhabited land;
in the past it had people    but it lost them through great troubles,

por batallas muy crueles    que hubo en la Cristiandad:
a esta llaman la Floresta    sin ventura y de pesar,
porque nunca caballero    en ella se acaeció entrar
que saliese sin gran daño    o desastre desigual.
Esta tierra es del marqués    de Mantua, la gran ciudad:
fasta Mantua son cien millas,    sin poblado ni lugar,
sino sola una ermita    que a seis millas de aquí está,
donde yo hago mi vida    por del mundo me apartar.
El más cercano poblado    a veinte millas está;
es una villa cercada    del ducado de Milán.
Ved lo que queréis, señor,    en que yo os pueda ayudar,
que por servicio de Dios    lo haré de voluntad,
y por vuestro acatamiento,    y por hacer caridad.
El marqués que aquesto oyera    comenzóle de rogar
que no recibiese pena    de con el cuerpo quedar,
mientras él y el escudero    el caballo van buscar
que allí cerca había dejado    en un prado a descansar.
Plúgole al ermitaño    allí haberlos de esperar:
el marqués y el escudero    el caballo van buscar:
por el camino do iban    comenzóle a preguntar:
—Dígasme, buen escudero,    si Dios te quiera guardar,
¿qué venía tu señor    por esta tierra buscar,
y por qué causa lo han muerto,    y quién le fuera a matar?
Respondió el escudero,    tal respuesta le fue a dar:
—Por la fe que debo a Dios    yo no lo puedo pensar,
porque no lo sé, señor:    lo que ví os quiero contar.
Estando dentro en París    en cortes del emperante,
el príncipe don Carloto    a mi señor envió a llamar.
Estuvieron en secreto    todo el día en su hablar;
cuando la noche cerró    ambos se fueron armar.
Cabalgaron a caballo,    salieron de la ciudad
armados de todas armas    a guisa de pelear.
Yo salí con Valdovinos    y con Carloto, un paje:
ayer hubo quince días    salimos de la ciudad.
Luego cuando aquí llegamos    a este bosque de pesar,
mi señor y don Carloto    mandaron nos esperar.
Solos se entraron los dos    por aquel espeso valle;
el paje estaba cansado,    gran sueño le fue a tomar;
yo pensando en Valdovinos    no podía reposar.
Apartéme del camino    en un árbol fui a pujar,
a todas partes miraba    cuando los vería tornar.

through very cruel battles    waged in Christendom:
it's called the Luckless    and Grievous Forest
because no knight has ever    happened to enter it
and come out without great injury    or some uncommon disaster.
The land belongs to the Marquess    of Mantua, that great city.
From here to Mantua it's a hundred miles,    without people or villages,
but only a single hermitage    located six miles from here,
where I spend my days    to separate myself from the world.
The closest inhabited spot    is twenty miles away;
it's a walled city    within the duchy of Milan.
Decide what you wish, sir,    so that I can help you,
for, in God's service,    I'll do so gladly,
both from respect for you    and as an act of charity."
When the marquess heard this,    he began to ask him
to be so good as    to remain with the body
while he and the squire    looked for his horse,
which he had left nearby    to rest in a meadow.
The hermit agreed    to await them there;
the marquess and the squire    went looking for the horse;
as they proceeded    he began to ask him:
"Tell me, good squire,    so may God keep you!
What was your master    seeking in this land,
and why was he killed,    and who killed him?"
The squire replied,    he made this answer:
"By the faith I owe to God,    I can't imagine it,
because I don't know, sir,    but I'll tell you what I saw.
While we were in Paris    at the emperor's court,
Prince Carloto    had my master sent for.
They remained in privacy,    talking all day;
when night fell,    they both donned armor.
They mounted horses    and left the city
fully armed    as if for combat.
I left with Valdovinos,    a page with Carloto;
yesterday was two weeks    since we left the city.
As soon as we got here    in this sorrowful forest,
my master and Don Carloto    ordered us to wait.
The two of them alone entered    that dense valley;
the page was weary    and fell into a deep sleep;
I, thinking of Valdovinos,    was unable to rest.
I drew aside from the path    and climbed a tree;
I gazed in all directions    to see them return.

A cabo de un gran rato    caballos oí relinchar,
vi venir tres caballeros,    mi señor no vi tornar.
Venían bañados en sangre,    luego vi mala señal;
el uno era don Carloto,    los dos no pude notar.
Con gran miedo que tenía    no les osé preguntar
do quedaba Valdovinos,    do le fueran a dejar,
mas abajéme del árbol,    entré por aquel pinar:
desque los vi trasponer    yo comencé de buscar
a mi señor Valdovinos,    mas no lo podía hallar:
el rastro de los caballos    no dejaba de mirar.
A la entrada de un llano,    al pasar de un arenal,
vi huella de otro caballo,    la cual me pareció mal;
vi mucha sangre por tierra,    de que me fui a espantar;
en la orilla del río    el caballo fui a hallar,
más adelante, no mucho,    a Valdovinos vi estar.
Boca abajo estaba en tierra,    y casi quería espirar,
todo cubierto de sangre    que apenas podía hablar.
Levantáralo de tierra,    comencéle de limpiar;
por señas me demandó    confesor fuese a buscar.
Esto es, noble señor,    lo que sé de este gran mal.
En estas cosas hablando    el caballo van topar,
cabalgó en él el marqués,    y a las ancas fuele a tomar:
a do quedó el ermitaño    presto tornado se han.
Desque hablaron un rato    acuerdo van a tomar
que se fuesen a la ermita,    y el cuerpo allá lo llevar.
Pónenlo encima el caballo,    nadie quiso cabalgar.
El ermitaño los guía,    comienzan de caminar;
llevan vía de la ermita    apriesa y no de vagar.
Deque allá hubieron llegado    el cuerpo van desarmar.
Quince lanzadas tenía,    cada una era mortal,
que de la menor de todas    ninguno podría escapar.
Cuando así lo vio el marqués    traspasóse de pesar,
a cabo de una gran pieza    un gran suspiro fue a dar.
Entró dentro en la capilla,    de rodillas se fue a hincar,
puso la mano en una ara    que estaba sobre el altar,
en los pies de un crucifijo    jurando, empezó de hablar:
—Juro por Dios poderoso,    por Santa María su Madre,
y al santo Sacramento    que aquí suelen celebrar,
de nunca peinar mis canas    ni las mis barbas cortar:
de no vestir otras ropas,    ni renovar mi calzar;
de no entrar en poblado,    ni las armas me quitar,

After a long while    I heard horses neigh;
I saw three horsemen coming,    I didn't see my master returning.
They were soaked with blood,    which I at once took as a bad sign;
one of them was Don Carloto,    I couldn't recognize the other two.
I was so afraid    that I didn't dare ask them
where Valdovinos was,    where they had left him;
but I descended from the tree    and entered that pine grove;
when they vanished from sight,    I began to seek
my master Valdovinos,    but couldn't find him;
I kept on observing    the track of the horses.
At the entrance to a plain,    crossing a sandy area,
I saw the hoofprints of another horse;    this looked bad to me;
I saw much blood on the ground,    which frightened me;
by the bank of the river    I found the horse;
further along, but not much,    I saw Valdovinos lying.
He was face down on the ground    and nearly about to die,
all covered with blood    and barely able to speak.
I raised him from the ground    and started to clean him;
in signs he asked me    to bring him a confessor.
That, noble lord, is    all I know of this great disaster."
While engaged in this discussion    they came across the horse;
the marquess mounted it    and the squire got on behind him;
they were soon back    where the hermit had remained.
After talking a while    they resolved
to go to the hermitage    and take the body there.
They placed it on the horse;    none of them wished to ride.
The hermit guided them    and they began walking;
they took the path to the hermitage    quickly, and not slowly.
When they reached it,    they took the armor off the body.
It had fifteen lance wounds,    each of them mortal;
the slightest of them all    nobody could survive.
When the marquess saw him like that,    he was smitten with grief;
after a long while    he heaved a mighty sigh.
He entered the chapel    and fell on his knees;
placing his hand on an altar stone    that lay on the altar,
at the feet of a crucifix    he began to speak this oath:
"I swear by God Almighty    and His Mother, St. Mary,
and by the Holy Sacrament    that is celebrated here,
never to comb my white hair    or trim my beard,
or change my clothes    or wear different shoes,
or enter an inhabited place    or remove my armor,

sino fuere una hora    para mi cuerpo limpiar;
de no comer a manteles,    ni a mesa me asentar,
fasta matar a Carloto    por justicia o pelear,
o morir en la demanda    manteniendo la verdad:
y si justicia me niegan    sobre esta tan gran maldad,
de con mi estado y persona    contra Francia guerrear,
y manteniendo la guerra    morir o vencer sin paz.
Y por este juramento    prometo de no enterrar
el cuerpo de Valdovinos    fasta su muerte vengar.
De que aquesto hubo jurado    mostró no sentir pesar;
rogando está al ermitaño    que le quisiese ayudar
para llevar aquel cuerpo    al más cercano lugar.
El ermitaño piadoso    su bestia le fue a dejar;
amortajaron el cuerpo,    en ella lo van a posar:
con las armas de Valdovinos    el marqués se fue armar:
cabalgara en su caballo,    comienza de caminar.
Camino llevan de la villa    que arriba oistes nombrar.
Con él iba el ermitaño    por el camino mostrar.
Antes que a la villa lleguen    una abadía van fallar
de la orden de San Bernardo    que en una montaña está,
a la bajada de un puerto    y a la entrada de un lugar.
Allá se fue el marqués    y allí acordó quedar
por estar más encubierto,    y el cuerpo en guarda dejar,
por hacelle un ataúd    y habello de embalsamar.
Al ermitaño rogaba    dineros quiera tomar;
desque dineros no quiso    sus ricas joyas le da:
no quiso ninguna cosa,    su bestia fue a demandar:
despidióse del marqués,    a Dios le fue encomendar.
Después de ser despedido    para su ermita se va;
por el camino do vuelve    a muchos topado ha
que el marqués iban buscando,    llorando por le hallar.
Muchos por él preguntaban,    las señales ciertas dan,
por las señas que le dieron    él conocido lo ha,
a todos les respondía:    —Yo vos digo de verdad,
que un hombre de tales señas,    que no sé quién es ni cuál,
dos días ha que le acompaño    sin saber adónde va;
dejélo en un abadía    que dicen de Flores Valle,
con un caballero muerto    que acaso fuera a fallar:
si allá quereis ir, señores,    fallaréislo de verdad.

except for an hour    to cleanse my body,
never to eat at a spread table    or sit down to table at all,
until I kill Carloto    by legal means or in combat,
or else die challenging him    in the interests of truth;
and if I'm denied justice    for this very great crime,
with my property and person    I shall war against France
and, sustaining the war,    die or conquer without peace.
And by this oath    I promise not to bury
the body of Valdovinos    until I avenge his death."
After swearing this oath    he seemed to grieve no longer;
he requested the hermit    to assist him
in taking the body    to the nearest village.
The compassionate hermit    loaned him his mount;
they wrapped the body in a shrowd    and placed it on the beast;
the marquess clad himself    in the armor of Valdovinos;
he mounted his horse    and set out on the journey.
They headed for the town    you've heard mentioned earlier.
With him went the hermit    to show him the way.
Before they reached the town,    they found an abbey
of the Order of St. Bernard    situated on a mountain
at the descent from a pass    and the entrance to a village.
There the marquess went    and there he resolved to stay
in order to remain out of sight    and leave the body under guard,
to make a coffin for it    and have it embalmed.
He asked the hermit    to accept money;
when he refused money,    he offered him his costly jewelry;
he wanted nothing,    but asked for his animal back;
he took leave of the marquess,    commending him to God.
After taking leave    he returned to his hermitage;
on his way back    he met with many men
who were seeking the marquess,    weeping as they sought him.
Many men asked about him,    giving an accurate description;
by the description they gave    he knew whom they meant
and replied to them all:    "I tell you in truth
that a man of that description    (I don't know his name or rank)
I have been accompanying two days,    not knowing where he was bound;
I left him at an abbey    called Vale of Flowers,
along with a dead knight    whom he had found by chance;
if you wish to go there, gentlemen,    you'll surely find him."

## 38. Romance del conde Dirlos

Estábase el conde Dirlos     sobrino de don Beltrane,
asentado en sus tierras     deleitándose en cazare,
cuando le vinieron cartas     de Carlos el emperante;
de las cartas placer hubo,     de las palabras pesare,
que lo que las cartas dicen     a él parece muy male:
—Rogar vos quiero, sobrino,     el buen francés naturale,
que lleguéis vuestros caballeros,     los que comen vuestro pane,
darles héis doble sueldo     del que les soledes dare;
dobles armas y caballos,     que bien menester lo hane;
darles héis el campo franco     de todo lo que ganarane,
partiros héis a los reinos     del rey moro Aliarde.
Deseximiento me ha dado,     a mí y a los doce pares,
grande mengua me sería,     que todos se hubiesen de andare;
no veo caballero en Francia     que mejor puedo enviare,
sino a vos el conde Dirlos,     esforzado en peleare.
El conde que esto oyó,     tomó tristeza y pesare;
no por miedo de los moros,     ni miedo de peleare,
mas tiene la mujer hermosa,     mochacha de poca edade,
tres años anduvo en armas     para con ella casare
y el año no era complido     a ella lo mandan apartare,
de que esto él pensaba     tomó dello gran pesare.
Triste estaba y pensativo,     no cesa de sospirare,
despide los falconeros;     los monteros manda pagare;
despide todos aquellos     con quien solía deleitarse.
No burla con la condesa     como solía burlare,
mas muy triste y pensativo     siempre le veían andare;
la condesa que esto vido     llorando empezó de hablare:
—Triste estades vos, el conde,     triste, lleno de pesare,
desta tan triste partida     para mí de tanto male.
Partir vos queréis, el conde,     a reinos del rey moro Aliarde;
dejáisme en tierras ajenas     sola y sin quien m'acompañe,
¿Cuántos años, el buen conde,     hacéis cuenta de tardare
y volverme a las tierras,     a las tierras de mi padre?
Vestirme de un paño negro,     este será mi llevare;
maldiré mi hermosura,     maldiré mi mocedade,
maldiré aquél triste día     que con vos quise casare.

## 38. Ballad of the Count of Irlos

The Count of Irlos,   nephew of Don Beltrán,
was on his estate   taking pleasure in the hunt,
when he received a letter   from Emperor Carlos;
he was glad of the letter,   but saddened by its contents,
for the message in the letter   seemed very bad to him:
"I wish to request of you, nephew,   good Frenchman that you are,
to assemble your knights,   those who eat your bread;
you'll give them twice the pay   that you usually do;
twice as many weapons and horses,   for they'll really need them;
you'll give them an open hand   on any spoils they win;
you shall depart for the realm   of the Moorish king Aliarde.
He has sent me a challenge,[17]   me and the twelve peers;
it would be a great detriment to me   if all were to go;
I see no knight in France   whom I might better send
than you, Count of Irlos,   courageous in combat."
When the count heard this,   it gave him sadness and grief,
not out of fear of the Moors   or fear of fighting,
but because he had a beautiful wife,   just a young girl;
he had borne arms three years   in order to marry her,
and it was not yet a full year later   that he was ordered to leave her;
when he reflected on this,   he felt immense sorrow.
He went about sad and pensive,   never ceasing to sigh;
he dismissed his falconers,   he had his huntsmen paid off;
he dismissed all those   with whom he was wont to take pleasure.
He didn't sport with the countess   as he had been accustomed to,
but very sad and pensive   he was always seen to be;
when the countess saw this,   she wept and began to speak:
"You are sad, count,   sad and full of grief
because of this sad parting,   which gives me such distress.
You're about to leave, count,   for the realm of the Moorish king Aliarde;
you're leaving me with other people   alone and unescorted.
How many years, good count,   do you expect to tarry,
sending me back to the lands,   the lands of my father?
Black cloth,   that shall be my garb;
I shall curse my beauty,   I shall curse my youth,
I shall curse the sad day   when I married you.

17. A conjecture from the context; the translator has failed to find *deseximiento* (or any of its possible variant forms) in any glossary or dictionary, no matter how specialized. Perhaps: "a declaration of war."

Mas si vos queredes, conde,    yo con vos quería andare;
más quiero perder la vida    que sin vos de ella gozare.
El conde, desque esto oyera,    empezóla de mirare,
con una voz amorosa    presto tal respuesta hace:
—No lloredes vos, condesa,    de mi partida no hayáis pesare;
no quedáis en tierra ajena,    sino en vuestra a vuestro mandare;
que antes que yo me parta,    todo vos lo quiero dare.
Podéis vender cualquier villa    y empeñar cualquier ciudad
como principal heredera    que nada vos pueden quitare.
Quedaréis encomendada    a mi tío don Beltrane
y a mi primo Gaiferos,    señor de París la grande;
quedaréis encomendada    a Oliveros y a Roldane,
al emperador y a los doce    que a una mesa comen pane,
porque los reinos son lejos    del Rey moro Aliarde,
que son cerca la Casa Santa    allende del nuestro mare,
siete años, la condesa,    todos siete me esperade;
si a los ocho no viniere,    a los nueve vos casade.
Seréis de veinte y siete años,    que es la mejor edade,
el que con vos casare, señora,    mis tierras tome en ajuare;
gozará de mujer hermosa,    rica y de gran linaje.
Bien es verdad, la condesa,    que comigo vos querría llevare,
mas yo voy para batallas    y no cierto para holgare.
Caballero que va en armas    de mujer no debe curare,
porque, con el bien que os quiero,    la honra habría de olvidare.
Mas aparejad, condesa,    mandad vos aparejare,
iréis comigo a las cortes,    a París esa ciudade.
Toquen, toquen, mis trompetas,    manden luego cabalgare.
Ya se parte el buen conde,    la condesa otro que tale.
La vuelta van de Parise,    apriesa, no de vagare;
cuando son a una jornada    de París esa ciudade,
el emperador que lo supo    a recebírselo sale.
Con él sale Oliveros,    con él sale don Roldane,
con él, Arderín de Ardeña    y Urgel de la fuerza grande;
con él, infante Guarinos,    almirante de la mare,
con él sale el esforzado    Reinaldos de Montalbane.
Con él van todos los Doce,    que a una mesa comen pane,
sino el infante Gaiferos    y el buen conde don Beltrane,
que salieron tres jornadas    más que todos adelante.
No quiso el emperador    que hobiesen de aposentare,
sino en sus reales palacios    posada les mandó dare.
Empiezan luego su partida,    apriesa, e no de vagare,

But if you wish, count,     I'd like to go with you;
I'd rather lose my life     than enjoy it without you."
When the count heard this,     he began to gaze at her;
in a loving voice     he quickly made this answer:
"Don't weep, countess,     don't grieve at my departure;
don't stay at another's home,     but in yours as your own mistress;
for before I leave     I intend to give you everything.
You can sell any town     or mortgage any city
as my chief heir,     from whom nothing can be taken.
You shall be entrusted     to my uncle, Don Beltrán,
and to my cousin Gaiferos,     lord of great Paris;
you shall be entrusted     to Oliveros and Roldán,
to the emperor and the twelve     who eat bread at one table;
because the realm is distant     of the Moorish king Aliarde,
which is near the Holy Sepulcher     beyond our sea,
seven years, countess,     wait for me a full seven years;
if I'm not back by the eighth,     remarry in the ninth.
You'll be twenty-seven,     which is the best age;
whoever marries you, lady,     let him take my land as a trousseau;
he'll enjoy a beautiful woman,     wealthy and of high ancestry.
It's true, countess,     that I'd like to take you with me,
but I'm going to do battle,     and certainly not to have fun.
A knight in his armor     shouldn't have to worry about a wife;
you see, I love you so much,     I might forget my honor.
But make ready, countess,     order your things made ready;
you'll go with me to the court,     to the city of Paris.
Blow, blow, my trumpets,     sound the signal to mount at once!"
Now the good count departs,     and the countess as well.
They head for Paris     quickly, and not slowly;
when they're one day's distance     from the city of Paris,
the emperor, who has learned this,     comes out to greet them.
With him comes Oliveros,     with him comes Don Roldán,
with him Alderín de Ardeña     and Urgel of great might,
with him Prince Guarinos,     admiral of the sea,
with him comes brave     Reinaldos of Montalván.
With him come all the twelve     who eat bread at one table,
except for Prince Gaiferos     and the good Count Beltrán,
who had left three days     ahead of all the rest.
The emperor refused     to have them lodged elsewhere,
but in his royal palace     he bade they be given rooms.
At once their departure begins,     quickly, and not slowly;

dale diez mil caballeros　de Francia más principales
y con mucha otra gente　y gran ejército reale;
el sueldo les paga junto　por siete años y mase.
Ya tomadas buenas armas,　caballos otro que tale,
enderezan su partida,　empiezan de cabalgare.
Cuando el buen conde Dirlos　ruega mucho al emperante
que él y todos los doce　se quisiesen ayuntare;
cuando todos fueron juntos　en la gran sala reale,
entra el conde y la condesa,　mano por mano se vane;
cuando son en medio de ellos　el conde empezó de hablare:
—A vos lo digo, mi tío,　el buen viejo don Beltrane,
y a vos infante Gaiferos　y a mi buen primo carnale,
y esto delante de todos　lo quiero mucho rogare,
y al muy alto emperador　que sepa mi voluntade:
cómo villas y castillos　y ciudades y lugares
los dejo a la condesa,　que nadie las pueda quitare;
mas como principal heredera　en ellas pueda mandare,
en vender cualquier villa　y empeñar cualquier ciudade,
de aquello que ella hiciere　todos se hayan de agradare.
Si por tiempo yo no viniere,　vosotros la queráis casare;
el marido que ella tome　mis tierras tome en ajuare.
Y a vos la encomiendo, tío,　en lugar de marido y padre,
y a vos, mi primo Gaiferos,　por mí la queráis honrare,
y encomiéndola a Oliveros　y encomiéndola a Roldane
y encomiéndola a los Doce　y a don Carlos el emperante.
Y a todos les place mucho　de aquello que el conde hace.
Ya se parte el buen conde　de París, esa ciudade,
la condesa que ir lo vido　jamás lo quiso dejare
hasta orillas de la mare　do se había de embarcare.
Con ella va don Gaiferos,　con ella va don Beltrane,
con ella va el esforzado　Reinaldos de Montalbane,
sin otros muchos caballeros　de Francia más principales.
A tan triste dispedida　el uno del otro hacen,
que si el conde iba triste,　la condesa mucho mase;
palabras se están diciendo,　que era dolor de escuchare;
el conorte que se daban　era continuo llorare.
Con gran dolor manda el conde　hacer vela y navegare,
como sin la condesa se vido　navegando por la mare,
movido de muy gran saña,　movido de gran pesare,
diciendo que por ningún tiempo　de ella lo harán apartare,
sacramento tiene hecho　sobre un libro misale

he gives him ten thousand horsemen,   the foremost in France,
with many other men    and a large royal army;
he pays them at one time    for seven years and more.
Now, with good weapons    and good horses, too,
they prepare to move out,    they begin to mount.
After the good Count of Irlos    insisted to the emperor
that he and all the twelve    dine with him,
when they were all assembled    in the royal great hall,
the count and countess entered,    walking hand in hand;
when they were in their midst,    the count began to speak:
"I say this to you, uncle,    good old man Don Beltrán,
and to you, Prince Gaiferos,    my good first cousin,
and in the presence of all here    I wish to make this request,
also of the lofty emperor,    who is to know my wishes:
that towns and castles,    cities and villages,
I leave to the countess    as inalienable property;
as chief heiress    she can do as she likes with them,
she can sell any town    or mortgage any city;
whatever she chooses to do,    everyone must agree to.
If I don't return in time,    please marry her off;
the husband she takes,    let him have my land as a trousseau.
I entrust her to you, uncle,    as if you were husband and father,
and to you, cousin Gaiferos;    honor her for my sake;
and I entrust her to Oliveros    and I entrust her to Roldán
and I entrust her to the twelve    and to Emperor Carlos."
And all were very pleased    with what the count had done.
Now the good count departs    from the city of Paris;
when the countess saw him go,    she refused to leave him
until they reached the coast,    where he was to embark.
With her went Don Gaiferos,    with her went Don Beltrán,
with her went the brave    Reinaldos of Montalván,
not to mention many other knights,    the foremost in France.
Such a sad farewell    the two of them make
that if the count was sad,    the countess was much more so;
they spoke words to each other    that were sorrowful to hear;
the comfort they gave each other    was continual weeping.
Very sadly the count gave orders    to set sail and depart;
when he found himself without the countess,    sailing on the sea,
agitated by very great fury,    agitated by great grief,
saying he wouldn't be separated from her    at any time,
he swore on oath    on a missal

de jamás volver en Francia,    ni en ella comer pane,
ni que nunca enviará carta    porque de él no sepan parte.
Siempre triste y pensativo,    puesto en pensamiento grande,
navegando sus jornadas    por la tempestosa mare,
llegado es a los reinos    del rey moro Aliarde,
ese gran soldán de Persia    con poderío muy grande.
Ya les estaban aguardando    a las orillas del mare,
cuando vino cerca tierra    las naves mandó llegare,
con un esfuerzo esforzado    los empieza de esforzare:
—Oh, esforzados caballeros,    oh mi compaña leale,
acuérdeseos que dejamos    nuestra tierra naturale,
de ellos dejamos mujeres,    de ellos hijos, de ellos padres
sólo para ganar honra    y no para ser cobardes;
pues, esforzados caballeros,    esforzad en peleare;
yo llevaré la delantera    y no me queráis dejare.
La morisma era tanta,    tierra no les dejan tomare;
el conde era esforzado    y discreto en peleare;
manda toda artillería    en las sus barcas posare,
con el ingenio que traía    empiézales de tirare;
los tiros eran tan fuertes,    por fuerza hacen lugare.
Veréis sacar los caballos    y muy apriesa cabalgare,
tan fuerte dan en los moros    que tierra les hacen dejare.
En tres años que el buen conde    entendió en peleare,
ganados tiene los reinos    del rey moro Aliarde.
Con todos sus caballeros    parte por iguales partes:
tan grande parte da al chico,    tanto le da como al grande.
Sólo él se retraía
armado de armas blancas    y cuentas para rezare
y tan triste vida hacía    que no se puede contare.
El soldán le hace tributo    y los reyes de allende el mare;
de los tributos que le daban,    a todos hacía parte;
a todos hace mandamiento    y a los mejores jurare,
ninguno sea osado    hombre a Francia enviare
y al que cartas enviase    luego le hará matare.
Quince años el conde estuvo,    siempre allende el mare,
que no escribió a la condesa    ni a su tío don Beltrane,
ni escribió a los Doce    ni menos al emperante.
Unos creían que era muerto,    otros anegado en mare.
Las barbas y los cabellos    nunca los quiso afeitare,
tiénelos hasta la cinta,    hasta la cinta y aun mase;
la cara mucho quemada    del mucho sol y del aire,

never to return to France,   or eat bread there,
or ever send a letter,   so they'd have no news of him.
Always sad and pensive,   lost in deep thought,
sailing each day   on the stormy sea,
he arrived at the realm   of the Moorish king Aliarde,
that great sultan of Persia   of such great might.
They were already expected   at the seashore;
when he came near land,   he ordered the ships assembled;
with a brave effort   he began to encourage them:
"O brave knights,   O loyal followers,
remember that we've left   our homeland,
some leaving wives,   some leaving sons, some fathers,
solely to win honor   and not be cowards;
well, then, brave knights,   strive to fight;
I'll be in the vanguard,   please don't desert me!"
There were so many Moors,   they weren't able to land;
the count was a brave   and prudent fighter;
he ordered all the artillery   placed in their launches;
with the weaponry he had   he began to fire on them;
the shots were so violent,   they were forced to yield ground.
Then you'd see them beach their horses   and quickly mount;
they attacked the Moors so hard   that they cleared the coast.
In the three years the good count   spent in combat,
he conquered the realm   of the Moorish king Aliarde.
With all his knights   he shares the booty equally:
the same amount he gives the little man, he gives the great.
He withdrew alone,
clad in white armor   and carrying prayer beads,
and he spent such sad days   that it can't be related.
The sultan sent him tribute,   as did the kings overseas;
the tribute they sent him   he shared with all;
he gave orders to all,   and had the chief men swear,
that no one should be so bold   as to send a man to France;
whoever sent a letter   he'd have killed at once.
Fifteen years the count stayed there,   overseas the whole time,
writing neither to the countess   nor to his uncle Beltrán,
nor to the twelve   nor even to the emperor.
Some thought he was dead,   others that he had drowned at sea.
He never cut   his beard or hair;
they came down to his waist,   to his waist and even below;
his face was deeply tanned   by all the sun and air,

con el gesto demudado  muy feroz y espantable.
Los quince años cumplidos,  deciséis quería entrare,
acostóse en su cama  con deseo de holgare;
pensando estaba, pensando  la triste vida que hace,
pensando en aquel tiempo  que solía festejare,
cuando justas y torneos  por la condesa solía armare.
Dormióse con pensamiento  y empezara de holgare,
cuando hace un triste sueño  para él de gran pesare:
que veía estar la condesa  en brazos de un infante.
Salto diera de la cama,  con un pensamiento grande;
gritando con altas voces,  no cesando de hablare:
—Toquen, toquen mis trompetas,  mi gente manden llegare.
Pensando que había moros,  todos llegados se hane;
desde que todos son llegados  llorando empezó a hablare:
—Oh, esforzados caballeros,  oh, mi compaña leale,
yo conozco aquél ejemplo  que dicen que es verdade,
que todo hombre nascido,  que es de hueso y de carne,
el mayor deseo que tenía  era en sus tierras holgare;
ya complidos son quince años  y en deciséis quiere entrare,
que somos en estos reinos  y estamos en soledade.
Quien tiene mujer hermosa,  vieja la ha de hallare;
el que dejó hijos pequeños  hallar los ha hombres grandes:
ni el padre conocerá el hijo,  ni el hijo menos al padre.
Hora es, mis caballeros,  de ir a Francia a holgare,
pues llevamos harta honra  y dineros mucho mase.
Lleguen, lleguen luego naves.  Mandenlas aparejare,
ordenemos capitanes,  para las tierras guardare.
Ya todo es aparejado,  ya empiezan a navegare,
cuando todos son llegados  a las orillas del mare,
llorando el conde de sus ojos  les empieza de hablare:
—Oh, esforzados caballeros,  oh, mi compaña leale,
una cosa rogarvos quiero,  no me la queráis negare;
quien secreto me tuviere  yo le he de gualardonare:
que todos hagáis juramento  sobre un libro misale,
que en parte ninguna que sea,  no me hayáis de nombrare,
porque con el gesto que traigo  ningunos me conoscerane,
mas viéndome con tanta gente  y ejercicio reale;
si vos demandan yo quien soy,  no les digáis la verdade,
mas decid que soy mensajero  que vengo de allende el mare,
que voy con una embajada  a don Carlos el emperante,
porque es hecho un mal suyo  y quiero ver si es verdade.

and with his haggard features    looked very fierce and frightful.
When the fifteen years were over,    the sixteenth about to begin,
he lay down on his bed,    wishing to relax;
he kept on thinking, thinking    about his sad existence,
thinking about the days    when he used to hold festivities,
when he used to organize jousts    and tourneys for the countess.
He fell asleep while thinking,    and was beginning to relax,
when he had a sad dream,    very grievous to him:
he saw the countess    in a prince's arms.
He jumped out of bed,    lost in thought;
he shouted loudly    and kept on saying:
"Blow, blow, my trumpets,    have my men assembled!"
Thinking there were Moors,    everyone assembled;
when they were all together,    he began to say, in tears:
"O brave knights,    O my loyal followers,
I know that saying,    which is supposed to be true,
that every man born    who is of flesh and blood
desires most of all    to enjoy himself at home;
fifteen years have now passed,    and the sixteenth is beginning,
since we came to this realm,    where we live in solitude.
Whoever has a beautiful wife    will find her old;
the man who left small sons    will find them grown men:
father won't recognize son,    nor the son the father.
It's time, my knights,    to return to pleasure in France,
for we've won plenty of honor    and even more money.
Let ships come, come at once.    Let thim be fitted out,
let's appoint commanders    to guard this territory."
Now everything is in readiness,    now they begin to sail;
when everyone was assembled    on the seashore,
the count, weeping,    began to address them:
"O brave knights,    O my loyal followers,
I want to make one request,    don't refuse it;
whoever keeps my identity a secret    I shall reward:
you are all to swear    on a missal
that, wherever it may be,    you won't speak my name,
so that, looking as I now do,    no one will recognize me,
seeing me with so many men    and a royal army;
if they ask you who I am,    don't tell them the truth,
but say I'm an envoy    coming from overseas
bearing a diplomatic message    for Emperor Carlos,
because he has suffered a loss    and I want to see if it's true."

Con el alegria que llevaban    de a Francia se tornare,
todos hacen sacramento    de tenerle poridade.
Embárcanse muy alegres,    empiezan de navegare;
el viento tienen muy fresco,    que placer es de mirare.
Allegados son en Francia,    en sus tierras naturales.
Cuando el conde ya se partiera,    empieza de caminare.
No va la vuelta de las cortes    de don Carlos el emperante,
mas la vuelta de sus tierras,    las que solía mandare.
Ya llegado que es a ellas,    por ellas empieza de andare,
andando por su camino,    una villa fue a hallare.
Llegádose había cerca    por con alguno hablare;
alzó los ojos en alto;    a la puerta del lugare
llorando de los sus ojos,    comenzara de hablare:
—Oh, esforzados caballeros,    de mi dolor habed pesare:
armas que mi padre puso,    mudadas las veo estare,
o es casada la condesa    o mis tierras van a male.
Allegóse a las puertas,    con gran enojo y pesare;
miró por entre las puertas,    gentes de armas vido estare;
llamando está uno de ellos,    el más viejo en antigüedade:
de la mano él lo toma    y empiézale de hablare:
–Por Dios te ruego, el portero,    me digas una verdade,
¿de quién son aquestas tierras,    quién las solía mandare?
—Pláceme, dijo el portero,    de deciros la verdade:
ellas eran del conde Dirlos    señor de aqueste lugare,
agora son de Celinos,    de Celinos el infante.
El conde desde que esto oyera,    vuelta se le ha la sangre;
con una voz demudada    otra vez le fue a hablare:
—Por Dios te ruego, hermano,    no te quieras enojare,
que este que agora me dices    tiempo habrá que te lo pague.
Dime si las heredó Celinos    o si las fue a mercare,
o si en juego de dados    si las fuera a ganare;
o si las tenía por fuerza,    que no las quiere tornare.
El portero que esto oyera,    presto le fue a hablare:
—No las heredó, señor,    que no le vinieren de linaje,
que hermanos tiene el conde,    aunque se querían male,
y sobrinos tiene muchos,    que las podían heredare;
ni menos las ha mercado,    que no las basta pagare,
que Irlos es muy gran ciudade    y muchas villas y lugares.
Cartas hizo contrahechas,    que al conde muerto lo hane,
por casar con la condesa    que era rica y de linaje;
y aun ella no casara    cierto a su voluntade,

With the joy they felt    at returning to France,
they all took an oath    to keep his identity secret.
They embarked with great cheer    and began to sail;
they had a very brisk wind,    a pleasure to behold.
They reached France,    their homeland.
When the count departed,    he began his journey.
He didn't head for the court    of Emperor Carlos,
but for his own estate,    which he used to govern.
Once he reached it,    he began to traverse it;
continuing onward,    he found a town.
He had drawn near it    in order to talk with someone;
he raised his eyes upward;    at the village gateway,
with tears in his eyes    he began to speak:
"O brave knights,    have pity on my sorrow:
the coat of arms my father affixed    I now see changed;
either the countess has remarried    or my estate has been ruined."
He came up to the gate    with great vexation and grief;
he looked inside the gate    and saw men-at-arms;
calling one of them,    the oldest one among them,
he took him by the hand    and began to address him:
"For the love of God, I ask you, gatekeeper,    to tell me true:
Whose is this land?    Who is wont to govern it?"
"Gladly," said the gatekeeper,    "will I tell you the truth:
It belonged to the Count of Irlos,    the lord of this place,
but now belongs to Celinos,    Prince Celinos."
When the count heard this,    he was violently agitated;
in a shaky voice    he spoke to him again:
"By God, I ask you, brother,    and please don't get angry,
since what you tell me now    I'll reward you for in the future:
Tell me whether Celinos inherited it    or purchased it,
or whether he won it    in a dice game,
or if he holds it by force    and doesn't want to return it."
When the gatekeeper heard this,    he said quickly:
"He didn't inherit it, sir,    it didn't come down in the family,
for the count has brothers,    though they didn't get along,
and has many nephews    who could have inherited it;
nor did he purchase it,    for he couldn't afford it,
Irlos being a big city    with many towns and villages.
He wrote a lying letter    saying the count had been killed,
in order to wed the countess,    who is rich and well-born;
what's more, she surely    wouldn't marry him voluntarily,

sino por fuerza de Oliveros    y a porfía de Roldane
y a ruego de Carlosmagno    de Francia rey emperante,
por casar bien a Celinos    y ponerle en buen lugare,
mas el casamiento han hecho    con una condición tale
que no allegáse a la condesa    ni a ella haya de llegare,
mas por él se desposara    ese paladín Roldane.
Ricas fiestas se hicieron    en Irlos esa ciudade,
gastos, galas y torneos    muchos de los doce Pares.
El conde de que esto oyera,    vuelto se le ha la sangre,
por mucho que disimulaba    no cesaba de sospirare,
diciéndole esto: —Hermano,    no te enojes de contare
quién fue en aquestas bodas    y quién no quiso estare.
—Señor, en ellas fue Oliveros    y el emperador y Roldane,
fue Belardos y Montesinos    y el gran conde don Grimalde
y otros muchos caballeros    de aquellos de los doce Pares;
pesó mucho a Gaiferos,    pesó mucho a don Beltrane,
más pesó a don Galvane    y al fuerte Meriane.
Ya que eran desposados,    misa les querían dare;
allegó un falconero    a don Carlos el emperante,
que venía de aquellas tierras,    de allá de allende el mare,
dijo que el conde era vivo    y que traía señale.
Plugo mucho a la condesa,    pesó mucho al infante,
porque en las grandes fiestas    hubo grande desbarate;
allá traen grandes pleitos    en las cortes del emperante,
por lo cual es vuelta Francia    y todos los doce Pares.
Ella dice que un año de tiempo    pidió antes de desposare
por enviar mensajeros    muchos allende la mare;
si el conde era ya muerto,    el casamiento fuese adelante;
si era vivo, bien sabía    que ella no podia casare.
Por ella responde Gaiferos,    Gaiferos y don Beltrane,
por Celinos era Oliveros,    Oliveros y Roldane;
creemos que es dada sentencia    o se quería dare
porque ayer hobimos cartas    de Carlos el emperante,
que quitemos aquellas armas    y pongamos las naturales
y que guardemos las tierras    por el conde don Beltrane,
que a ninguno de Celinos    en ellas no pueda entrare.
El conde desque esto oyera,    movido de gran pesare
vuelve riendas al caballo;    en el lugar no quiso entrare,
mas allá en un verde prado    su gente mandó llegare;
con una voz muy humilde    les empieza de hablare:
—Oh, esforzados caballeros,    oh, mi compaña leale,

but through pressure from Oliveros,   Roldán's insistence,
and the request of Charlemagne,   the emperor of France,
who wish Celinos to marry well   and attain a lofty position;
but they've arranged the marriage   with this condition:
that he doesn't approach the countess   and mustn't come near her;
instead, the paladin Roldán   will wed her by proxy.
Costly feasts have been held   in the city of Irlos,
with expensive finery and tourneys,   by many of the twelve peers."
When the count heard this,   he was violently agitated;
as much as he concealed his emotion,   he kept on sighing,
saying this: "Brother,   may it not vex you to relate
who was at that wedding   and who refused to attend!"
"Sir, Oliveros was there   and the emperor and Roldán,
Belardos and Montesinos were there   and the great Count Grimalde,
and many other knights   from among the twelve peers;
it deeply grieved Gaiferos,   it deeply grieved Don Beltrán;
it grieved even more Don Galván   and powerful Merián.
After they were married,   a mass was to be sung for them;
a falconer approached   Emperor Carlos,
coming from those lands   across the sea;
he said the count was alive,   and he brought proof of it.
The countess was delighted,   the prince was dismayed
that at the grand celebration   there was such a disturbance;
then great law disputes arose   at the emperor's court,
by which France is in turmoil,   as are all twelve peers.
She said that, before the ceremony,   she requested a year's time
in order to send messengers,   many, across the sea;
if the count was dead,   the marriage could proceed;
if he was alive, it was clear   that she couldn't get married.
Gaiferos spoke up on her behalf,   Gaiferos and Don Beltrán;
Oliveros was on Celinos's side,   Oliveros and Roldán;
we think the decision has been handed down,   or is about to be,
because yesterday we got a letter   from Emperor Carlos,
telling us to doff this armor   and don everyday armor,
and guard the land   for Count Beltrán,
so that none of Celinos's people   can enter it."
When the count heard this,   agitated by great grief,
he turned his horse around;   he didn't want to enter the village,
but there on a green meadow   he ordered his men to assemble;
in very humble tones   he began to address them:
"O brave knights,   O my loyal followers,

del consejo que os pidiere    bueno me lo queráis dare:
si me consejáis que vaya    a las cortes del emperante,
o que mate a Celinos,    a Celinos el infante,
volveremos en allende    do seguros podemos estare.
Caballeros que esto oyeron,    presto tal respuesta hacen:
—Calledes, conde, calledes,    conde, no digáis a tale,
no miréis a vuestra gana,    mas mirad a don Beltrane
y esos buenos caballeros,    que tanta honra vos hacen;
si vos matáis a Celinos,    dirán que fuistes cobarde.
Si no, que váis a las cortes    de Carlos el emperante,
conosceréis quien bien os quiere    y quien os quiere male;
por bueno que es Celinos,    vos sois de tan buen linaje
y tenéis tantas tierras    y dineros que gastare;
nosotros vos prometemos,    con sacramento leale,
que somos diez mil caballeros    y franceses naturales
que por vos perder la vida    y cuanto tenemos gastare,
quitando al emperadore    contra cualquier otro grande.
El conde desque esto oyera    respuesta ninguna hace;
da d'espuelas al caballo,    va por el camino adelante;
la vuelta va de París,    como aquel que bien la sabe;
cuando fue a una jornada    de las cortes del emperante,
otras vez llega a los suyos    y les empieza de hablare:
—Esforzados caballeros,    una cosa os quiero rogare:
siempre tomé vuestro consejo,    el mío queráis tomare,
porque si entro en París    con ejército reale
saldrá por mí el emperador    con todos los principales;
si no me conoce de vista,    conocerme ha en el hablare
y así no sabré de cierto    todo mi bien y mi male.
El que no tiene dineros    yo le daré que gastare;
los unos vuelvan a casa,    los otros pasen adelante,
los otros en derredor    pasad en villas y lugares;
yo solo con cien caballeros    entraré en la ciudade,
de noche y oscurecido,    que nadie de mí sepa parte.
Vosotros en ocho días    podréis poco a poco entrare,
hallarme'is en los palacios    de mi tío don Beltrane,
aparejarvos he posada    y dineros que gastare.
Todos fueron muy contentos    pues al conde así le place.
Noche era oscurecida,    cerca diez horas o mase,
cuando entró el conde Dirlos    en París esa ciudade,

I shall ask you for advice    and I want it to be good:
whether you advise me to go    to the emperor's court
or to kill Celinos,    Prince Celinos,
from there we'll return    to a place that's safe for us."
When the knights heard this,    they quickly made answer:
"Be still, count, be still,    count, don't say such things;
don't consider your desires,    but consider Don Beltrán
and those good knights    who are doing you such honor;
if you kill Celinos,    they'll say you were a coward.
Instead, if you go to the court    of Emperor Carlos,
you'll know who wishes you well    and who wishes you ill;
as distinguished as Celinos is,    your ancestry is very great
and you possess much land    and money to spend;
we promise you    with a loyal oath
that we are ten thousand horsemen,    native-born Frenchmen,
who will lose our lives for you    and spend everything we have,
protecting the emperor    against any other great man."[18]
When the count heard this,    he made no answer;
he spurred his horse    and proceeded on his way;
he headed for Paris,    like one familiar with the way there;
when he was one day's distance    from the emperor's court,
he turned to his men once more    and began to address them:
"Brave knights,    I make one request of you:
I've always taken your advice,    now take mine,
because if I enter Paris    with a royal army,
the emperor will come out to meet me    with all the chief men;
if he doesn't know me by sight,    he'll know me by my voice,
and so I won't learn for sure    where I stand, for good or bad.
Those who have no money,    I'll give you some to spend;
some of you go home,    the others keep on going;
others, in the vicinity,    go into towns and villages;
I with only a hundred horsemen    will enter the city,
in the darkness of night,    so no one knows about me.
In a week all of you    can enter gradually;
you'll find me in the palace    of my uncle, Don Beltrán;
I'll have lodgings ready for you    and money to spend."
They were all very satisfied,    since that was the count's desire.
It was nighttime and dark,    about ten or later,
when the Count of Irlos entered    the city of Paris;

---

18. Or: "opposing any great man, except the emperor."

derecho va a los palacios    de su tío don Beltrane,
a lo cual atravesaban    por medio de la ciudade.
Vido asomar tantas hachas,    gente d'armas mucho mase,
por do él pasar había,    por allí van a pasare.
El conde de que los vido    los suyos manda apartare;
desque todos son pasados,    el postrero fue a llamare:
—Por Dios te ruego, escudero,    me digas una verdade:
¿quién son esta gente d'armas,    que agora van por ciudade?
El escudero que esto oyera,    tal respuesta le fue a dare:
—Señor, la condesa Dirlos    viene del palacio reale
sobre un pleito que traía    con Oliveros y Roldane;
los que la llevan en medio    son Roldán y don Beltrane,
aquellos que van zagueros    donde tantas lumbres vane,
son el infante Gaiferos    y el fuerte Meriane.
El conde que esto oyera    de la ciudad él se sale,
debajo de una espesura    para cabe los adarves,
diciendo está a los suyos:    —No es hora de entrare,
que desde que sean apeados    tornarán a cabalgare.
Yo quiero entrar en hora    que de mí no sepan parte.
Allí están razonando    d'armas y de hechos grandes
hasta la medianoche,    los gallos querían cantare.
Vuelven riendas a los caballos    y entran en la ciudade.
La vuelta van de los palacios    del buen conde don Beltrane,
antes de llegar a ellos    de dos calles y aún mase,
tantas cadenas hay puestas    que ellos no pueden pasare;
lanzas les ponen a los pechos    no cesando de hablare:
—Vuelta, vuelta, caballeros,    que por aquí no hay pasaje;
que aquí están los palacios    del buen conde don Beltrane,
enemigo de Oliveros,    enemigo de Roldane,
enemigo de Belardos,    y de Celinos el infante.
El conde desde que esto oyera,    presto tal respuesta hace:
—Ruégote, el caballero,    que me quieras escuchare:
anda ve y dile luego    a tu señor don Beltrane
que aquí está un mensajero    que viene allende el mare;
cartas traigo del conde Dirlos,    su buen sobrino carnale.
El caballero con placer    empieza de aguijare,
presto las nuevas le daba    al buen conde don Beltrane,
el cual ya se acostaba    en su cámara reale.
Desque tal nueva oyera,    tornóse a vestir y calzare;
caballeros alderredor    trecientos trae por guardarle;
hachas muchas encendidas    al patín hizo bajare,

he went straight to the palace    of his uncle, Don Beltrán,
to which the way led    through the center of town.
He saw many torches appear,    and even more men-at-arms;
the route he had to take,    that is where they passed.
When the count saw them,    he ordered his men to withdraw;
after they had all passed,    he called the rearmost man:
"By God, I ask you, squire,    to tell me the truth:
Who are these men-at-arms    who are now crossing the city?"
When the squire heard this,    he made this answer:
"Sir, the Countess of Irlos    is coming from the royal palace,
where she's involved in a case    against Oliveros and Roldán;
those who have her in their midst    are Roldán and Don Beltrán;
those who follow behind,    where all those lights are,
are Prince Gaiferos    and the powerful Merián."
When the count heard this,    he left the city;
within a thicket    beside the city walls
he said to his men:    "It's not the right time to enter,
for after they dismount    they'll mount again.
I want to enter at a time    when they won't notice me."
They stayed there discussing    arms and great exploits
until midnight,    when the cocks were about to crow.
They turned their horses around    and entered the city.
They headed for the palace    of good Count Beltrán;
before arriving there,    for two streets or more
there were so many chains strung    that they couldn't pass;
lances were put to their chests    with the incessant words:
"Turn back, turn back, knights,    there's no passage here;
for this is the palace    of good Count Beltrán,
enemy of Oliveros,    enemy of Roldán,
enemy of Belardos    and of Prince Celinos."
When the count heard this,    he quickly made answer:
"I ask you, knight,    to deign to hear me out:
go tell at once    to your master, Don Beltrán,
that a messenger is here,    come from across the sea;
I have a letter from the Count of Irlos,    his good nephew."
With pleasure the knight    began to spur his horse;
quickly he brought the news    to good Count Beltrán,
who was already in bed    in his princely chamber.
When he heard this news,    he donned his clothes and shoes again;
he called three hundred knights    around him as a guard;
he had many lighted torches    sent down to the patio,

mandó que al mensajero    solo lo dejen entrare;
cuando fue en el patín    con la mucha claridade,
mirando le está mirando    viéndole como salvaje,
como el que está espantado    a él no se osa llegare;
bajito el conde le habla    dándole muchas señales;
conoscióle don Beltrán    entonces en el hablare
y con los brazos abiertos    corre para abrazarle,
diciéndole está, "sobrino",    no cesando de sospirare.
El conde le está rogando    que nadie d'él sepa parte.
Envían presto a las plazas,    carnecerías otro que tale
para mercarles de cena    y mándales aparejare.
Mandan que a sus caballeros    todos les dejen entrare,
que les tomen los caballos    y los hagan bien pensare.
Abren muy grandes estudios,    mándanlos aposentare;
allí entra el conde y los suyos,    ningún otro dejan entrare
porque no conozcan el conde    ni d'él supiesen parte.
Veréis todos los del palacio    unos con otros hablare:
—Si es este el conde Dirlos,    o ¿quién otro puede estare?,
según el rescibimiento    la ha hecho don Beltrane.
Oído lo ha la condesa    a las voces que dan grandes;
mandó llamar sus doncellas    y encomienza de hablare:
—¿Qué es aquesto, mis doncellas,    no me lo queráis negare,
que esta noche tanta gente    por el palacio siento andare?
Decidme, ¿do es el señor,    el mi tío don Beltrane,
si quizá dentro en mis tierras    Roldán ha hecho algun male?
Las doncellas que lo oyeran    atal respuesta le hacen:
—Lo que vos sentís, señora,    no son nuevas de pesare;
es venido un caballero,    así proprio como salvaje;
muchos caballeros con él;    gran acatamiento le hacen.
Muy rica cena le guisa    el buen conde don Beltrane;
unos dicen que es mensajero    que viene de allende el mare;
otros, que es el conde Dirlos,    nuestro señor naturale.
Allá se han encerrado    que nadie no puede entrare,
según ven el aparejo    creen todos que es verdade.
La condesa que esto oyera    de la cama fue a saltare;
apriesa demanda el vestido,    apriesa demanda el calzare,
muchas damas y doncellas    empiezan de aguijare;
a las puertas de los estudios,    grandes golpes manda dare,
llamando a don Beltrane    que dentro la mande entrare;
no quería el conde Dirlos    que la dejasen entrare;
don Beltrán salió a la puerta,    no cesando de hablare:

and ordered that the messenger    be admitted alone;
when he was in the patio    with all the light around,
he studied him closely,    seeing him look so wild;
like one who is frightened,    he didn't dare approach him;
the count spoke to him quietly,    giving him identifying signs;
Don Beltrán recognized him    then from his speech,
and with open arms    ran to embrace him,
calling him nephew    and sighing constantly.
The count asked him    not to reveal his identity.
Quickly they send to the markets    and to the butchers' shops
to buy food for dinner,    which he ordered to be prepared.
The order was given for all    his knights to be admitted;
their horses were to be taken    and well fed.
Very large apartments are opened    and lodging is arranged for them;
there the count and his men enter,    no one else is admitted,
so the count won't be recognized    and his doings won't be known.
Then you'd see everyone in the palace    talking to one another:
"Is this the Count of Irlos?    Who else can it be,
to judge by the welcome    Don Beltrán gave him?"
The countess heard this,    their voices were so loud;
she sent for her maidens    and began to speak:
"What's this, my maidens?    Don't refuse to tell me
why tonight I hear so many people    walking in the palace.
Tell me, where is the master,    my uncle Don Beltrán?
Has Roldán perhaps done    some damage to my estate?"
When the maidens heard this,    they made this answer:
"What you hear, my lady,    is not unhappy news;
a knight has come    who looks just like a savage,
many horsemen with him;    they pay him great respect.
Good Count Beltrán    is having a fine dinner cooked for him;
some say he's an envoy    come from overseas;
others that he's the Count of Irlos,    our liege lord.
They've shut themselves in there    and no one is admitted;
to judge by the preparations    everyone thinks that's the case."
When the countess heard this,    she jumped out of bed;
quickly she asked for her clothes,    quickly she asked for her shoes;
many ladies and damsels    begin to stir briskly;
at the doors to the apartments    she bids them knock loudly,
calling to Don Beltrán    to have her admitted;
the Count of Irlos refused    to have her let in;
Don Beltrán came to the door,    not ceasing to say:

—¿Qué es esto, señora prima,   no tengáis priesa tan grande,
que aún no sé bien las nuevas   que el mensajero me trae,
porque es de tierras ajenas   y no entiendo el lenguaje.
Mas la condesa por esto   no quiere sino entrare,
que mensajero de su marido   ella le quiere honrare;
de la mano la entraba,   ese conde don Beltrane,
de que ella es de dentro   al mensajero empieza de mirare;
él mirar no la osaba   y no cesa de suspirar;
meneando la cabeza,   los cabellos ponía a la faz;
desde que la condesa oyera   a todos callar y no hablare,
con viva voz muy humilde   empieza de razonare:
—Por Dios vos ruego, mi tío,   por Dios vos quiero rogare,
pues que este mensajero   viene de tan luengas partes
que si no terná dineros   ni tuviere que gastare,
decid si nada le falta,   no cese de demandare;
pagarle hemos su gente,   darle hemos que gastare;
pues viene por mi señor   yo no la puedo faltare;
a él y a todos los suyos,   aunque fuesen mucho mase.
Estas palabras hablando,   no cesaba de llorare;
mancilla hubo su marido   con el amor que le tiene grande,
pensando de consolarla,   acordó de la abrazare
y con los brazos abiertos   iba para la tomare.
La condesa espantada   púsose tras don Beltrane;
el conde con grandes sospiros   comenzóle de hablare:
—No fuyades, la condesa,   ni os queráis espantare;
que yo soy el conde Dirlos,   vuestro marido carnale,
estos son aquellos brazos   en que solíades holgare.
Con las manos se aparta   los cabellos de la hace.
Conosciólo la condesa   entonces en el hablare,
en sus brazos ella se echa,   no cesando de llorare:
—¿Qu'es aquesto, mi señor?,   ¿quién vos hizo ser salvaje?
No es este aquel gesto   que vos teníades ante;
quítenvos aquestas armas,   otras luego os quieran dare;
traigan de aquellos vestidos,   que solíades llevare.
Ya les paraban las mesas,   ya les daban a cenare,
cuando empezó la condesa   a decir y hablare:
—Cierto paresce, señor,   que lo hacemos muy male,
que el conde está ya en sus tierras   y en la su heredade,
que no avisemos aquellos   que su honra quieren mirare;

"What's this, lady cousin?   Don't be in such a hurry,
for I still don't know the news    the messenger brings me,
because he's from foreign lands    and I don't understand the language."
But, even so, the countess    insisted on going in,
for she wished to do honor    to a messenger from her husband;
Count Beltrán    led her in by the hand;
once she was inside,    she began to study the messenger;
he didn't dare look at her    and he kept on sighing;
tossing his head,    he covered his face with his hair;
when the countess observed    that they were all silent and not talking,
very humbly but briskly    she began to speak:
"For the love of God, I beg you, uncle,    by God I beseech you,
since this messenger    comes from so far away,
in case he has no money    or anything to spend,
ask him if he lacks anything,    don't cease asking him;
we shall pay his men on his behalf,    we'll give him spending money;
since he comes on my lord's errand,    I can do no less,
for him and all his followers,    even if they were much more numerous."
Speaking these words,    she wept constantly;
her husband felt compassion,    for he loved her so much;[19]
intending to comfort her,    he resolved to embrace her;
with open arms    he went to grasp her.
The countess, frightened,    retreated behind Don Beltrán;
the count, sighing deeply,    began to address her:
"Don't run away, countess,    and don't be frightened,
for I am the Count of Irlos,    your lawful husband,
and these are the arms    in which you used to rest."
With his hands he pushed    the hair away from his face.
Then the countess knew him    by his speech;
she threw herself into his arms,    weeping constantly:
"What's this, my lord?   Who turned you into a savage?
This isn't the appearance    you formerly had;
take off this armor,    let them give you another suit at once;
let them bring those garments    you used to wear."
Now they were setting the tables,    now they were serving their dinner,
when the countess began    to speak and say:
"It surely seems, lord,    that we're acting most improperly,
now that the count is home    and possesses his lands again,
not to inform those    who are bound to honor him;

---

19. Or: "because she loved him so much."

no lo digo aun por Gaiferos    ni por su hermano Meriane,
sino por el esforzado    Reinaldos de Montalbane:
bien sabedes, señor tío,    cuánto se quiso mostrare,
siendo siempre con nosotros    contra el paladín Roldane.
Llaman luego dos caballeros    de aquesos más principales:
el uno envían a Gaiferos,    otro a Reinaldos de Montalbane.
Apriesa viene Gaiferos,    apriesa y no de vagare;
desque vido la condesa    en brazos de aquel salvaje,
a ellos se le allega    y empezóles de hablare;
desde que el conde lo vido,    levantóse abrazarle.
Desde que se han conoscido,    grande acatamiento se hacen.
Ya puestas eran las mesas,    ya les daban a cenare,
la condesa lo servía    y estaba siempre delante,
cuando llegó don Reinaldos,    Reinaldos de Montalbane,
y desde que el conde le vido,    hubo un placer muy grande;
con una voz amorosa    le empezara de hablare:
—Oh, esforzado conde Dirlos,    de vuestra venida me place,
aunque agora vuestros pleitos    mejor se podrán librare.
Mas si yo fuera creido,    fueran hechos antes de vos llegare,
o no me hallárades vivo    o al paladín Roldane.
El conde, desde que esto oyera,    grandes mercedes le hace,
diciendo juramento ha hecho    sobre un libro misale
de jamás se quitar las armas    ni con la condesa holgare,
hasta que haya cumplido    toda la su voluntade.
El concierto que ellos tienen    por mejor y naturale
es que en el otro día,    cuando yante el emperante,
vaya el conde a palacio    por la mano le besare.
Toda la noche pasaron    descansando en hablare;
cuando vino el otro día    a la hora del yantare,
cabalgara el conde Dirlos;    muy leales armas trae
y encima un collar de oro    y una ropa rozagante.
Sólo con cien caballeros,    que no quieren llevar mase,
a la parte izquierda Gaiferos,    a la derecha don Beltrane,
viénense a los palacios    de Carlos el emperante;
cuantos grandes allí hallan    acatamiento le hacen
por honra de don Gaiferos,    que era suya la ciudade;
cuando son a la gran sala,    hallan allí al emperante
asentado a la mesa,    que le daban a yantare,
con él está Oliveros,    con él está don Roldane,
con él está Valdovinos    y Celinos el infante,
con él estaban muchos grandes    de Francia la naturale.

I don't even mean Gaiferos   or his brother Merián,
but the brave   Reinaldos of Montalván:
you're well aware, lord uncle,   how great a help he was,
being always on our side   against the paladin Roldán."
At once they summon two knights   among the highest-ranking;
they send one to Gaiferos,   the other to Reinaldos of Montalván.
Gaiferos arrives quickly,   quickly, and not slowly;
when he saw the countess   in the arms of that savage,
he approached them   and began to address them;
as soon as the count saw him,   he arose to embrace him.
After recognizing each other,   they showed each other great respect.
Now the tables were fully set,   now dinner was served;
the countess served it   and was constantly active,
when Don Reinaldos arrived,   Reinaldos of Montalván;
when the count saw him,   he was greatly delighted;
in affectionate tones   he began to address him:
"O brave Count of Irlos,   I'm pleased at your coming,
and now your lawsuits   will be settled more easily.
But if it had been up to me,   they would have been before you came,
or else either I or the paladin Roldán   would now be dead."
When the count heard this,   he thanked him profusely,
saying he had sworn an oath   on a missal
never to doff his armor   or sport with the countess
until all his wishes   had been satisfied.
The plan they considered   best and most proper
was that, the following day,   at the emperor's midday meal,
the count should go to the palace   to kiss his hand.
They spent the whole night   in relaxed conversation;
when the next day came,   at the time of the midday meal,
the Count of Irlos mounted;   he wore excellent armor
and, on top, a gold necklace   and a magnificent robe.
With only a hundred horseman,   he didn't want to take more,
Gaiferos on the left side,   Don Beltrán on the right,
he rode to the palace   of Emperor Carlos;
all the grandees they found there   showed their respect
in honor of Gaiferos,   for the city was his;
when they reached the great hall,   they found the emperor there
seated at table   being served his meal;
with him was Oliveros,   with him was Don Roldán,
with him was Valdovinos,   and Prince Celinos,
with him were many grandees   of their homeland France.

El entrando por la sala    grande reverencia hacen,
saludan al emperador    los tres juntos a la pare;
desde que don Roldán los vido,    presto se fue a levantare,
apriesa demanda a Celinos    no cesando de hablare:
—Cabalgad presto, Celinos,    no estéis más en la ciudade,
que quiero perder la vida,    si bien miráis las señales,
si aquel no es el conde Dirlos    que viene como salvaje.
Yo quedaré por vos, primo,    a lo que querrán demandare.
Ya cabalga Celinos    y sale de la ciudad,
con él va gran gente d'armas    por haberlo de guardare.
El conde y don Gaiferos    lléganse al emperante,
la mano besarle quiere    y él no se la quiere dare;
mas está muy maravillado,    diciendo: —¿Quién puede estare?
El conde que así lo vido    empezóle de hablare:
—No se maraville vuestra alteza,    que no es de maravillare,
que quien dijo que era muerto    mentira dijo y no verdade;
señor, yo soy el conde Dirlos,    vuestro servidor leale,
mas los malos caballeros    siempre presumen el male.
Conoscido lo han todos    entonces en el hablare,
levantóse el emperador    y empezó de abrazarle
y mandó salir a todos    y las puertas bien cerrare;
sólo queda Oliveros    y el paladin Roldane,
el conde Dirlos y Gaiferos    y el buen viejo don Beltrane.
Asentóse el emperador    y a todos manda posare,
entonces con voz humilde    le empezó de hablare:
—Esforzado conde Dirlos,    de vuestra venida me place,
aunque vuestro enojo    no es de tener pesare,
porque no hay cargo ninguno    ni vergüenza otro que tale,
que si casó la condesa    no cierto a su voluntade,
sino a porfía mía    y a ruegos de don Roldane,
y con tantas condiciones    que sería largo contare
por do siempre ha mostrado    teneros amor muy grande.
Si ha errado Celinos,    hízolo con mocedade
en escrebir que érades muerto,    pues que no era verdade;
mas por eso nunca quise    a ella dejar tocare,
ni menos a los desposorios    a él no dejé estare,
mas por él fue presentado    ese paladín Roldane;
mas la culpa, conde, es vuestra    y a vos os la debéis dare:
para ser vos tan discreto,    esforzado y de linaje
dejastes mujer hermosa,    moza de poca edade;

Entering the great hall,    they bowed deeply;
all three together    saluted the emperor;
when Don Roldán saw them,    he arose rapidly
and quickly spoke to Celinos,    addressing him constantly:
"To horse at once, Celinos!    Stay in the city no longer,
for I wish to die    (if you observe him closely)
if that's not the Count of Irlos    looking like a savage!
I'll be here for you, cousin,    to answer their demands."
Now Celinos mounts    and leaves the city;
with him go many men-at-arms    to protect him.
The count and Don Gaiferos    approach the emperor;
the count wants to kiss his hand,    but he refuses to give it;
instead, in great amazement,    he says: "Who can this be?"
When the count saw him that way,    he began to address him:
"Don't be amazed, Your Highness,    there's no cause for amazement,
for the man who said I was dead    spoke lies, not truth;
lord, I am the Count of Irlos,    your faithful servant,
but evil knights    always assume that evil has occurred."
Then they all recognized him    by his speech;
the emperor arose    and began to embrace him;
he ordered everyone to leave    and the doors to be securely locked;
only Oliveros remained    and the paladin Roldán,
the Count of Irlos and Gaiferos,    and the good old man Beltrán.
The emperor sat down    and bade them all be seated;
then in humble tones    he began to address them:
"Brave Count of Irlos,    I'm pleased at your coming;
the vexation you've suffered    is not one to grieve over,
because there's been no crime    or shame, either,
for if the countess married,    it was against her will;
it was at my insistence    and Don Roldán's request,
and with so many conditions,    it would take long to count them,
by which she steadily showed    she loved you very much.
If Celinos has done wrong,    blame it on his youth,
when he wrote that you were dead,    since it wasn't so;
but, for all that, I never allowed    her to be touched,
and the wedding    I didn't let him attend,
but this paladin Roldán    stood proxy for him;
the fault, count, lies with you,    and you should blame yourself:
though so prudent,    brave and well-born,
you left behind a beautiful wife,    a girl not very old;

y de vista no la visitastes,    de cartas la debíades visitare.
Si supiera que a la partida    llevábades tan gran pesare
n'os enviara yo, el conde,    que otros pudiera enviare,
mas por ser vos buen caballero    sólo a vos quise enviare.
El conde de que esto oyera    atal respuesta le hace:
—Calle, calle, vuestra alteza,    buen señor, no diga tale,
que no cabe quejar de Celinos    por ser de tan poca edade,
que con tales caballeros    yo me costumbro honrare;
mas por él está aquí Oliveros    y por él está don Roldane,
que son buenos caballeros    y los tengo yo por tales;
¡consentir ellos tal carta    y consentir tan gran maldade!
o me tenían en poco,    o me tienen por cobarde,
que sabiendo que era vivo,    no se lo osaría demandare.
Por eso suplico a vuestra alteza    campo me quiera otorgare,
pues por el pleito tomaban    el campo pueden aceptare.
Si quieren uno por uno,    o los dos juntos a la pare,
no perjudicando a los míos    aunque hay hartos de linaje
que esto y mucho más qu'esto    recaudo bastan a dare,
porque conozcan que sin parientes,    amigos no me han de faltare:
tomaré al esforzado    Reinaldos de Montalbane.
Don Roldán que esto oyera    con gran enojo y pesare,
no por lo que el conde dijo,    que con razón lo veía estare,
mas en nombrarle Reinaldos    vuelta se le ha la sangre,
porque los que mal le quieren    cuando le quieren facer pesare,
luego le dan por los ojos    Reinaldos de Montalbane.
Movido de muy gran saña,    luego habló don Roldane:
—Soy contento, el conde Dirlos,    y tomad este mi guante,
y agradeced que sois venido    tan presto sin más tardare,
que a pesar de quien pesara    yo los hiciera casare,
sacando a don Gaiferos,    sobrino del emperante.
—Calledes, dijo Gaiferos,    Roldán, no digáis tale;
por ser soberbio y descortés    mal vos quieren los Doce Pares,
que otros tan buenos como vos    defienden la otra parte,
que yo faltar no les puedo    ni dejar pasar lo tale,
aunque mi primo es Celinos,    hijo de hermana de madre,
bien sabéis que el conde Dirlos    es hijo de hermano de padre,
por ser hermano de padre    no le tengo de faltare,
ni porque no pase la vuestra,    que a todos ventaja queréis llevare.
El conde Dirlos el guante toma    y de la sala se sale,
tras él guía Gaiferos    y tras él va don Beltrane.

you didn't visit her in person,    so you should have sent her letters.
If I had known when you left    you would grieve so,
I wouldn't have sent you, count,    for I could have sent others;
but because you're a good knight    I wanted to send only you."
When the count heard this,    he made this answer:
"Be still, be still, Your Highness,    good lord, don't say such things;
there's no cause to accuse Celinos    since he's so young,
for to such knights    my custom is to show honor;
but, in his place, Oliveros is here,    and Don Roldán as well,
who are good knights,    and I consider them as such;
that they should tolerate such a letter    and such great wickedness!
Either they held me cheap    or they thought I was a coward,
if, knowing I was alive,    they thought I wouldn't dare seek redress.
Therefore I beseech Your Highness    to grant me combat with them;
if they agreed to the lawsuit,    they can accept the challenge.
If they want to fight one at a time    or both together:
without belittling my followers,    of whom plenty are nobly born
and are sufficient to give surety    for this and much more,
so that they know I'm not without    relatives or friends,
I shall take as my second the brave    Reinaldos of Montalván."
When Don Roldán heard this,    he was angry and grieved,
not for what the count said,    for he saw he was right,
but at the mention of Reinaldos    he was violently agitated,
because when those who wished him ill    wanted to give him grief,
they'd immediately throw up to him    Reinaldos of Montalván.
Stirred by very great rage,    Don Roldán said at once:
"I'm contented, Count of Irlos;    take this glove of mine,
and give thanks that you've come    so soon with no more delay,
for, no matter who objected,    I would have seen them wed,
except for Don Gaiferos,    the emperor's nephew."
"Be still," said Gaiferos,    "Roldán, don't say such things;
because you're haughty and rude,    the twelve peers dislike you,
for others as good as you    uphold the opposite viewpoint,
and I can't fail them    or allow such things to happen;
even if Celinos is my cousin,    my mother's sister's son,
you know the Count of Irlos    is my father's brother's son;
because it's my father's brother    I can't let him down,
also so you won't get your way,    for you wish to outdo everyone."
The Count of Irlos took the glove    and left the hall;
behind him went Gaiferos,    and behind him Don Beltrán.

Triste está el emperador,    haciendo llantos muy grandes,
viendo a Francia revuelta    y a todos los Doce Pares;
desque Reinaldos lo supo    hubo de ello placer grande,
al conde palabras decía,    mostrando tener voluntade:
—Esforzado conde Dirlos,    de lo que habéis hecho me place
y muy mucho más del campo    contra Oliveros y Roldane;
una cosa rogar vos quiero:    no me la queráis negare,
pues no es principal Oliveros    ni menos don Roldane,
sin perjudicar vuestra honra    con cualquier podéis peleare;
tomad vos a Oliveros    y dejadme a don Roldane.
—Pláceme, dijo el conde,    Reinaldos, pues a vos place.
Desque supieron las nuevas    los grandes y principales,
que es venido el conde Dirlos    y que está ya en la ciudad,
veréis parientes y amigos    qué grandes fiestas le hacen:
los que a don Roldán mal quieren    al conde Dirlos hacen parte,
por lo cual toda la Francia    en armas veréis estare,
mas si los Doce quisieran,    bien los podían paciguare;
mas ninguno por paz se pone,    todos hacen parcilidade,
sino el arzobispo Turpín,    de Francia cardenale,
sobrino del emperador    en esfuerzo principale;
sólo aquél se ponía,    si los podía apaciguare,
mas ellos escuchar no quieren,    tanto s'an mala voluntade.
Veréis ir dueñas y doncellas    a unos y otros rogare,
ni por ruegos ni por cosas    no los pueden apaciguare;
sobre todos mostraba saña    el esforzado Meriane,
hermano del conde Dirlos    y hermano de Durandarte,
aunque por diferencias    no se solían hablare,
de que sabe lo que ha dicho    en el palacio reale,
que si el conde más tardara    el casamiento hiciera pasare
a pesar de todos ellos    y a pesar de don Beltrane.
Por esto cartas envía    con palabras de pesare,
que aquello que él ha dicho    no lo basta hacer verdade,
que aunque el conde no viniera    había quien lo demandare.
El emperador que lo supo,    muy grandes llantos que hace,
por perdida dan a Francia    y a toda la cristiandade;
dicen que alguna de las partes    con moros se irá ayuntare.
Triste iba y pensativo,    no cesando el suspirare,
mas los buenos consejeros    aprovechan a la necesidade;
consejan al emperador    el remedio que ha de tomare:
que mande tocar las trompetas    y a todos mande juntare

The emperor is sad    and makes loud lament,
seeing France in turmoil,    and all the twelve peers;
when Reinaldos learned of this,    he was delighted,
and spoke to the count    in a display of good will:
"Brave Count of Irlos,    I like what you've done,
and I like much more the challenge    to Oliveros and Roldán;
one thing I wish to ask of you,    don't refuse me:
since Oliveros and Roldán    aren't the chief defendants,
with no loss to your honor    you can fight either one;
you take Oliveros    and leave Don Roldán to me."
"Agreed," said that count,    "if that's your wish, Reinaldos."
When the news was learned    by the grandees and magnates
that the Count of Irlos had returned    and was already in town,
you'd have seen his relatives and friends    holding great celebrations:
those who wished Don Roldán ill    took the side of the Count of Irlos,
so that you would have seen    all of France up in arms;
if the twelve had wished,    they could have pacified them,
but no one speaks up for peace,    they all form factions,
except for Archbishop Turpín    cardinal of France,
nephew to the emperor    and eminently courageous;
he alone offered his services    to try and pacify them,
but they refused to listen,    their ill will was so great.
You'd have seen ladies and maidens    begging both sides,
but neither prayers nor material things    could pacify them;
especially furious was    the brave Merián,
brother of the Count of Irlos    and brother of Durandarte,
even though their quarrels    kept them from speaking to each other,
after he heard what Roldán said    in the royal palace,
that if the count had tarried longer,    he'd have forced the marriage
in spite of everyone    and in spite of Don Beltrán.
Therefore he sent a letter    with grievous words,
stating that, what he said,    he couldn't have accomplished,
for even if the count hadn't come,    someone would have opposed it.
When the emperor learned this,    he lamented loudly;
France was given up as lost,    and all of Christendom;
they said one of the factions    would ally itself with Moors.
He went about sad and pensive,    sighing constantly,
but good counselors    are helpful in time of need;
they counsel the emperor    as to a cure for the situation:
he should bid the trumpets blow    and assemble everyone;

y al que luego no viniere    por traidor lo mande dare,
que le quitará las tierras    y le mandará desterrare.
Mas todos son muy leales,    que todos juntos se hane,
el emperador en medio de ellos    llorando empezó de hablare:
—Esforzados caballeros,    y los mis primos carnales,
entre vosotros no hay diferencia,    vosotros las queréis buscare;
todos sois muy esforzados,    todos primos e de linaje;
acuérdeseos de morire    y que a Dios hacéis pesare:
no solo en perder a vosotros,    mas a toda la cristiandade.
Una cosa rogar os quiero,    no os queráis enojare,
que sin mis leis de Francia    campo no se puede dare;
de tal campo no soy contento,    ni a mí cierto me place
porque yo no veo causa    porque lo haya de dare;
ni hay vergüenza ni injuria    que a ninguno se pueda dare,
ni al conde han enojado    Oliveros ni Roldane
ni el conde a ellos menos,    porque se hayan de matare.
De ayudar a sus amigos    ya usanza es atale.
Si Celinos ha errado    con amor e mocedade,
pues no ha tocado a la condesa,    no ha hecho tanto male,
que de ello merezca muerte    ni se la deben de dare.
Ya sabemos que el conde Dirlos    es esforzado y de linaje
y de los grandes señores    que en Francia comen pane;
que quien a él enojara,    él le basta a enojare,
aunque fuese el mejor caballero    que en el mundo se hallase.
Mas porque sea escarmiento    a otros hombres de linaje,
que ninguno sea osado    ni pueda hacerlo tale,
si estimará su honra    en esto no osará entrare,
que mengüemos a Celinos    por villano y no de linaje,
que en el número de los Doce    no se haya de contare,
ni quando el conde fuere en cortes,    Celinos no pueda estare
ni do fuere la condesa    él no pueda habitare
y esta honra, el conde Dirlos,    para siempre os la darane.
Don Roldán desde que esto oyera,    presto tal respuesta hace:
—Más quiero perder la vida,    que tal haya de pasare.
El conde Dirlos que lo oyera,    presto se fue a levantare
y con una voz muy alta    empezara de hablare:
—Pues requier'os, don Roldán,    por mí y el de Montalbane,
que de hoy en los tres días    en campo hayáis de estare,
si no, a vos y a Oliveros    daros hemos por cobardes.
—Pláceme, dijo Roldán,    y aun si queredes antes.

whoever failed to appear    he should brand a traitor,
whose lands would be forfeit    and who would be exiled.
But all were very faithful,    they all assembled;
the emperor in their midst    began to say tearfully:
"Brave knights    and my own cousins,
there's no real dispute between you,    you're creating it;
you're all very brave,    all well-born cousins;
remember you may die    and grieve God:
not only you will be lost,    but all of Christendom.
I wish to make one request,    please don't be angry,
for without my French laws    a challenge cannot take place;
I'm not pleased by this challenge,    nor, surely, do I like it,
because I see no reason    why it should occur;
there was no shame or insult    that anyone could receive;
Oliveros and Roldán    haven't vexed the count,
nor the count them,    so badly as to kill each other.
To aid one's friends    is a long-standing custom.
If Celinos did wrong    through love and youth,
he never touched the countess    and did no harm
that merits his death,    nor should he be killed.
We already know the Count of Irlos    is brave and highly born,
one of the great lords    who eat bread in France;
whoever vexed him,    he'd suffice to vex him back,
even if it were the best knight    to be found in the world.
But, to make this a lesson    to other well-born men,
so that no one is so bold    as to do such things
(if he esteems his honor    he won't dare do them),
let us demote Celinos    to a commoner of no ancestry,
so that he longer counts    among the number of the twelve;
and whenever the count is at court,    Celinos is not to be there,
nor may he remain    anywhere in the countess's presence;
and this honor, Count of Irlos,    will always be shown you."
When Don Roldán heard this,    he quickly made this answer:
"I'd rather lose my life    than allow this to occur!"
When the Count of Irlos heard this,    he swiftly arose
and very loudly    began to speak:
"Then I challenge you, Don Roldán,    in my name and his of Montalván,
to appear in the field of combat    three days from today;
otherwise we shall proclaim    you and Oliveros cowards."
"Agreed," said Roldán,    "and earlier if you like."

Veréis llantos en el palacio,    que al cielo quieren llegare,
dueñas y grandes señoras,    casadas y por casare,
a pies de maridos e hijos    las veréis arrodillare.
Gaiferos fue el primero    que ha mancilla de su madre,
ansí mesmo don Berltrán    de su hermana carnale,
don Roldán de su esposa,    que tan tristes llantos hace.
Tíranse entonces todos    y vánse asentare,
los valedores hablando    a voz alta y sin parare:
—Mejor es, buenos caballeros,    vos hayamos apaciguare,
pues no hay cargo ninguno    que todo se haya de dejare.
Entonces dijo Roldane    que es contento y que le place
con esta condición    y esto se quiere aturare,
porque Celinos es muchacho    de quince años y no mase,
y no es para las armas    ni aún para peleare,
que fasta veinte y cinco años    y fasta en aquella edade,
que en el número de los Doce    no se haya de contare,
ni en la mesa redonda    menos pueda comer pane,
ni donde fuere el conde y la condesa    Celinos no pueda estare;
desde que fuere de veinte años    o puesto en mejor edade,
si estimare su honra,    que lo pueda demandare,
y que entonces por las armas    cada cual defienda su parte,
porque no diga Celinos    que era de menor edade.
Todos fueron muy contentos    y a ambas partes les place,
entonces el emperador    a todos los hace abrazare;
todos quedan muy contentos,    todos quedan muy iguales.
Otro día el emperador,    muy real sala les hace,
a damas y caballeros    convídalos a yantare;
el conde se afeita las barbas,    los cabellos otro que tale;
la condesa en las fiestas    sale muy rica y triunfante;
los mestresalas que servían    de parte del emperante,
el uno es don Roldán    y Reinaldos de Montalbane,
por dar mas avinenteza    que hobiesen de hablare;
cuando hobieron yantado,    antes de bailar ni danzare
se levantó el conde Dirlos    delante todos los grandes
y al emperador entregó    de las villas y lugares
las llaves de lo ganado    del rey moro Aliarde,
por lo cual el emperador    de ello le da muy gran parte
y él, a sus caballeros,    grandes mercedes les hace.
Los Doce tenían en mucho    la gran victoria que trae;
de allí quedó con gran honra    y mayor prosperidade.

Then you'd see weeping in the palace    that seemed to reach the sky;
women and great ladies,    married and still single,
you'd see kneeling    at the feet of husbands and sons.
Gaiferos was the first    who took pity on his mother;
Don Beltrán likewise    on his own sister,
Don Roldán on his bride,    who was weeping so sadly.
Then everyone drew aside    and went to sit down,
the protective males speaking    loud and nonstop:
"It's better, good knights,    for us to pacify you;
since there was no real crime,    let the whole thing be dropped."
Then Roldán said    he was satisfied and pleased,
on one condition,    which should be adhered to:
since Celinos was a boy    of fifteen, not older,
and wasn't adept in arms,    or able to fight as yet:
until he was twenty-five,    until he was that age,
he shouldn't be counted    among the number of the twelve,
nor allowed to eat bread    at the round table,
and Celinos could not be    where the count and countess were;
after he was twenty    or had reached his majority,
if he esteemed his honor    he could seek redress,
and then through combat    each man could aid his party,
so that Celinos might not say    he was under age.
Everyone was very contented    and both sides agreed;
then the emperor    bade them all embrace;
they were all quite satisfied,    and no one had an advantage.
The next day, the emperor    prepared a truly royal feast;
ladies and knights    he invited to a midday meal;
the count trimmed his beard    and his hair as well;
the countess came to the feast    well dressed and triumphant;
the chief waiters who served    on the emperor's behalf
were Don Roldán    and Reinaldos of Montalván
to give more opportunity    for speaking;
after the meal,    before the dancing,
the Count of Irlos arose    in front of all the grandees
and handed over to the emperor    the keys of the towns
and villages he had won    from the Moorish king Aliarde,
for which the emperor    gave him a big share of the conquest;
to him and to his knights    he gave great thanks.
The twelve thought highly    of his great victory;
from then on, he enjoyed great honor    and greater prosperity.

## 39. Romance de Montesinos

—Cata Francia, Montesinos,    cata París la ciudad,
cata las aguas de Duero,    do van a dar en la mar;
cata palacios del rey,    cata los de don Beltrán,
y aquella que ves más alta    y que está en mejor lugar
es la casa de Tomillas,    mi enemigo mortal.
Por su lengua difamada    me mandó el rey desterrar,
y he pasado a causa de esto    mucha sed, calor y hambre,
trayendo los pies descalzos,    las uñas corriendo sangre.
A la triste madre tuya    por testigo puedo dar,
que te parió en una fuente    sin tener en que te echar.
Yo triste quité mi sayo    para haber de cobijarte;
ella me dijo llorando    por te ver tan mal pasar:
—Tomes este niño, conde,    y lléveslo a cristianar;
llamédesle Montesinos,    Montesinos le llamad.
Montesinos, que lo oyera,    los ojos volvió a su padre;
las rodillas por el suelo    empezóle de rogar
le quisiese dar licencia,    que en París quiere pasar,
y tomar sueldo del rey    si se lo quisiere dar,
por vengarse de Tomillas,    su enemigo mortal;
que si sueldo del rey toma    todo se puede vengar.
Ya que despedirse quieren,    a su padre fue a rogar
que a la triste de su madre    él la quiera consolar,
y de su parte le diga    que a Tomillas va buscar.
—Pláceme, dijera el conde,    hijo, por te contentar.
Ya se parte Montesinos    para en París entrar,
y en entrando por las puertas    luego quiso preguntar
por los palacios del rey,    que se los quieran mostrar.
Los que se lo oían decir    d'él se empiezan a burlar;
viéndolo tan mal vestido,    piensan que es loco o truhán;
en fin, muéstranle el palacio,    por ver qué quiere buscar:
sube alto en el palacio,    entró en la sala real,
halló que comía el rey,    don Tomillas a la par.
Mucha gente está en la sala,    por él no quieren mirar.
Desque hubieron ya comido,    al ajedrez van a jugar
solos el rey y Tomillas    sin nadie a ellos hablar,
si no fuera Montesinos,    que llegó a los mirar;
mas el falso de Tomillas,    en quien nunca hubo verdad,
jugara una treta falsa,    donde no pudo callar

# 39. Ballad of Montesinos

"Behold France, Montesinos,   behold the city of Paris,
behold the waters of the Duero   where they flow into the sea;
behold the king's palaces,   behold those of Don Beltrán,
and the tallest house you see,   the one best situated,
is the house of Tomillas,   my mortal enemy.
Because of his slanderous tongue   the king had me exiled,
and for that reason I've suffered   much thirst, heat, and hunger,
my feet unshod,   my nails bleeding.
Your unhappy mother   I can call to witness;
she bore you at a spring   and had no swaddling clothes.
I, sad man, took off my cloak   to cover you with;
she said to me, weeping   to see you in such distress:
'Take this boy, count,   and have him baptized;
call him Montesinos,   Montesinos name him.'"
When Montesinos heard this,   he turned his eyes to his father;
kneeling on the ground,   he began to beseech him
to give him permission   to go to Paris
and accept the king's pay   if he took him into his service,
in order to take revenge on Tomillas,   his mortal enemy;
for in the king's service   everything can be avenged.
Now that they were about to part,   he asked his father
to be so good as to comfort   his unhappy mother
and tell her for him   that he was looking for Tomillas.
"Gladly," said the count,   "to satisfy you, son."
Now Montesinos departs   to enter Paris;
entering its gates,   he immediately asked
to be shown the way   to the king's palace.
Those who heard him ask   began to laugh at him;
seeing him so poorly dressed,   they took him for a madman or rogue;
finally they showed him the palace   to see what he was after:
he walked upstairs into the palace   and entered the royal hall;
he found the king dining   and Tomillas with him.
There were many people in the hall   who paid no heed to him.
When the meal was over,   a chess game was begun
by only the king and Tomillas,   and no one spoke to them,
except for Montesinos,   who drew near to watch them;
but that devious Tomillas,   in whom truth never resided,
cheated at one move,   which noble Montesinos

el noble de Montesinos,    y publica su maldad.
Don Tomillas, que esto oyera,    con muy gran riguridad
levantara la su mano,    un bofetón le fue a dar.
Montesinos con el brazo    el golpe le fue a tomar,
y echó mano al tablero,    y a don Tomillas fue a dar
un tal golpe en la cabeza,    que le hubo de matar.
Murió el perverso dañado,    sin valerle su maldad.
Alborótanse los grandes    cuantos en la sala están:
prendieron a Montesinos    y queríanlo matar,
sino que el rey mandó a todos    que no le hiciesen mal,
porque él quería saber    quien le dio tan gran osar;
que no sin algún misterio    él no osara tal pensar.
Cuando el rey le interrogara,    él dijera la verdad:
—Sepa tu real Alteza,    soy tu nieto natural;
hijo soy de vuestra hija,    la que hicisteis desterrar
con el conde don Grimaltos,    vuestro servidor leal,
y por falsa invención    le quisiste maltratar;
mas agora vuestra Alteza    de ello se puede informar;
que el falso de don Tomillas    sepan si dijo verdad,
y si pena yo merezco,    buen rey, mandádmela dar,
y también si no la tengo    que me mandásedes soltar,
y al buen conde y la condesa    los mandéis ir a buscar,
y les tornéis a sus tierras    como solía gobernar.
Cuando el rey aquesto oyera,    no quiso más escuchar.
Aunque veía ser él su nieto,    quiso saber la verdad:
supo que don Tomillas    ordenó aquella maldad,
porque tuvo envidia    viéndole en prosperidad.
Cuando el rey la verdad supo,    al conde hizo ir a buscar:
gente de a pie y de a caballo    iban para le acompañar,
y damas por la condesa    como solía llevar.
Llegado junto a París,    dentro no quieren entrar,
porque cuando d'él salieron    los dos fueron a jurar
que las puertas de París    nunca las vieran pasar.
Cuando el rey aquello supo,    luego mandó derribar
un pedazo de la cerca    por do pudiesen pasar
sin quebrar el juramento    que ellos fueron a jurar.
Lleváronlos al palacio    con mucha solemnidad,
hácenlos muy ricas fiestas    cuantos en la corte están.
Caballeros, dueñas, damas    los vienen a visitar,
y el rey delante de todos,    por mayor honra les dar,
les dijo que había sabido    como era todo maldad

couldn't overlook    but proclaimed his wrongdoing.
When Don Tomillas heard this,    with great severity
he raised his hand    to give him a slap.
Montesinos intercepted the blow    with his arm
and, seizing the chessboard,    gave Don Tomillas
such a blow on the head    that he killed him.
The accursed evildoer died,    his wickedness was no protection.
All the grandees in the hall    were in a commotion;
they apprehended Montesinos    and were about to kill him;
but the king ordered everyone    to do him no harm,
because he wanted to know    who gave him such daring,
for without some hidden cause    he wouldn't have dared to contemplate it.
When the king questioned him,    he told him the truth:
"Your royal Highness should know    I'm your own grandson;
I'm the son of your daughter,    whom you had banished
along with Count Grimaltos,    your faithful servant,
and wished to mistreat    because of a lying, made-up story;
but now Your Highness    can learn the truth of the case;
let them inquire whether false    Don Tomillas spoke the truth,
and if I deserve punishment,    good king, order me to suffer it;
but if I don't deserve it,    order me set free,
and send for    the good count and countess,
and restore to them the lands    they used to govern."
When the king heard this,    he wished to listen no further.
Though he saw it was his grandson,    he wished to know the truth:
he learned that Don Tomillas    had committed that crime
because he was envious,    seeing him in prosperity.
When the king learned the truth,    he sent for the count:
men on foot and on horse    went out to escort him,
and ladies for the countess    as she used to have.
Arriving near Paris,    they didn't want to enter,
because when they left it    the couple had sworn
that the gates of Paris    would never see them pass.
When the king learned this,    at once he ordered a section
of the city wall demolished    through which they could pass
without violating the oath    they had sworn.
They were brought to the palace    with great ceremony;
everyone in the court    greeted them effusively.
Knights, women, ladies    came to visit them,
and, in front of all, the king,    to show them greater honor,
told them he had learned    it had all been a criminal act,

lo que dijo don Tomillas    cuando lo hizo desterrar:
y porque sea mas creído    allí les tornó a afirmar
todo lo que antes tenían,    y el gobierno general,
y que después de sus días    el reino haya de heredar
el noble de Montesinos,    y así lo mandó firmar.

## 40. "De Mérida sale el palmero"

De Mérida sale el palmero,    de Mérida, esa ciudade;
los pies llevaba descalzos,    las uñas corriendo sangre;
una esclavina trae rota,    que no valía un reale,
y debajo traía otra,    bien valía una ciudade,
que ni rey ni emperador    no alcanzaba otra tale.
Camino lleva derecho    de París, esa ciudade;
ni pregunta por mesón,    ni menos por hospital,
pregunta por los palacios    del rey Carlos do estáe.
Un portero está a la puerta,    empezóle de hablare:
—Dijésesme tú, el portero,    el rey Carlos ¿dónde estáe?
El portero, que lo vido,    mucho maravillado se hae
cómo un romero tan pobre    por el rey va a preguntare.
—Digádemeslo, señor,    de eso no tengáis pesare.
—En misa estaba, palmero,    allá en San Juan de Letrane,
que dice misa un arzobispo,    y la oficia un cardenale.
El palmero, que lo oyera,    íbase para San Juane;
en entrando por la puerta,    bien veréis lo que haráe:
humillóse a Dios del cielo    y a Santa María, su madre,
humillóse al arzobispo,    humillóse al cardenale,
porque decía la misa,    no porque merecía mase,
humillóse al emperador    y a su corona reale,
humillóse a los doce    que a una mesa comen pane.
No se humilla a Oliveros,    ni menos a don Roldane,
porque un sobrino que tienen    en poder de moros estáe,
y pudiéndolo hacer,    no le van a rescatare.
Desque aquesto vio Oliveros,    desque aquesto vio Roldane,
sacan ambos las espadas,    para el palmero se vane.
El palmero con su bordón    su cuerpo van mamparare.
Allí hablara el buen rey,    bien oiréis lo que diráe:
—Tate, tate, Oliveros,    tate, tate, don Roldane,
o este palmero es loco,    o viene de sangre reale.
Tomárale por la mano,    y empiézale de hablare:

all that Don Tomillas had said    when he had them exiled.
So it would be believed no more,    he reconfirmed their possession
of all their former property,    and their full control of it,
promising that after he died    the kingdom would be inherited
by noble Montesinos;    and he had his orders signed.

## 40. "From Mérida the Pilgrim Sets Out"

From Mérida the pilgrim sets out,    from the city of Mérida;
his feet were bare,    his nails were bleeding;
he wore a torn short cape    not worth one *real*,
but beneath it he wore another    well worth an entire city,
for neither king nor emperor    could afford one like it.
He headed straight    for the city of Paris;
he didn't ask for an inn,    or a hospice, either;
he asked for the palace    of King Carlos, where he dwelt.
A guard is at the door,    he began to address him:
"Tell me, doorkeeper,    where is King Carlos?"
When the doorkeeper saw him,    he was quite astonished
to see such a poor pilgrim    asking for the king.
"Tell me, sir,    don't be grieved by my question."
"He's at mass, pilgrim,    there at St. John Lateran;
an archbishop is saying mass    and a cardinal the office.
When the pilgrim heard this,    he went to St. John's;
after entering the door,    you shall see what he did:
he knelt to God in heaven    and to His Mother, St. Mary;
he knelt to the archbishop,    he knelt to the cardinal
because he was saying mass,    not that he had any special merit;
he knelt to the emperor    and his royal crown,
he knelt to the twelve    who eat bread at one table.
He didn't kneel to Oliveros    or to Don Roldán, either,
because they had a nephew    in Moorish captivity
and, though they might have,    they hadn't gone to rescue him.
When Oliveros saw this,    when Roldán saw this,
they both drew their swords    and walked toward the pilgrim.
With his staff the pilgrim    protected his body.
Then the good king spoke,    you shall hear what he said:
"Easy, easy, Oliveros!    Easy, easy, Don Roldán!
Either this pilgrim is crazy,    or else he's of noble blood."
He took him by the hand    and began to address him:

—Dígasme tú, el palmero,   no me niegues la verdade,
¿en qué año y en qué mes   pasaste aguas de la mare?
—En el mes de mayo, señor,   yo las fuera a pasare;
porque yo me estaba un día   a orillas de la mare,
en el huerto de mi padre   por haberme de holgare,
cautiváronme los moros,   pasáronme allende el mare,
a la infanta de Sansueña   me fueron a presentare;
la infanta, desque me vido,   de mí se fue a enamorare.
La vida que yo tenía,   rey, quiero vos la contare:
en la su mesa comía,   y en su cama me iba a echare.
Allí hablara el buen rey,   bien oiréis lo que diráe:
—Tal cautividad como ésa   quien quiera la tomáre.
Dígasme tú, el palmerico,   si la iría yo a ganare.
—No vades allá, el buen rey,   buen rey, no vades alláe,
porque Mérida es muy fuerte,   bien se vos defenderáe.
Trescientos castillos tiene,   que es cosa de los mirare,
que el menor de todos ellos   bien se os defenderáe.
Allí hablara Oliveros,   allí habló don Roldane:
—Miente, señor, el palmero,   miente y no dice verdade,
que en Mérida no hay cien castillos,   ni noventa, a mi pensare,
y estos que Mérida tiene   no tiene quien los defensare,
que ni tenían señor,   ni menos quien los guardare.
Desque esto oyó el palmero,   movido con gran pesare,
alzó su mano derecha,   dio un bofetón a Roldane.
Allí hablara el rey,   con furia y con gran pesare:
—Tomadle, la mi justicia,   y llevédeslo ahorcare.
Tomado lo ha la justicia   para haberlo de justiciare
y aun allá al pie de la horca   el palmero fuera hablare:
—¡Oh mal hubieses, rey Carlos!   Dios te quiera hacer male,
que un hijo solo que tienes   tú le mandas ahorcare.
Oídolo había la reina,   que se le paró a mirare;
—Déjeslo, la justicia,   no le queráis hacer male,
que si él era mi hijo   encubrir no se podráe,
que en un lado ha de tener   un extremado lunare.
Ya le llevan a la reina,   ya se lo van a llevare;
desnúdanle una esclavina   que no valía un reale,
ya le desnudaban otra   que valía una ciudade;
halládole han al infante,   hallado le han la señale.
Alegrías se hicieron   no hay quien las pueda contare.

"Tell me, pilgrim,    don't refuse to tell the truth,
in what year and what month    did you cross the sea?"
"In the month of May, sire,    I crossed it;
because I was standing one day    by the seashore
in my father's orchard    for my amusement,
when Moors captured me    and took me over the sea;
where they made a gift of me    to the princess of Sansueña;
when the princess saw me,    she fell in love with me.
The life I lived,    king, I shall relate to you:
I ate at her table    and would lie down on her bed."
Then the good king spoke,    you shall hear what he said:
"A captivity like that    anyone would accept!
Tell me, young pilgrim,    whether I should go and win it."
"Don't go there, good king,    good king, don't go there,
because Mérida is well fortified,    and will defend itself well.
It has three hundred castles    marvelous to behold,
for the smallest of them    will defend itself well against you."
Then Oliveros spoke up,    then Don Roldán spoke:
"Sire, the pilgrim lies,    he lies and speaks untruth,
for there aren't a hundred castles in Mérida,    or ninety, I believe,
and the ones Mérida does have    have no one to defend them,
for they have neither a lord    or anyone to guard them."
When the pilgrim heard this,    stirred with great grief,
he raised his right hand    and slapped Roldán.
then the king said    furiously and greatly grieved:
"Seize him, officers,    and take him to be hanged!"
The officers seized him    in order to execute him,
and at the very foot of the gallows    the pilgrim said:
"Oh, may evil befall you, King Carlos!    May God punish you,
for the only son you have    you sentence to be hanged!"
The queen heard this    and stopped to observe him:
"Release him, officers,    do him no harm,
for if he's my son,    it can't be concealed,
because on one side he must have    a very large birthmark."
Now they take him to the queen,    now they take him to her;
they strip him of a short cape    that isn't worth one *real*,
they strip him of another    that is worth an entire city;
they've discovered the prince,    they've found his birthmark.
They rejoiced so greatly,    no one could describe it.

## 41. Romance de la linda Melisenda

Todas las gentes dormían    en las que Dios había parte;
mas no duerme Melisenda,    la hija del emperante,
que amores del conde Ayuelos    no la dejan reposar.
Salto diera de la cama    como la parió su madre;
vistiérase una alcandora,    no hallando su brial;
vase para los palacios    donde sus damas están;
dando palmadas en ellas    las empezó de llamar:
—Si dormides, mis doncellas,    si dormides, recordad;
las que sabedes de amores    consejo me queráis dar;
las que de amor non sabedes    tengádesme poridad;
amores del conde Ayuelos    no me dejan reposar.
Allí hablara una vieja,    vieja es de antigua edad:
—Mientras sois moza, mi fija,    placer vos querades dar,
que si esperáis a vejez    no vos querrá un rapaz.
Desque esto oyó Melisenda,    empezó de caminar;
vase para los palacios    donde el conde ha de hallar,
a sombra va de tejados,    que no la conosca nadie.
Encontró con Fernandinos,    el alguacil de su padre.
—¿Qué es aquesto, Melisenda?    Esto ¿qué podría estar?
¡O vos tenéis mal de amores    o os queréis loca tornar!
—Que no tengo mal de amores    ni tengo por quién penar,
mas cuando yo era pequeña    tuve una enfermedad;
prometí tener novenas    allá en san Juan de Letrán;
las dueñas iban de día,    doncellas agora van.
Desque esto oyera Fernando    puso fin a su hablar;
la infanta, mal enojada,    queriendo dél se vengar:
—Prestásesme, ora, Fernando,    prestásesme tu puñal,
que miedo me tengo, miedo,    de los perros de la calle.
Tomó el puñal por la punta,    los cabos le fuera a dar;
diérale tal puñalada    que en el suelo muerto cae.
Allí murió Fernandinos,    el alguacil de su padre;
y ella toma su camino,    donde el conde ha de hallar;
las puertas halló cerradas,    no halla por dónde entrar;
con arte de encantamiento    ábrelas de par en par;
siete antorchas que allí arden    todas las fuera a apagar.
Despertado se había el conde    con un dolor atán grande:
—¡Ay, válasme, Dios del cielo    y Santa María su madre!
¿Si serán mis enemigos    que me vienen a matar,

## 41. Ballad of Beautiful Melisenda

Everyone was asleep    in whom God had a share,
but Melisenda didn't sleep,    the emperor's daughter,
because her love for Count Ayuelos    didn't let her rest.
She jumped out of bed    naked as the day she was born;
she put on a simple shift,    not finding her gown;
she went to the palace    where her ladies resided;
tapping at their door,    she began to call to them:
"If you're asleep, my maidens,    if you're asleep, awake;
those who know of love,    please counsel me;
those who don't know of love,    keep my secret;
love for Count Ayuelos    gives me no rest."
Then an old woman spoke up,    an old woman of great age:
"While you're young, my girl,    take all the pleasure you can,
for if you wait till old age,    young men won't want you."
When Melisenda heard this,    she began to walk;
she went to the palace    where she could find the count,
walking in the shadow of roofs    to avoid being recognized.
She met Fernandinos,    her father's constable.
"What's this, Melisenda?    What can this be?
Either you're lovesick    or you're about to go mad!"
"I'm not lovesick    and I have no one to pine for,
but when I was small    I had a malady;
I promised to hold novenas    in St. John Lateran;
mature women go by day,    maidens go at this hour."
When Fernando heard this,    he said no more;
the princess, very angry,    wishing revenge on him:
"Fernando, now lend me,    lend me your dagger,
for I'm afraid, afraid    of the dogs in the street."
He took the dagger by the point    and gave her the handle;
she gave him such a blow    that he fell dead to the ground.
There Fernandinos died,    her father's constable;
and she resumes her path    in search of the count;
she found the doors locked    and no way in;
by magic arts    she opened them wide;
seven torches burned there,    all of which she extinguished.
The count awoke    with a feeling of great sorrow:
"Ah, stand by me, God in heaven    and Your Mother, St. Mary!
Can it be my enemies    coming to kill me,

o eran los mis pecados    que me vienen a tentar?
La Melisenda discreta    le empezara de hablar:
—Yo no so tus enemigos    que te vienen a matar,
ni eran los tus pecados    que te vienen a tentar;
mas era una morica,    morica de allén la mare;
mi cuerpo tengo tan blanco    como un fino cristal;
mis dientes tan menudicos,    menudos como la sal;
mi boca tan colorada    como un fino coral.
Allí fablara el buen conde,    tal respuesta le fue a dar:
—Juramento tengo hecho    y en un libro misal,
que mujer que a mí demande    nunca mi cuerpo negalle,
si no era a la Melisenda,    la hija del emperante.
Entonces la Melisenda    comenzolo de besar
y en las tinieblas oscuras    de Venus es su jugar.
Quando vino la mañana,    que quería alborear,
hizo abrir las sus ventanas    por la morica mirar;
vido que era Melisenda    y empezole de hablar:
—¡Señora, cuán bueno fuera    a esta noche yo me matar,
antes que haber cometido    aqueste tan grande mal!
Fuérase al emperador    por habérselo de contar;
las rodillas por el suelo,    le comienza de hablar:
—Una nueva vos traía    dolorosa de contar;
mas catad aquí mi espada    que en mí lo podréis vengar;
que esta noche Melisenda    en mis palacios fue a entrar,
siete antorchas que allí ardían    todas las fuera a apagar;
díjome que era morica,    morica de allén la mar,
y que venía conmigo    a dormir y a folgar,
y entonces yo, desdichado,    cabe mí la dejé echar.
Allí fabló el emperador,    tal respuesta le fue a dar:
—Tira, tira allá tu espada,    que no te quiero fer mal;
mas si tú la quieres, conde,    por mujer se te dará.
—Pláceme, dijera el conde,    pláceme de voluntad;
lo que vuestra alteza mande    veisme aquí a vuestro mandar.
Hacen venir un obispo    para habellos de desposar;
ricas fiestas se hicieron    con mucha solemnidad.


## 42. Romance del moro Calaínos

Ya cabalga Calaínos    a la sombra de una oliva,
el pie tiene en el estribo,    cabalga de gallardía.

or is it my devils   coming to tempt me?"
Prudent Melisenda   began to address him:
"I am not your enemies   coming to kill you,
nor your devils   coming to tempt you;
I'm a Moorish girl,   a Moor from overseas;
my body is as white   as a clear crystal;
my teeth are as tiny,   tiny as grains of salt;
my lips are as red   as fine coral."
Then the good count spoke,   he made this answer:
"I've sworn an oath   on a missal
that if a woman wants me   I'll never refuse her my body,
except for Melisenda,   the emperor's daughter."
The Melisenda   began to kiss him,
and in the dark shadows   their game was that of Venus.
When morning came   and day was about to break,
he had his windows opened   so he could see the Moor;
he saw it was Melisenda   and began to address her:
"Lady, how good it would have been   to kill myself last night
before having committed   such a great crime!"
He went to the emperor   to tell him about it;
kneeling on the floor,   he began to address him:
"I bring you some news   sorrowful to relate;
but here is my sword   so you can avenge yourself for it;
you see, last night Melisenda   entered my palace;
seven torches burned there,   all of which she extinguished;
she said she was a Moorish girl,   a Moor from overseas,
and that she had come to sleep   and frolic with me;
then I, unlucky man,   let her lie down beside me."
Then the emperor spoke,   he made this answer:
"Throw away your sword,   I have no wish to harm you;
but if you want her, count,   you may have her as your wife."
"I consent," said the count,   "I consent gladly;
whatever Your Highness orders,   I'm ready to comply."
They sent for a bishop   to marry them;
a grand celebration was made   with great ceremony.

## 42. Ballad of the Moor Calaínos

Now Calaínos mounts   in the shade of an olive tree;
he puts his foot in the stirrup   and rides gallantly.

Mirando estaba a Sansueña,     al arrabal con la villa,
por ver si vería algún moro     a quien preguntar podría.
Por los palacios venía     la linda infanta Sevilla;
vido estar un moro viejo     que a ella guardar solía.
Calaínos que lo vido     llegado allá se había;
las palabras que le dijo     con amor y cortesía:
—Por Alá te ruego, moro,     así te alargue la vida,
que me muestres los palacios     donde mi vida vivía,
de quien triste soy cautivo,     y por quien pena tenía,
que cierto por sus amores     creo yo perder la vida;
mas si por ella la pierdo     no se llamará perdida,
que quien muere por tal dama     desque muerto tiene vida.
Mas porque me entiendas, moro,     por quien preguntado había,
es la mas hermosa dama     de toda la Morería,
sepas que a ella la llaman     la grande infanta Sevilla.
Las razones que pasaban     Sevilla bien las oía:
púsose a una ventana,     hermosa a maravilla,
con muy ricos atavíos,     los mejores que tenía.
Ella era tan hermosa,     otra su par no la había.
Calaínos que la vido     de esta suerte le decía:
—Cartas te traigo, señora,     de un señor a quien servía:
creo que es el rey tu padre     porque Almanzor se decía:
descende de la ventana,     sabrás la mensajería.
Sevilla cuando lo oyera     presto de allí descendía:
apeóse Calaínos,     gran reverencia le hacía.
La dama cuando esto vido     tal pregunta le hacía:
—¿Quién sois vos el caballero,     que mi padre acá os envía?
—Calaínos soy, señora,     Calaínos el de Arabía,
señor de los Montes Claros.     De Constantina la llana,
y de las tierras del Turco     yo gran tributo llevaba,
y el Preste Juan de las Indias     siempre parias me enviaba,
y el Soldán de Babilonia     a mi mandar siempre estaba:
reyes y príncipes moros     siempre señor me llamaban,
sino es el rey vuestro padre,     que yo a su mandado estaba,
no porque le he menester,     mas por nuevas que me daban
que tenía una hija     a quien Sevilla llamaban,
que era más linda mujer     que cuantas moras se hallan.
Por vos le serví cinco años     sin sueldo ni sin soldada;
él a mí no me la dio,     ni yo se la demandaba.
Por tus amores, Sevilla,     pasé yo la mar salada,
porque he de perder la vida     o has de ser mi enamorada.

He observed Sansueña,   the outskirts and the town,
to see if he could find any Moor   of whom he might inquire.
Through the palace came   the lovely princess Sevilla;
he saw an old Moor there   who always guarded her.
When Calaínos saw him,   he approached him;
the words he spoke to him   showed love and courtesy:
"By Allah I beg you, Moor   (so may He lengthen your days!),
to show me the palace   where my darling resides,
whose sad captive I am,   the one for whom I pine,
for surely from love of her   I think I'll lose my life;
but if I lose it for her,   I won't count it as lost,
for he who dies for such a lady   gains life after death.
But, so you understand, Moor,   for whom I'm inquiring,
she's the most beautiful lady   in all of Moorish lands;
know that she is called   the great princess Sevilla."
Sevilla clearly heard   their conversation;
she stood by a window,   marvelously lovely,
with very costly adornments,   the best she owned.
She was so beautiful   she had no equal.
When Calaínos saw her,   he addressed her as follows:
"I bring you a letter, lady,   from a lord whom I served:
I think it's your father, the king,   for his name was Almanzor;
come down from the window   and you'll hear the message."
When Sevilla heard this,   she quickly came down from there;
Calaínos dismounted   and bowed deeply to her.
When the lady saw this,   she asked him this question:
"What knight are you   that my father sends here?"
"I am Calaínos, lady,   Calaínos of Arabia,
lord of Montes Claros.   From Constantine of the plain
and from the lands of the Turk   I received much tribute,
and Prester John of the Indies   always sent me tribute,
and the sultan of Babylonia   was always at my command;
Moorish kings and princes   always called me their lord,
except for the king, your father,   for I was at his command,
not because I had to be   but because of the news I heard
that he had a daughter   named Sevilla
who was the loveliest woman   of all the Moors in the world.
For you I served him five years   without pay or wages;
he didn't give me any   and I never asked him for any.
For love of you, Sevilla,   I crossed the salt sea,
because either I must die   or you must be my sweetheart."

Cuando Sevilla esto oyera    esta respuesta le daba:
—Calaínos, Calaínos,    de aqueso yo no sé nada,
que siete amas me criaron,    seis moras y una cristiana.
Las moras me daban leche,    la otra me aconsejaba;
según que me aconsejaba    bien mostraba ser cristiana.
Diérame muy buen consejo,    y a mí bien se me acordaba
que jamás yo prometiese    de nadie ser enamorada,
hasta que primero hubiese    algún buen dote o arras.
Calaínos que esto oyera    esta respuesta le daba:
—Bien podéis pedir, señora,    que no se os negará nada:
si queréis castillos fuertes,    ciudades en tierra llana,
o si queréis plata u oro    o moneda amonedada.
Y Sevilla, aquestos dones,    como no los estimaba,
respondióle: si quería    tenella por namorada,
que vaya dentro a París,    que en medio de Francia estaba,
y le traiga tres cabezas    cuales ella demandaba,
y que si aquesto hiciese    sería su enamorada.
Calaínos cuando oyó    lo que ella le demandaba
respondióle muy alegre,    aunque él se maravillaba
dejar villas y castillos    y los dones que le daba
por pedirle tres cabezas    que no le costarán nada:
dijo que las señalase,    o diga cómo se llaman.
Luego la infanta Sevilla    se las empezó a nombrar:
la una es de Oliveros,    la otra de don Roldán,
la otra del esforzado    Reinaldos de Montalván.
Ya señalados los hombres    a quien había de buscar,
despídese Calaínos    con muy cortés hablar:
—Déme la mano, tu Alteza,    que se la quiero besar,
y la fe y prometimiento    de comigo te casar,
cuando traiga las cabezas    que quesiste demandar.
—Pláceme, dijo, de grado    y de buena voluntad.
Allí se toman las manos,    la fe se hubieron de dar
que el uno ni el otro    no se pudiesen casar
hasta que el buen Calaínos    de allá hubiese de tornar,
y que si otra cosa fuese    la enviaría avisar.
Ya se parte Calaínos,    ya se parte, ya se va:
hace broslar sus pendones    y en todos una señal;
cubiertos de ricas lunas,    teñidas en sangre van.
En camino es Calaínos    a los franceses buscar:
andando jornadas ciertas    a París llegado ha.
En la guardia de París    cabe San Juan de Letrán,

When Sevilla heard this,   she made this answer:
"Calaínos, Calaínos,   I know nothing of all that,
for seven nurses raised me,   six Moors and one Christian.
The Moorish ones gave me milk,   the other one instructed me;
from the way she instructed me   it was clear she was a Christian.
She gave me much good advice,   whereby I firmly resolved
never to promise   to be anyone's sweetheart
until he first had   some good dowry or bride gift."
When Calaínos heard this,   he made this answer:
"You may well request it, lady,   for nothing will be denied you:
whether you want fortified castles,   cities on the plain,
or whether you want silver or gold   or coined money."
But Sevilla, as if   she spurned such gifts,
replied that if he wanted   to have her for a sweetheart,
he must go to Paris,   in the center of France,
and bring her three heads,   the ones she requested,
and if he did that   she'd be his sweetheart.
When Calaínos heard   what she demanded of him,
he replied very cheerfully,   though he was astonished
that she'd pass up towns and castles   and the gifts he offered
and ask instead for three heads   that would cost him nothing:
he asked her to describe them   or name their owners.
Then Princess Sevilla   began to name them:
one was that of Oliveros,   the second that of Don Roldán,
the third that of the brave   Reinaldos de Montalván.
Knowing the specific men   he had to seek,
Calaínos took leave   with a very courtly speech:
"Give me your hand, Your Highness,   so I can kiss it,
and your pledge and promise   to marry me
when I bring the heads   you deigned to ask for."
"I consent," she said, "gladly   and with the best will."
Then they held hands   and pledged each other
that neither one   would marry
until good Calaínos   returned from there,
and if anything else occurred   he'd send her word of it.
Now Calaínos departs,   now he departs, now he leaves;
he had his pennants embroidered   with an emblem on each;
covered with rich crescents,   they were dyed blood-red.
Calaínos is on his way   to seek the Frenchmen;
traveling set daily distances,   he has reached Paris.
At the Parisian guard post,   beside St. John Lateran,

allí levantó su seña   y empezara de hablar:
—Tañan luego esas trompetas   como quien va a cabalgar,
porque me sientan los doce   que dentro en París están.
El emperador aquel día   había salido a cazar:
con él iba Oliveros,   con él iba don Roldán,
con él iba el esforzado   Reinaldos de Montalván;
también el Dardín Dardeña   y el buen viejo don Beltrán,
y ese Gastón y Claros   con el romano Final:
también iba Valdovinos,   y Urgel en fuerzas sin par,
y también iba Guarinos,   almirante de la mar.
El emperador entre ellos   empezara de hablar:
—Escuchad, mis caballeros,   que tañen a cabalgar.
Ellos estando escuchando   vieron un moro pasar;
armado va a la morisca,   empiézanle de llamar,
y ya que es llegado el moro   do el emperador está,
el emperador que lo vido   empezóle a preguntar:
—Di, ¿adónde vas tú, el moro?   ¿cómo en Francia osaste entrar?
¡Grande osadía tuviste   de hasta París llegar!
El moro cuando esto oyó   tal respuesta le fue a dar:
—Vo a buscar al emperante   de Francia la natural,
que le traigo una embajada   de un moro principal,
a quien sirvo de trompeta,   y tengo por capitán.
El emperador que esto oyó   luego lo fue a demandar
que dijese qué quería,   por qué a él iba a buscar;
que él es el emperador Carlos   de Francia la natural.
El moro cuando lo supo   empezóle de hablar:
—Señor, sepa tu Alteza   y tu corona imperial,
que ese moro Calaínos,   señor, me ha enviado acá,
desafiando a tu Alteza   y a todos los doce pares,
que salgan lanza por lanza   para con él pelear.
Señor, veis allí su seña,   donde los ha de aguardar;
perdóneme vuestra Alteza,   que respuesta le vo a dar.
Cuando fue partido el moro   el emperador fue a hablar:
—¡Cuando yo era mancebo,   que armas solía llevar,
nunca moro fue osado   de en toda Francia asomar;
mas agora que soy viejo   a París los veo llegar!
No es mengua de mí solo   pues no puedo pelear,
mas es mengua de Oliveros,   y asimesmo de Roldán;

there he raised his standard    and began to speak:
"Blow those trumpets at once    to announce a rider,
so that the twelve hear of me,    they who are in Paris!"
That day the emperor    had gone out hunting;
with him went Oliveros,    with him went Don Roldán,
with him went the brave    Reinaldos of Montalván;
also Dardín of Ardeña    and the good old man Don Beltrán,
and Gastón and Claros    with the Roman Final;
Valdovinos was there, too,    and Urgel of matchless strength,
and also Guarinos,    admiral of the sea.
In their midst the emperor    began to speak:
"Listen, my knights,    the trumpets are blowing 'To horse!'"
While they were listening    they saw a Moor ride by;
his arms were in Moorish style;    they began to call to him,
and when the Moor drew near    where the emperor was,
the emperor, seeing him,    began to question him:
"Tell me, where are you off to, Moor?    How did you dare enter France?
You were very bold    to come all the way to Paris!"
When the Moor heard this,    he made this answer:
"I'm seeking the emperor    of goodly France,[20]
for I bring him a message    from an eminent Moor,
whom I serve as a trumpeter    and consider my captain."
When the emperor heard this,    he at once requested him
to state his wishes    and why he was seeking him,
for he was Emperor Carlos    of goodly France.
When the Moor learned this,    he began to address him:
"Sire, I inform Your Highness    and your imperial crown
that the Moor Calaínos    sent me here, sire,
to challenge Your Highness    and all twelve peers
to ride out lance by lance    to fight with him.
Sire, there you see his standard    where he'll await them;
give me leave, Your Highness,    for I'm going to report to him."
After the Moor left them,    the emperor spoke:
"When I was younger    and used to bear arms,
no Moor was ever bold enough    to show his face anywhere in France;
but now that I'm old    I see them reaching Paris!
It's not the fault of me alone,    since I can no longer fight,
it's the fault of Oliveros    and of Roldán as well,

---

20. Literally, "France the homeland," though it isn't the speaker's homeland. Here *natural* is a mechanical formula, just as a king is called "good" even when committing atrocities.

mengua de todos los doce,    y de cuantos aquí están.
Por Dios a Roldán me llamen    porque se vaya a pelear
con el moro de la enguardia    y lo haga de allí quitar:
que lo traiga muerto o preso,    porque se haya de acordar
de cómo viene a París    para me desafiar.
Don Roldán cuando esto oyera    empiézale de hablar:
—Excusado es, señor,    de enviarme a pelear,
porque tenéis caballeros    a quien podéis enviar,
que cuando son entre damas    bien se saben alabar,
que aunque vengan dos mil moros    uno los esperará,
cuando son en la batalla    véolos tornar atrás.
Todos los doce callaron    si no el menor de edad,
al cual llaman Valdovinos,    en el esfuerzo muy grande;
las palabras que dijera    eran con riguridad:
—Mucho estoy maravillado    de vos, señor don Roldán,
que amengüéis todos los doce    vos que los habíades de honrar:
si no fuérades mi tío    con vos me fuera a matar,
porque entre todos los doce    ninguno podéis nombrar,
que lo que dice de boca    no lo sepa hacer verdad.
Levantóse con enojo    ese paladín Roldán;
Valdovinos que esto vido    también se fue a levantar,
el emperador entre ellos    por el enojo quitar.
Ellos en aquesto estando,    Valdovinos fue a llamar
a los mozos que traía;    por las armas fue a enviar.
El emperador que esto vido    empezóle de rogar
que le hiciese un placer,    que no fuese a pelear,
porque el moro era esforzado,    podríale maltratar,
—que aunque ánimo tengáis    la fuerza os podría faltar,
y el moro es diestro en armas,    vezado a pelear.
Valdovinos que esto oyó    empezóse a desviar
diciendo al emperador    licencia le fuese a dar,
y que si él no se la diese    que él se la quería tomar.
Cuando el emperador vido    que no lo podía excusar,
cuando llegaron sus armas    él mesmo le ayudó a armar:
diole licencia que fuese    con el moro a pelear.
Ya se parte Valdovinos,    ya se parte, ya se va,
ya es llegado a la guardia    do Calaínos está.
Calaínos que lo vido    empezóle así de hablar:
—Bien vengáis el francesico,    de Francia la natural,
si queréis vivir comigo    por paje os quiero llevar;
llevaros he a mis tierras    do placer podáis tomar.

the fault of all the twelve    and everyone present here.
For the love of God, summon Roldán    so he can go and fight
with that Moor at the guard post    and drive him off;
let him bring him dead or a prisoner,    so that he'll remember
the way he came to Paris    to challenge me!"
When Don Roldán heard this,    he began to address him:
"Sire, it's needless    to send me to fight
when you have knights    whom you can send;
when they're with the ladies    they know how to boast
that even if two thousand Moors come,    they'll await them single-handed;
but when they're in battle    I see them retreat."
All the twelve were silent    except for the youngest,
the one named Valdovinos,    of very great courage;
the words he uttered    were spoken sternly:
"I'm very surprised    at you, lord Don Roldán,
for belittling all the twelve,    you who should honor them;
if you weren't my uncle    I'd go and fight with you,
because among all the twelve    you can't name one
who doesn't uphold    that which his lips utter."
The paladin Roldán    arose in anger;
when Valdovinos saw this,    he arose as well;
the emperor stepped between them    to calm their anger.
At that point    Valdovinos called
the lads he had brought,    and sent them for his armor.
When the emperor saw this,    he began to beseech him,
as a favor to him,    not to go out and fight,
because the Moor was courageous    and could injure him:
"Even though you're brave,    your strength may give out,
while the Moor is skillful in arms    and a seasoned warrior."
When Valdovinos heard this,    he began to ride away,
asking the emperor    to give him leave to go,
and if he wouldn't give it,    he himself would take it.
After the emperor saw    he couldn't prevent it,
when his armor arrived    he himself helped him don it;
he gave him leave to go    and fight the Moor.
Now Valdovinos departs,    now he departs, now he leaves,
now he has reached the guard post    where Calaínos waits.
When Calaínos saw him,    he began to address him thus:
"Welcome, little Frenchman    from goodly France;
if you wish to live with me,    I'll take you as a page;
I'll take you to my country,    where you can find pleasure."

Valdovinos que esto oyera   tal respuesta le fue a dar:
—Calaínos, Calaínos,  no debíades así de hablar,
que antes que de aquí me vaya  yo os lo tengo de mostrar
que aquí moriréis primero  que por paje me tomar.
Cuando el moro aquesto oyera  empezó así de hablar:
—Tórnate, el francesico,  a París, esa ciudad.
que si esa porfía tienes  caro te habrá de costar,
porque quien entra en mis manos  nunca puede bien librar.
Cuando el mancebo esto oyera  tornóle a porfiar
que se aparejase presto  que con él se ha de matar.
Cuando el moro vio al mancebo  de tal suerte porfiar,
díjole: —Vente, cristiano,  presto para me encontrar,
que antes que de aquí te vayas  conocerás la verdad,
que te fuera muy mejor  comigo no pelear.
Vanse el uno para el otro,  tan recio que es de espantar.
A los primeros encuentros  el mancebo en tierra está.
El moro cuando esto vido  luego se fue apear;
sacó un alfanje muy rico  para habelle de matar;
mas antes que le hiriese  le empezó de preguntar
quién o cómo se llamaba,  y si es de los doce pares.
El mancebo estando en esto  luego dijo la verdad,
que le llaman Valdovinos,  sobrino de don Roldán.
Cuando el moro tal oyó  empezóle de hablar:
—Por ser de tan pocos días,  y de esfuerzo singular
yo te quiero dar la vida,  y no te quiero matar;
mas quiérote llevar preso  porque te venga a buscar
tu buen pariente Oliveros,  y ese tu tío don Roldán,
y ese otro muy esforzado  Reinaldos de Montalván,
que por esos tres ha sido  mi venida a pelear.
Don Roldán allá do estaba  no hace sino sospirar,
viendo que el moro ha vencido  a Valdovinos el infante.
Sin más hablar con ninguno  don Roldán luego se parte;
íbase para la guardia  para aquel moro matar.
El moro cuando lo vido  empezóle a preguntar
quién es o cómo se llama,  o si era de los doce pares.
Don Roldán cuando esto oyó  respondiérale muy mal:
—Esa razón, perro moro,  tú no me la has de tomar,
porque a ese a quien tú tienes  yo te lo haré soltar:
presto aparéjate, moro,  y empieza de pelear.
Vanse el uno para el otro  con un esfuerzo muy grande:
danse tan recios encuentros  que el moro caído ha;

When Valdovinos heard this,   he made this answer:
"Calaínos, Calaínos,   you shouldn't say such things,
for before I leave this spot   I will prove to you
that you'll die here before   taking me as your page."
When the Moor heard this,   he began to speak thus:
"Return, little Frenchman,   to the city of Paris,
for if you insist on this,   it will cost you dearly,
for whoever falls into my hands   can never escape."
When the lad heard this,   he insisted again
that he ready himself quickly,   for he had to fight with him.
When the Moor saw the lad   so insistent,
he said: "Come quickly,   Christian, and encounter me,
for before you leave this spot   you'll know the truth:
that it would have been much better for you   not to fight me."
They charged each other   so violently, it was frightening.
At their first clash   the lad was on the ground:
When the Moor saw this,   he dismounted at once;
he drew a very costly scimitar   to kill him with,
but before he struck him   he began to ask him
who he was, what his name was,   and if he was one of the twelve peers.
The lad, situated as he was,   told him the truth at once,
that his name was Valdovinos,   nephew of Don Roldán.
When the Moor heard this,   he began to address him:
"Because you are so young   and already so very brave,
I wish to spare your life   and do not wish to kill you;
but I want to take you prisoner,   so you'll be looked for
by your good relative Oliveros   and your uncle, Don Roldán,
and that other very brave man,   Reinaldos of Montalván,
for it was to find those three   that I came here to fight."
Where Don Roldán stood   he did nothing but sigh,
seeing that the Moor had overcome   Prince Valdovinos.
Saying no more to anyone,   Don Roldán left at once,
heading for the guard post   to kill that Moor.
When the Moor saw him,   he began to ask him
who he was, what his name was,   and if he was one of the twelve peers.
When Don Roldán heard this,   he replied spitefully:
"That information, Moorish dog,   you shall not get from me,
because the man you hold   I shall make you release;
get ready quickly, Moor,   and begin to fight."
They charged each other   with mighty courage,
their clash was so violent   that the Moor fell;

Roldán que al moro vio en tierra    luego se fue apear:
—Dime tú, traidor de moro,    no me lo quieras negar:
¿cómo tú fuiste osado    de en toda Francia parar,
ni al buen viejo emperador,    ni a los doce desafiar?
¿Cuál diablo te engañó    cerca de París llegar?
El moro cuando esto oyera    tal respuesta le fue a dar:
—Tengo una cativa mora,    mujer de muy gran linaje:
requeríla yo de amores,    y ella me fue a demandar
que le diese tres cabezas    de París, esa ciudad:
que si éstas yo le llevo    comigo había de casar;
la una es de Oliveros,    la otra de don Roldán,
la otra del esforzado    Reinaldos de Montalván.
Don Roldán cuando esto oyera    así le empezó de hablar:
—¡Mujer que tal te pedía    cierto te quería mal,
porque esas no son cabezas    que tú las puedes cortar!
mas porque a ti sea castigo,    y otro se haya de guardar
de desafiar a los doce,    ni venirlos a buscar,
echó mano a un estoque    para el moro matar.
La cabeza de los hombros    luego se la fue a cortar:
llevóla al emperador    y fuésela a presentar.
Los doce cuando esto vieron    toman placer singular
en ver así muerto al moro,    y por tal mengua le dar.
También trajo a Valdovinos    que él mismo lo fue a soltar.
Así murió Calaínos    en Francia la natural,
por manos del esforzado,    el buen paladín Roldán.

when Roldán saw the Moor on the ground,   he dismounted at once:
"Tell me, traitor of a Moor,   and don't refuse to answer,
how were you so bold   as to appear anywhere in France
and challenge the good old Emperor   and the twelve?
What devil tricked you   into approaching Paris?"
When the Moor heard this,   he made this answer:
"I have a captive Moorish woman,   a woman of lofty birth;
I wooed her   and she requested of me
to bring her three heads   from the city of Paris,
and if I brought them   she'd marry me;
one was that of Oliveros,   the second that of Don Roldán,
the third that of the brave   Reinaldos of Montalván."
When Don Roldán heard this,   he began to address him thus:
"The woman who asked you for that   surely wished you ill,
because those aren't heads   a man like you can cut off!
But as a lesson to you,   and so that others refrain
from challenging the twelve   or coming to find them,"
he laid his hand to a rapier   to kill the Moor.
At once he cut off   his head from his shoulders;
he brought it to the emperor   and made him a present of it.
When the twelve saw this,   they were immensely pleased
to see the Moor killed that way,   and his honor so abated.
He also brought Valdovinos,   whom he himself had released.
Thus died Calaínos   in goodly France
at the hands of the brave,   good paladin Roldán.

# Otros romances

## 43. Romance de la reina Elena

—Reina Elena, reina Elena,   ¡Dios prospere tu alto estado!
si mandáis alguna cosa   veisme aquí a vuestro mandado.
—Bien vengades vos, París,   París el enamorado.
París, ¿dónde vais camino,   dónde tenéis vuestro trato?
—Por la mar ando, señora,   hecho un terrible cosario;
traigo un navío muy rico,   de plata y oro cargado,
llévolo a presentar   a ese buen rey castellano.
Respondiérale la reina,   de esta suerte le ha hablado:
—Tal navío como aquése   razón era de mirarlo.
Respondiérale París   muy cortés y mesurado:
—El navío y yo, señora,   somos a vuestro mandado.
—Gran placer tengo, París,   como venís bien criado.
—Vayádeslo a ver, señora,   veréis cómo va cargado.
—Pláceme, dijo la reina,   por hacer vuestro mandado.
Con trescientas de sus damas   a la mar se había llegado.
Echó la compuerta París   hasta que hubieron entrado;
desque todos fueron dentro   bien oiréis lo que ha mandado:
—¡Alcen áncoras, tiendan velas!   Y a la reina se ha llevado.
Lunes era, caballeros,   un día fuerte y aciago,
cuando entró por la sala   aquese rey Menelao,
mesándose las sus barbas,   fuertemente sospirando,
sus ojos tornados fuentes,   de la su boca hablando:
—¡Reina Elena, reina Elena,   quién de mí os ha apartado,
aquese traidor París,   el señor de los troyanos
con las sus palabras falsas   malamente os ha engañado!

# Miscellaneous Ballads

## 43. Ballad of Queen Helen

"Queen Helen, Queen Helen,   God prosper your noble state!
Whatever you command,   here I am at your orders."
"Welcome, Paris,   Paris the lover!
Paris, where are you off to?   Where do you live your life?"
"I ply the seas, lady,   I've become a fearful corsair;[21]
I have a very costly ship   laden with silver and gold,
which I'm bringing as a gift   for the good king of Castile."
The queen answered him,   addressing him as follows:
"A ship like that   would be interesting to inspect."
Paris replied   most courteously and temperately:
"The ship and I, my lady,   are at your disposal."
"I'm very pleased, Paris,   to find you so polite."
"Come to see it, lady,   come to see its cargo."
"Gladly," said the queen,   "to do your bidding."
With three hundred of her ladies   she arrived at the sea.
Paris slammed the hatch shut   as soon as they boarded the ship;
when they were all on board,   you'll hear the order he gave:
"Hoist anchor! Spread sail!"   And he abducted the queen.
It was a Monday, gentlemen,   a heavy, fateful day,
when King Menelaus   entered the great hall
tearing his beard   and sighing loudly,
his eyes having become fountains,   and saying with his lips:
"Queen Helen, Queen Helen,   who has separated us?
That treacherous Paris,   the lord of the Trojans,
with his lying words   has deceived you grossly!"

---

21. The word also means "a transporter of merchandise," but that meaning doesn't
seem to sit well with the adjective *terrible*.

Cuán bien se lo consolaba    don Agamenón su hermano:
—No lloredes vos, el rey,    no hagades tan gran llanto,
que llorar y sollozar    a las mujeres es dado:
a un tal rey como vos,    con el espada en la mano.
Yo os ayudaré, señor,    con treinta mil de caballo,
yo seré capitán de ellos,    y los iré ordenando,
por las tierras donde fuere    iré hiriendo y matando:
la villa que se me diere    haréla yo derribar,
y la que tomare por armas    esa sembraré de sal,
mataré las criaturas    y cuantos en ella están,
y de esta manera iremos    hasta el Troya allegar.
—Buen consejo es ése, hermano,    y así lo quiero tomar.
Ya se sale el buen rey    por la ciudad a pasear,
con trompetas y añafiles    comienzan a pregonar:
quien quisiere ganar sueldo    de grado se lo darán.
Tanta viene de la gente    que era cosa de espantar.
Arman naos y galeras,    comiénzanse de embarcar.
Agamenón los guiaba,    todos van a su mandar.
Por las tierras donde iban,    van haciendo mucho mal.
Andando noches y días    a Troya van a llegar;
los troyanos que lo saben    las puertas mandan cerrar.
Agamenón que esto vido    mandó apercebir su real,
pone en orden su gente    cómo había de estar.
Los troyanos eran muchos,    bien repara su ciudad.
Otro día de mañana    la comienzan de escalar,
derriban el primer paño,    de dentro quieren entrar,
si no fuera por don Héctor    que allí se fue a hallar;
con él estaba Troilo    y el esforzado Picar.
París esfuerza su gente    que empiezan de desmayar;
las voces eran tan grandes    que al cielo quieren llegar.
Matan tantos de los griegos    que no los saben contar.
Más venían de otra parte    que no hay cuento ni par;
entrado se han por Troya,    ya la empiezan a robar,
prenden al rey y a la reina    y al esforzado Picar.
Matan a Troilo y a Héctor    sin ninguna piedad,
y al gran duque de Troya    ponen en captividad,
y sacan a la reina Elena,    pónenla en su libertad.
Todos le besan las manos    como a reina natural.
Preso llevan a París    con mucha riguridad,
tres pascuas que hay en el año    le sacan a justiciar,
sácanle ambos los ojos,    los ojos de la su faz,

How greatly his brother    Don Agamemnon consoled him!
"Don't weep, king,    don't make such great lament,
for weeping and sobbing    is womanly;
a king such as you    should take up his sword.
I shall help you, sire,    with thirty thousand horse;
I shall be their leader    and shall command them;
on land, wherever it may be,    I shall strike and kill;
any town that surrenders to me    I shall have demolished,
and the one I conquer by arms    I shall sow with salt,
kill the infants    and everyone in it,
and we'll continue that way    till we reach Troy."
"That's good advice, brother,    and I accept it."
Now the good king goes out    to march through the city;
with trumpets and clarions    they begin to announce
that whoever wishes to earn pay    will receive it from them gladly.
So many men respond    that it was an awesome sight.
They fitted out ships and galleys    and began to embark.
Agamemnon led them,    everyone did his bidding.
In the territory they crossed    they did great damage.
Proceeding night and day,    they arrived at Troy;
when the Trojans found out,    they had the gates locked.
When Agamemnon saw this,    he ordered his camp pitched,
and organized his men    as he wanted them.
The Trojans were numerous    and guarded their city well.
The following morning    they began to scale the walls;
they made the first breach    and tried to enter,
but were prevented by Don Hector,    who was stationed there;
with him was Troilus    and brave Picar.
Paris encouraged his men,    who began to lose heart;
the shouts were so loud    they nearly reached the sky.
They killed so many of the Greeks    that they couldn't count them.
More came from another direction,    who were beyond counting;
they entered Troy    and began to pillage it;
they captured the king and queen    and brave Picar.
They killed Troilus and Hector,    showing no mercy,
and took prisoner    the grand duke of Troy;
they rescued Queen Helen    and set her free.
Everyone kissed her hands    as their lawful queen.
They captured Paris,    guarding him strictly;
on the three chief holidays    they took him out and flogged him;
they put out both his eyes,    the eyes in his face,

córtanle el pie del estribo,    la mano del gavilán,
treinta quintales de hierro    a sus pies mandan echar,
y el agua hasta la cinta    por que pierda el cabalgar.

## 44. Romance de Tarquino y Lucrecia

Aquel rey de los romanos    que Tarquino se llamaba
enamoróse de Lucrecia,    la noble y casta romana,
y para dormir con ella    una gran traición pensaba.
Vase muy secretamente    a donde Lucrecia estaba;
cuando en su casa le vido    como a rey le aposentaba.
A hora de medianoche    Tarquino se levantaba.
Vase por el aposento    a donde Lucrecia estaba,
a la cuál halló durmiendo    de tal traición descuidada.
En llegando cerca de ella    desenvainó su espada
y a los pechos se la puso;    de esta manera le habla:
—Yo soy aquel rey Tarquino,    rey de Roma la nombrada,
el amor que yo te tengo    las entrañas me traspasa;
si cumples mi voluntad    serás rica y estimada,
si no, yo te mataré    con el cruel espada.
—Eso no haré yo, el rey,    sí la vida me costara,
que más la quiero perder    que no vivir deshonrada.
Como vido el rey Tarquino    que la muerte no bastaba,
acordó otra traición,    con ella la amenazaba:
—Si no cumples mi deseo,    como yo te lo rogaba,
yo te mataré, Lucrecia,    con un negro de tu casa,
y desque muerto lo tenga    echarlo he en la tu cama;
yo diré por toda Roma    que ambos juntos os tomara.
Después que aquesto oyó Lucrecia    que tan gran traición pensaba,
cumplióle su voluntad    por no ser tan deshonrada.
Desque Tarquino hubo hecho    lo que tanto deseaba,
muy alegre y muy contento    para Roma se tornaba.
Lucrecia quedó muy triste    en verse tan deshonrada;
enviara muy apriesa    con un siervo de su casa
a llamar a su marido    porque allá en Roma estaba.
Cuando ante sí lo vido    de esta manera le habla:
—¡Oh!, mi amado Colatino,    ya es perdida la mi fama,
que pisadas de hombre ajeno    han hollado la tu cama:
el soberbio rey Tarquino    vino anoche a tu posada,
recibíle como a rey    y dejóme violada.

they cut off his stirrup foot    and his hawk-bearing hand;
three tons of iron    they attached to his feet;
he was in water to his waist,    so he'd lose his ability to ride.

# 44. Ballad of Tarquin and Lucrece

That king of the Romans    who was named Tarquin
fell in love with Lucrece,    the noble, chaste Roman woman,
and in order to sleep with her    planned great treachery.
He went in great secrecy    to Lucrece's home;
when she found him in her house,    she lodged him as befits a king.
At the midnight hour    Tarquin arose.
He went to the room    where Lucrece was
and found her sleeping,    not suspecting such treachery.
Approaching her,    he unsheathed his sword
and put it to her breast,    then spoke to her as follows:
"I am King Tarquin,    king of renowned Rome;
my love for you    pierces my vitals;
if you do my will,    you'll be rich and esteemed;
if not, I'll kill you    with my cruel sword."
"I won't do it, king,    even if it costs my life,
for I'd rather lose it    than live in dishonor."
When King Tarquin saw    that the menace of death wasn't sufficient,
he resolved on another evil course,    with which he threatened her:
"If you don't do my will,    as I've asked you to,
I'll kill you, Lucrece,    along with one of your black slaves,
and after I kill him    I'll place him in your bed;
I'll tell everyone in Rome    I caught the two of you together.
When Lucrece heard this,    the great evil he planned,
she let him have his will    to avoid such a dishonor.
After Tarquin had done    what he so desired,
very cheerfully and contentedly    he returned to Rome.
Lucrece was very sad    to find herself thus dishonored;
very quickly she sent word    by one of her slaves
to summon her husband    who was yonder in Rome.
When she saw him before her,    she addressed him thus:
"O beloved Collatinus,    my reputation is now gone,
for another man's feet    have left tracks in your bed:
haughty King Tarquin    came last night to your dwelling;
I welcomed him royally    and he left me violated.

Yo me daré tal castigo    como adúltera malvada
porque ninguna matrona    por mi ejemplo sea mala.
Estas palabras diciendo    echa mano de una espada
que muy secreta traía    debajo de la su falda,
y a los pechos se la pone    que lástima era mirarla.
Luego allí, en aquel momento,    muerta cae la romana.
Su marido, que la viera,    amargamente lloraba;
sacóle de la herida    aquella sangrienta espada,
y en su mano la tenía    y a los sus dioses juraba
de matar el rey Tarquino    y quemarle la su casa.
En un monumento negro    el cuerpo a Roma llevaba
y púsolo descubierto    en medio de una gran plaza,
de los sus ojos llorando    de la su boca hablaba:
—¡Oh, romanos!, ¡Oh, romanos!    doleos de mi triste fama,
que el soberbio rey Tarquino    ha forzado esta romana
y por esta gran deshonra    ella misma se matara.
Ayudádmela a vengar    su muerte tan desastrada.
Desque esto vido el pueblo    todos en uno se armaron
y se van para el palacio    donde el rey Tarquino estaba,
dándole mortales heridas,    y quemáronle su casa.

## 45. Romance de Virgilios

Mandó el rey prender Virgilios    y a buen recaudo poner
por una traición que hizo    en los palacios del rey:
porque forzó una doncella    llamada doña Isabel.
Siete años lo tuvo preso,    sin que se acordase de él,
y un domingo estando en misa    mientes se le vino de él.
—Mis caballeros, Virgilios,    ¿qué se había hecho de él?
Allí habló un caballero    que a Virgilios quiere bien:
—Preso lo tiene tu alteza    y en tus cárceles lo tien.
—Via comer, mis caballeros,    caballeros, via comer,
después que hayamos comido    a Virgilios vamos ver.
Allí hablara la reina:    —Yo no comeré sin él.
A las cárceles se van    adonde Virgilios es.
—¿Qué hacéis aquí, Virgilios?    Virgilios ¿aquí qué hacéis?
—Señor, peino mis cabellos    y las mis barbas también:
aquí me fueron nacidas,    aquí me han encanecer,
que hoy se cumplen siete años    que me mandaste prender.
—Calles, calles tú, Virgilios,    que tres faltan para diez.

I shall punish myself    like a wicked adulteress,
so that no matron    will do wrong by my example."
Saying these words,    she seized a sword
that she was secretly keeping    beneath her skirt,
and thrust iti into her breast,    a pitiful sight to see!
There at once, that very moment,    the Roman woman fell dead.
Her husband, seeing her,    wept bitterly;
he took from her wound    that bloodstained sword
and, holding it in his hand,    he swore to his gods
to kill King Tarquin    and burn down his house.
In a black coffin    he brought the body to Rome
and placed it, uncovered,    in the middle of a large square;
weeping tears,    he said with his lips:
"O Romans, O Romans,    grieve for my sad honor,
for haughty King Tarquin    has raped this Roman lady,
and because she was so dishonored    she killed herself.
Help me avenge    her disastrous death!"
When the people saw this,    they all took up arms together
and went to the palace    where King Tarquin resided;
they gave him mortal wounds    and burned down his house.

# 45. Ballad of Vergil

The king ordered Vergil arrested    and well guarded
for an evil act he committed    in the king's palace:
because he seduced a maiden    named Doña Isabel.
He kept him in prison seven years,    never thinking of him,
but one Sunday, at mass,    he remembered about him.
"My knights: Vergil,    what has become of him?"
Then a knight spoke up    who wished Vergil well:
"Your Highness, you've imprisoned him    and are holding him in your dungeons."
"Go and eat, knights,    knights, go and eat;
after we've eaten    let's go see Vergil."
Then the queen spoke up:    "I won't eat without him."
They went to the dungeons    where Vergil was kept.
"What do you do here, Vergil?    Vergil, what do you do here?"
"Sire, I comb my hair    and my beard as well:
here they grew,    here they shall turn gray,
for today is seven years    since you ordered me arrested."
"Be silent, be silent, Vergil,    for that's three less than ten."

—Señor, si manda tu alteza,　toda mi vida estaré.
—Virgilios, por tu paciencia　conmigo irás a comer.
—Rotos tengo mis vestidos,　no estoy para parecer.
—Yo te los daré, Virgilios,　yo dártelos mandaré.
Plugo a los caballeros　y a las doncellas también;
mucho más plugo a una dueña　llamada doña Isabel.
Ya llaman un arzobispo,　ya la desposan con él.
Tomárala por la mano　y llévasela a un vergel.

## 46. Lanzarote y el orgulloso

Nunca fuera caballero　de damas tan bien servido
como fuera Lanzarote　cuando de Bretaña vino,
que dueñas curaban de él,　doncellas del su rocino.
Esa dueña Quintañona,　ésa le escanciaba el vino,
la linda reina Ginebra　se lo acostaba consigo;
y estando al mejor sabor,　que sueño no había dormido,
la reina toda turbada　un pleito ha conmovido:
—Lanzarote, Lanzarote,　si antes hubieras venido,
no hablara el orgulloso　las palabras que había dicho,
que a pesar de vos, señor,　se acostaría conmigo.
Ya se arma Lanzarote　de gran pesar conmovido,
despídese de su amiga,　pregunta por el camino.
Topó con el orgulloso　debajo de un verde pino,
combátense de las lanzas,　a las hachas han venido.
Ya desmaya el orgulloso,　ya cae en tierra tendido.
Cortárale la cabeza,　sin hacer ningún partido;
vuélvese para su amiga　donde fue bien recibido.

## 47. Romance del conde Alarcos y de la infanta Solisa

Retraída está la infanta,　bien así como solía,
viviendo muy descontenta　de la vida que tenía,
viendo que ya se pasaba　toda la flor de su vida,
y que el rey no la casaba,　ni tal cuidado tenía.
Entre sí estaba pensando　a quien se descubriría,
acordó llamar al rey　como otras veces solía,

"Sire, if Your Highness orders,    I'll stay here all my life."
"Vergil, because of your patience    you'll come and dine with me."
"My clothes are torn,    and I can't show up like this."
"I'll give you some, Vergil,    I'll order some given to you."
The knights were pleased,    and the damsels as well;
But much more pleased was a lady    named Doña Isabel.
Now they summon an archbishop,    now they marry her to him.
He took her by the hand    and led her to an orchard.

## 46. Lancelot and the Prideful Knight

Never was a knight    so well served by ladies
as Lancelot was    when he came from Brittany,
for women tended to him,    and maidens to his steed.[22]
Lady Quintanoña    poured the wine for him,
lovely Queen Guinevere    had him lie down beside her;
enjoying their greatest delight,    before sleep had overtaken them,
the queen, in great agitation,    laid a complaint before him:
"Lancelot, Lancelot,    if you had come sooner,
the prideful knight wouldn't have    spoken as he did,
saying that, in spite of you, sir,    he'd lie with me."
Now Lancelot dons his armor,    stirred by deep grief;
he takes leave of his mistress    and asks the way.
He came across the prideful one    beneath a green pine;
they battle with lances,    then with battleaxes.
Now the prideful one loses heart,    now he falls on the ground full-length.
He cut off his head,    offering no quarter;
he returned to his mistress,    where he was warmly welcomed.

## 47. Ballad of Count Alarcos and Princess Solisa

The princess was solitary,    as was her wont,
very dissatisfied    with the life she was leading,
seeing that her prime of life    was already passing,
and that the king didn't marry her off    and wasn't concerned to.
Wondering silently    to whom to reveal her thoughts,
she resolved to call the king    as she had done in the past,

---

22. *Rocino* normally means "nag," but obviously not here.

por decirle su secreto    y la intención que tenía.
Vino el rey siendo llamado,    que no tardó su venida:
vídola estar apartada,    sola está sin compañía;
su lindo gesto mostraba    ser más triste que solía.
Conociera luego el rey    el enojo que tenía.
—¿Qué es aquesto, la infanta?    ¿qué es aquesto, hija mía?
Contadme vuestros enojos,    no toméis malenconía,
que sabiendo la verdad    todo se remediaría.
—Menester será, buen rey,    remediar la vida mía,
que a vos quedó encomendada    de la madre que tenía.
Dédesme, buen rey, marido,    que mi edad ya lo pedía:
con vergüenza os lo demando,    no con gana que tenía,
que aquestos cuidados tales    a vos, rey, pertenecían.
Escuchada su demanda,    el buen rey le respondía:
—Esa culpa, la infanta,    vuestra era, que no mía,
que ya fuórades casada    con el príncipe de Hungría.
No quesistes escuchar    la embajada que os venía,
pues acá en las nuestras cortes,    hija, mal recaudo había,
porque en todos los mis reinos    vuestro par igual no había,
sino era el conde Alarcos,    hijos y mujer tenía.
—Convidaldo vos, el rey,    al conde Alarcos un día,
y después que hayáis comido    decilde de parte mía,
decilde que se acuerde    de la fe que dél tenía,
la cual él me prometió,    que yo no se la pedía,
de ser siempre mi marido,    yo que su mujer sería.
Yo fui de ello muy contenta    y que no me arrepentía.
Si casó con la condesa,    que mirase lo que hacía,
que por él no me casé    con el príncipe de Hungría:
si casó con la condesa,    dél es culpa, que no mía.
Perdiera el rey en oírlo    el sentido que tenía,
mas después en sí tornado    con enojo respondía:
—¡No son estos los consejos    que vuestra madre os decía!
¡Muy mal mirastes, infanta,    do estaba la honra mía!
Si verdad es todo eso    vuestra honra ya es perdida:
no podéis vos ser casada    siendo la condesa viva.
Si se hace el casamiento    por razón o por justicia,
en el decir de las gentes    por mala seréis tenida.
Dadme vos, hija, consejo,    que el mío no bastaría,
que ya es muerta vuestra madre    a quien consejo pedía.
—Yo os lo daré, buen rey,    de este poco que tenía:
mate el conde a la condesa,    que nadie no lo sabría,

to tell him her secret wish    and what she had in mind.
Summoned, the king came,    he didn't delay his coming;
he saw her remaining aloof,    alone without company;
her lovely face showed    she was sadder than usual.
At once the king knew    what she was irritated about.
"What's this, princess?    What's this, my daughter?
Tell me what's troubling you,    don't be melancholy,
for when the truth is known    everything will come out all right."
"It will be necessary, good king,    to improve my life,
which was entrusted to you    by my mother.
Good king, give me a husband,    for my years demand it;
I request it for my honor,    not because I yearn for it,
for such concerns    pertain to you, king."
Hearing her request,    the good king replied:
"The fault, princess,    is yours, not mine,
or you'd already be wed    to the crown prince of Hungary.
You refused to listen to    the envoys that came to you,
since here at our court,    daughter, they were ill received;
because in my whole kingdom    there is no proper match for you
except Count Alarcos,    who had a wife and children."
"Invite him, king,    invite Count Alarcos some day,
and after you have dined    tell him from me,
tell him to remember    the troth he plighted me,
which he promised me,    for it wasn't I who asked for it,
to be my husband forever,    and I his wife.
I was very contented with that    and didn't regret it.
If he married the countess,    let him look to the consequences,
because it was for his sake I refused    the prince of Hungary;
if he married the countess,    it's his fault, not mine."
Hearing her, the king    was stunned,
but, coming around again,    he replied angrily:
"This isn't the advice    your mother used to give you!
Princess, you have very little concern    for my honor!
If all this is true,    your honor is already lost:
you can't be married    while the countess is alive.
If their marriage was performed    rightly and duly,
in the people's gossip    you'll be called a bad woman.
Daughter, give me advice,    my own doesn't suffice,
for now your mother is dead,    whom I used to ask for counsel."
"I'll give it to you, good king,    out of the little I have;
let the count kill the countess,    so no one is the wiser,

y eche fama que ella es muerta   de un cierto mal que tenía,
y tratarse ha el casamiento   como cosa no sabida.
De esta manera, buen rey,   mi honra se guardaría.
De allí se salía el rey,   no con placer que tenía;
lleno va de pensamientos   con la nueva que sabía;
vido estar al conde Alarcos   entre muchos, que decía:
—¿Qué aprovecha, caballeros,   amar y servir amiga,
que son servicios perdidos   donde firmeza no había?
No pueden por mí decir   aquesto que yo decía,
que en el tiempo que yo serví   una que tanto quería,
si muy bien la quise entonces,   agora más la quería;
mas por mí pueden decir   quien bien ama tarde olvida.
Estas palabras diciendo   vido al buen rey que venía,
y hablando con el rey   de entre todos se salía.
Dijo el buen rey al conde   hablando con cortesía:
—Convidaros quiero, conde,   por mañana en aquel día,
que queráis comer conmigo   por tenerme compañía.
—Que se haga de buen grado   lo que su Alteza decía;
beso sus reales manos   por la buena cortesía:
detenerme he aquí mañana,   aunque estaba de partida,
que la condesa me espera   según la carta me envía.
Otro día de mañana   el rey de misa salía;
asentóse luego a comer,   no por gana que tenía,
sino por hablar al conde   lo que hablarle quería.
Allí fueron bien servidos   como a rey pertenecía.
Después que hubieron comido,   toda la gente salida,
quedóse el rey con el conde   en la tabla do comía.
Empezó de hablar el rey   la embajada que traía:
—Unas nuevas traigo, conde,   que de ellas no me placía,
por las cuales yo me quejo   de vuestra descortesía.
Prometistes a la infanta   lo que ella no vos pedía,
de siempre ser su marido,   y a ella que le placía.
Si otras cosas pasastes   no entro en esa porfía.
Otra cosa os digo, conde,   de que más os pesaría:
que matéis a la condesa   que cumple a la honra mía:
echéis fama que ella es muerta   de cierto mal que tenía,
y tratarse ha el casamiento   como cosa no sabida,
porque no sea deshonrada   hija que tanto quería.
Oídas estas razones   el buen conde respondía:
—No puedo negar, el rey,   lo que la infanta decía,
sino que otorgo ser verdad   todo cuanto me pedía.

and announce that she died    of some infirmity she had;
and the marriage is to be regarded    as nonexistent.
In this way, good king,    my honor will be preserved."
The king went out,    and wasn't pleased;
he was deep in thought    over the news he had heard;
he saw Count Alarcos    in a large group, saying:
"Gentlemen, what's the good    of loving and serving a sweetheart
when your services are wasted    if love isn't constant?
It can't be said of me,    what I have just stated,
for in the days when I wooed    the one woman I loved,
if I loved her then,    I love her much more now;
what can be said of me is:    'Who loves truly, is slow to forget.'"
Speaking these words,    he saw the good king coming;
talking with the king,    he left the group he was in.
The good king said to the count,    speaking courteously:
"I wish to invite you, count,    for tomorrow,
to dine with me    and keep me company."
"Let Your Highness's command    be complied with gladly;
I kiss your royal hands    for this kind courtesy;
tomorrow I'll remain here,    though I was about to leave,
because the countess is expecting me,    from the letter she sent."
The following morning    the king came out of mass;
then he sat down to eat,    not because he was hungry,
but to tell the count    what he had to say to him.
There they were well served    as befits a king.
After they had eaten,    and everyone else was gone,
the king and the count remained    at the table where they had dined.
The king began to relate    the errand he had:
"I bear some news, count,    which doesn't please me,
in which I complain    of your ungracious behavior.
You promised the princess    something she didn't ask you for,
to be her husband always,    to which she consented.
If you acted otherwise,    I won't argue about it.
I have another order, count,    which will grieve you more:
to kill the countess,    for so it behooves my honor:
give out the word she died    of a certain illness she had,
and the marriage is to be regarded    as nonexistent,
so that the daughter I love so much    won't be dishonored."
Hearing that declaration,    the good count replied:
"I can't deny, king,    what the princess says;
rather, I grant it's true,    all that she asks of me.

Por miedo de vos, el rey,    no casé con quien debía,
no pensé que vuestra Alteza    en ello consentiría:
de casar con la infanta    yo, señor, bien casaría;
mas matar a la condesa,    señor rey, no lo haría,
porque no debe morir    la que mal no merecía.
—De morir tiene, el buen conde,    por salvar la honra mía,
pues no mirastes primero    lo que mirar se debía.
Si no muere la condesa    a vos costará la vida.
Por la honra de los reyes    muchos sin culpa morían,
por que muera la condesa    no es mucha maravilla.
—Yo la mataré, buen rey,    mas no será la culpa mía:
vos os avendréis con Dios    en fin de vuestra vida,
y prometo a vuestra Alteza,    a fe de caballería,
que me tengan por traidor    si lo dicho no cumplía
de matar a la condesa,    aunque mal no merecía.
Buen rey, si me dais licencia    yo luego me partiría.
—Vayáis con Dios, el buen conde,    ordenad vuestra partida.
Llorando se parte el conde,    llorando sin alegría;
llorando por la condesa,    que más que a sí la quería.
Llorando también el conde    por tres hijos que tenía,
el uno era de teta,    que la condesa lo cría,
que no quería mamar    de tres amas que tenía
sino era de su madre    porque bien la conocía;
los otros eran pequeños,    poco sentido tenían.
Antes que llegase el conde    estas razones decía:
—¡Quién podrá mirar, condesa,    vuestra cara de alegría,
que saldréis a recebirme    a la fin de vuestra vida!
Yo soy el triste culpado,    esta culpa toda es mía.
En diciendo estas palabras    la condesa ya salía,
que un paje le había dicho    como el conde ya venía.
Vido la condesa al conde    la tristeza que tenía,
vióle los ojos llorosos    que hinchados los tenía
de llorar por el camino    mirando el bien que perdía.
Dijo la condesa al conde:    ¡Bien vengáis, bien de mi vida!
¿Qué habéis, el conde Alarcos?    ¿por qué lloráis, vida mía,
que venís tan demudado    que cierto no os conocía?
No parece vuestra cara    ni el gesto que ser solía;
dadme parte del enojo    como dais de la alegría.
¡Decídmelo luego, conde,    no matéis la vida mía!
—Yo vos lo diré, condesa,    cuando la hora sería.
—Si no me lo decís, conde,    cierto yo reventaría.

Out of fear of you, king,   I failed to marry the woman I should have;
I didn't think Your Highness   would consent to it;
as for marrying the princess,   sire, I'd do so readily,
but to kill the countess,   king! I won't do it,
because a blameless woman   doesn't deserve to die."
"Die she must, good count,   to save my honor,
since you had no regard at first   for your proper duty.
If the countess doesn't die,   it will cost you your life.
For the honor of kings   many die who have no blame;
if the countess dies now,   it's nothing to be surprised at."
"I'll kill her, good king,   but it won't be my fault:
you'll account for it to God   at the end of your life,
and I promise Your Highness,   on my faith as a knight:
let me be called a traitor   if I don't do what you say
and kill the countess,   though she deserves no harm.
Good king, if you permit,   I'll leave right away."
"Go with God, good count,   arrange your departure."
Weeping, the count left,   weeping and without joy,
weeping for the countess,   whom he loved more than himself.
The count also wept   for his three children,
one not yet weaned,   whom the countess was nursing,
since he refused the milk   of three wetnurses he had,
but wanted only his mother's   because he recognized her;
the others were small   and were still very childish.
Before the count got home,   he said to himself:
"How, countess, can I behold   your happy face
when you come out to greet me,   since I know your life is over?
I am the wretched man at fault,   the blame is all mine."
As he spoke those words,   the countess was already coming out,
for a page had told her   that the count was coming.
The countess saw that the count   was very sad,
she saw his moist eyes,   which were swollen
from his weeping on the way   for the joy he was losing.
The countess said to the count:   "Welcome, darling!
What's wrong, Count Alarcos?   Why weeping, my love?
Why do you look so pale   I can't even recognize you?
It's not like your face   or your usual expression;
let me share the trouble   as you let me share your joy!
Tell me at once, count,   don't kill me!"
"I'll tell you, countess,   when the time comes."
"If you don't tell me, count,   I'll surely burst."

—No me fatiguéis, señora,    que no es la hora venida.
Cenemos luego, condesa,    de aqueso que en casa había.
—Aparejado está, conde,    como otras veces solía.
Sentóse el conde a la mesa,    no cenaba ni podía,
con sus hijos al costado,    que muy mucho los quería.
Echóse sobre los hombros;    hizo como que dormía;
de lágrimas de sus ojos    toda la mesa cubría.
Mirándolo la condesa,    que la causa no sabía,
no le preguntaba nada,    que no osaba ni podía.
Levantóse luego el conde,    dijo que dormir quería;
dijo también la condesa    que ella también dormiría;
mas entre ellos no había sueño,    si la verdad se decía.
Vanse el conde y la condesa    a dormir donde solían:
dejan los niños de fuera    que el conde no los quería:
lleváronse el más chiquito,    el que la condesa cría:
cierra el conde la puerta,    lo que hacer no solía.
Empezó de hablar el conde    con dolor y con mancilla:
—¡Oh desdichada condesa,    grande fue la tu desdicha!
—No só desdichada, el conde,    por dichosa me tenía
sólo en ser vuestra mujer:    esta fue gran dicha mía.
—¡Si bien lo sabéis, condesa,    esa fue vuestra desdicha!
Sabed que en tiempo pasado    yo amé a quien servía,
la cual era la infanta.    Por desdicha vuestra y mía
prometí casar con ella;    y a ella que le placía,
demándame por marido    por la fe que me tenía.
Puédelo muy bien hacer    de razón y de justicia:
díjomelo el rey su padre    porque de ella lo sabía.
Otra cosa manda el rey    que toca en el alma mía:
manda que muráis, condesa,    a la fin de vuestra vida,
que no puede tener honra    siendo vos, condesa, viva.
Desque esto oyó la condesa    cayó en tierra amortecida:
mas después en sí tornada    estas palabras decía:
—¡Pagos son de mis servicios,    conde, con que yo os servía!
si no me matáis, el conde,    yo bien os consejaría:
enviédesme a mis tierras    que a mi padre me ternía;
yo criaré vuestros hijos    mejor que la que vernía,
yo os mantendré castidad    como siempre os mantenía.
—De morir habéis, condesa,    en antes que venga el día.
—¡Bien parece, el conde Alarcos,    yo ser sola en esta vida;
porque tengo el padre viejo,    mi madre ya es fallecida,
y mataron a mi hermano,    el buen conde don García,

"Don't weary me, lady,   it's not time yet.
Let's dine at once, lady,   on what we have in the house."
"It's all prepared, count,   as on other occasions."
The count sat down at table,   but was unable to eat;
beside him were his children,   whom he loved dearly.
He slumped down   and seemed to be asleep;
with the tears from his eyes   he covered the whole table.
The countess, observing him   and not knowing the reason,
asked him no questions;   she didn't dare, she couldn't.
Then the count arose,   saying he wanted to sleep;
the countess, too,   said she'd go to bed;
but neither one could sleep   if truth were to be told.
The count and countess went   to bed in their usual room;
they left the children outside the room,   the count didn't want them there,
they took along the smallest one,   whom the countess was nursing;
the count locked the door,   which he wasn't wont to do.
The count began to speak   with sorrow and compassion:
"O unfortunate countess,   great is your misfortune!"
"I'm not unfortunate, count,   I consider myself fortunate
merely to be your wife:   that's my great good fortune."
"If you only knew, countess,   it's your misfortune!
Know that, in the past,   I loved the lady I served,
I mean the princess.   To your misfortune and mine,
I promised to marry her,   and she consented;
now she wants me for a husband   because of my vow to her.
She can easily bring it about   rightly and duly;
her father, the king, told me of it   upon learning it from her.
The king has ordered something diffierent,   which touches my soul:
he orders that you die, lady,   and end your days,
for he cannot have honor   while you're alive, countess."
When the countess heard this,   she fell to the floor in a faint;
after she had come to,   she spoke these words:
"A fine reward for the services   I performed for you, count!
If you don't kill me, count,   I can advise you well:
send me to my home,   where my father will take care of me;
I'll raise your children   better than your new wife would,
I'll be a chaste wife to you,   as I always have been."
"You've got to die, countess,   before the break of day."
"Clearly, Count Alarcos,   I'm all alone in the world,
because my father is old   and my mother already dead,
and my brother was killed,   the good Count García,

que el rey lo mandó matar    por miedo que dél tenía!
No me pesa de mi muerte,    porque yo morir tenía,
mas pésame de mis hijos,    que pierden mi compañía:
hacémelos venir, conde,    y verán mi despedida.
—No los veréis más, condesa,    en días de vuestra vida:
abrazad este chiquito,    que aqueste es el que os perdía.
Pésame de vos, condesa,    cuanto pesar me podía.
No os puedo valer, señora,    que más me va que la vida;
encomendáos a Dios    que esto hacerse tenía.
—Dejéisme decir, buen conde,    una oración que sabía.
—Decidla presto, condesa,    enantes que venga el día.
—Presto la habré dicho, conde,    no estaré un Ave María.
Hincó las rodillas en tierra,    esta oración decía:
«En las tus manos, Señor,    encomiendo el alma mía:
»no me juzgues mis pecados    según que yo merecía,
»mas según tu gran piedad    y la tu gracia infinita.»
—Acabada es ya, buen conde,    la oración que sabía;
encomiéndoos esos hijos    que entre vos y mí había,
y rogad a Dios por mí    mientra tuvierdes vida,
que a ello sois obligado    pues que sin culpa moría.
Dédesme acá ese hijo,    mamará por despedida.
—No lo despertéis, condesa,    dejaldo estar, que dormía,
sino que os demando perdón    porque ya viene el día.
—A vos yo perdono, conde,    por el amor que os tenía;
mas yo no perdono al rey,    ni a la infanta su hija,
sino que queden citados    delante la alta justicia,
que allá vayan a juicio    dentro de los treinta días.
Estas palabras diciendo    el conde se apercebía:
echóle por la garganta    una toca que tenía,
apretó con las dos manos    con la fuerza que podía:
no le aflojó la garganta    mientras que vida tenía.
Cuando ya la vido el conde    traspasada y fallecida,
desnudóle los vestidos    y las ropas que tenía:
echóla encima la cama,    cubrióla como solía;
desnudóse a su costado,    obra de un Ave María:
levantóse dando voces    a la gente que tenía:
—¡Socorré, mis escuderos,    que la condesa se fina!
Hallan la condesa muerta    los que a socorrer venían.
Así murió la condesa,    sin razón y sin justicia;

for the king had him killed   because he was afraid of him!
I'm not sorry about my own death,   since I had to die sometime,
but I'm sorry for my children,   who are losing my attentions:
let them in here, count,   to see my departing!"
"You'll never see them again, countess,   in your life;
embrace this little one,   for he's the one who destroyed you.[23]
I'm sorry for you, countess,   as sorry as I can be.
I can't protect you, lady,   for more than my life is at stake;
commend yourself to God,   for this has to be done."
"Good count, let me recite   a prayer that I know."
"Say it quickly, countess,   before day breaks."
"I'll say it quickly, count,   in less time than a 'Hail, Mary.'"
She knelt on the floor   and recited this prayer:
"'Into Your hands, O Lord,   I commend my soul;
do not judge my sins   in accordance with my deserts,
but in accordance with Your great mercy   and infinite grace.'
Good count, I have now finished   the prayer that I knew;
I entrust to you the children   we have had together;
pray to God for me   as long as you live;
you're obliged to do so   since I die blameless.
Give me that child   to nurse for the very last time."
"Don't awaken him, countess,   let him go on sleeping;
only, I ask your forgiveness,   because day is coming."
"I forgive you, count,   because of my love for you;
but I don't forgive the king   or his daughter, the princess;
rather, let them be haled   before God's court
and be judged there   within thirty days!"
As she spoke those words,   the count was readying himself;
he wrapped around her throat   a turban she had
and squeezed with both hands   as hard as he could;
he didn't slacken his hold   while she still lived.
When the count saw that she   was still and dead,
he stripped her of the gown   and clothes she wore;
he placed her on the bed   and covered her as usual;
he undressed and lay down beside her   in the time it takes to say a "Hail, Mary";
he arose, shouting   to his men:
"Help, squires,   the countess is dying!"
Those who came to his aid   found the countess dead.
Thus died the countess   unjustly and unduly;

23. Perhaps: "the one who is losing you."

mas también todos murieron    dentro de los treinta días.
Los doce días pasados    la infanta ya moría;
el rey a los veinte y cinco,    el conde al treinteno día,
allá fueron a dar cuenta    a la justicia divina.
Acá nos dé Dios su gracia,    y allá la gloria cumplida.

## 48. Romance de Espinelo

Muy malo estaba Espinelo,    en una cama yacía,
los bancos eran de oro,    las tablas de plata fina,
los colchones en que duerme    eran de holanda muy rica,
las sábanas que le cubren    en el agua no se vían,
la colcha que encima tiene    sembrada de perlería;
a su cabecera asiste    Mataleona, su amiga,
con las plumas de un pavón    la su cara le resfría.
Estando en este solaz    tal demanda le hacía:
—Espinelo, Espinelo,    ¡cómo naciste en buen día!
El día en que tú naciste    la luna estaba crecida,
ni un punto le faltaba,    ni un punto le fallecía.
Contásesme tú, Espinelo,    contásesme la tu vida.
—Yo te la diré, señora,    con amor y cortesía:
mi padre era de Francia,    mi madre de Lombardía;
mi padre con su poder    a toda Francia regía.
Mi madre como señora    una ley introducía:
que mujer que dos pariese    de un parto y en un día,
que la den por alevosa    y la quemen por justicia,
o la echen a la mar,    porque adulterado había.
Quiso Dios y mi ventura    que ella dos hijos paría
de un parto y en una hora    que por deshonra tenía.
Fuérase a tomar consejo    con tan loca fantasía
a una cautiva mora,    sabia en nigromancía.
—¿Qué me aconsejas tú, mora,    por salvar la honra mía?
Respondiérale: —Señora,    yo de parecer sería
que tomases a tu hijo,    el que se te antojaría,
y lo eches en la mar    en un arca de valía
bien embetunada toda,    con mucho oro y joyería,
porque quien al niño hallase    de criarlo holgaría.
Cayera la suerte en mí,    y en la gran mar me ponía,
la cual estando muy brava    arrebatado me había

but all the others, too, died   within thirty days.
After twelve days had passed   the princess was already dead;
the king after twenty-five,   the count on the thirtieth day;
then they went to make reckoning   to divine justice.
God give us His grace here on earth   and eternal glory after death!

# 48. Ballad of Espinelo

Espinelo was very ill,   he lay in bed;
its uprights were off gold,   its crossboards of pure silver;
the mattresses on which he slept   were of the finest Holland cloth;
the sheets that covered him   were invisible in water;
the bedspread on top   was spangled with pearls;
present at his bedside   was his sweetheart Mataleona;
with peacock feathers   she fanned his face.
While he was taking that ease,   she made this request of him:
"Espinelo, Espinelo,   lucky the day when you were born!
On the day you were born   the moon was full,
not lacking one jot,   not missing one tittle.
Tell me, Espinelo,   tell me your life story."
"I'll tell it to you, lady,   lovingly and courteously:
my father was from France,   my mother from Lombardy;
with his power my father   ruled all of France.
As queen, my mother   instituted a law saying
that any woman bearing two children   at one birth, in one day,
should be adjudged unfaithful   and executed by burning
or thrown into the sea,   because she committed adultery.
God and my luck would have it   that she bore two sons
at one birth, in one hour,   which she held to be a dishonor.
Prey to such a mad whim,   she went for advice
to a captive Moorish woman   learned in necromancy.
'What do you advise me, Moor,   to save my honor?'
She answered: 'My lady,   my advice is
to take one son,   either one you choose,
and throw him in the sea   inside a valuable chest
that is well coated with tar,   with much gold and jewelry,
so that whoever finds the boy   will be pleased to raise him.'
The lot fell to me,   and she placed me on the high seas;
the sea, being very stormy,   swept me away

y púsome en tierra firme,    con el furor que traía,
a la sombra de una mata    que por nombre espino había,
que por eso me pusieron    de Espinelo nombradía.
Marineros navegando    halláronme en aquel día,
lleváronme a presentar    al gran soldán de Suría.
El soldán no tenía hijos,    por su hijo me tenía;
el soldán agora es muerto.    Yo por el soldán regía.

## 49. Romance de la infantina

A cazar va el caballero,    a cazar como solía,
los perros lleva cansados,    el halcón perdido había;
arrimárase a un roble,    alto es a maravilla;
en una rama más alta,    vido estar una infantina,
cabellos de su cabeza    todo el roble cubrían.
—No te espantes, caballero,    ni tengas tamaña grima.
Fija soy yo del buen rey    y de la reina de Castilla,
siete fadas me fadaron    en brazos de una ama mía,
que andase los siete años    sola en esta montiña.
Hoy se cumplían los siete años,    o mañana en aquel día;
por Dios te ruego, caballero,    llévesme en tu compañía,
si quisieres, por mujer,    si no, sea por amiga.
—Esperéisme vos, señora,    hasta mañana aquel día,
iré yo tomar consejo    de una madre que tenía.
La niña le respondiera    y estas palabras decía:
—¡Oh, malhaya el caballero    que sola deja la niña!
Él se va a tomar consejo,    y ella queda en la montiña.
Aconsejóle su madre    que la tomase por amiga.
Cuando volvió el caballero    no la hallara en la montiña:
vídola que la llevaban    con muy gran caballería.
El caballero, desque la vido,    en el suelo se caía;
desque en sí hubo tornado,    estas palabras decía:
—Caballero que tal pierde,    muy grande pena merecía:
yo mismo seré el alcalde,    yo me seré la justicia:
que le corten pies y manos    y lo arrastren por la villa.

and brought me to dry land    in its great fury,
in the shade of a shrub    called *espino*,[24]
and for that reason I was given    the name Espinelo.
Seamen sailing    found me that day,
and brought me as a gift    to the great sultan of Syria.
The sultan had no sons,    he adopted me;
now the sultan is dead,    and I rule in his place."

## 49. Ballad of the Young Princess

The knight rides out hunting,    hunting as is his wont;
his hounds are weary,    he has lost his falcon;
he leaned against an oak    that was wondrously tall;
on a very high bough    he saw a young princess;
the hair of her head    covered the entire oak.
"Don't be frightened, knight,    don't be so horrified!
I'm the daughter of the good king    and queen of Castile;
seven fairies enchanted me    when I was in my nurses' arms,
making me spend seven years    alone in this forest.
Today the seven years are up,    today or tomorrow;
for the love of God, I beg you, knight,    to take me with you,
as your wife, if you wish,    or else even as a mistress."
"Wait for me, my lady,    until tomorrow,
while I go for advice    from my mother."
The girl replied,    speaking these words:
"Oh, accursed be the knight    who leaves a girl alone!"
He goes to get advice,    she remains in the forest.
His mother advised him    to take her as a mistress.
When the knight returned,    he didn't find her in the forest;
he saw her being carried off    by many horsemen.
When the knight saw this,    he fell to the ground;
when he regained his senses,    he spoke these words:
"A knight who sustains such a loss    deserves a great punishment:
I'll be my own judge,    and my own executioner;
let my feet and hands be cut off    and let me be dragged through town!"[25]

---

24. Hawthorn or blackthorn.    25. In the Spanish, the last line is in the third person, but this would have sounded too forced in English; moreover, some versions of the ballad actually have *me* in place of the *le* and *lo*.

## 50. El conde Arnaldos

¡Quién hubiese tal ventura    sobre las aguas del mar,
como hubo el conde Arnaldos    la mañana de San Juan!
Con un falcón en la mano    la caza iba a cazar,
vio venir una galera    que a tierra quiere llegar.
Las velas traía de seda,    la ejércia de un cendal,
marinero que la manda    diciendo viene un cantar
que la mar facía en calma,    los vientos hace amainar,
los peces que andan 'nel hondo    arriba los hace andar,
las aves que andan volando    en el mástil las face posar.
Allí fabló el conde Arnaldos,    bien oiréis lo que dirá:
—Por Dios te ruego, marinero,    dígasme ora ese cantar.
Respondióle el marinero,    tal respuesta le fue a dar:
—Yo no digo esta canción    sino a quien conmigo va.

## 51. Romance del prisionero

Por el mes era de mayo,    cuando hace la calor,
cuando canta la calandria    y responde el ruiseñor,
cuando los enamorados    van a servir al amor,
sino yo, triste cuitado,    que vivo en esta prisión,
que ni sé cuándo es de día,    ni cuándo las noches son,
sino por una avecilla    que me cantaba al albor.
Matómela un ballestero    ¡Déle Dios mal galardón!
Cabellos de mi cabeza    lléganme al corvejón,
los cabellos de mi barba    por manteles tengo yo,
las uñas de las mis manos    por cuchillo tajador.
Si lo hacía el buen rey,    hácelo como señor,
si lo hace el carcelero,    hácelo como traidor.
Mas quien agora me diese    un pájaro hablador,
siquiera fuese calandria,    o tordico, o ruiseñor,
criado fuese entre damas    y avezado a la razón,
que me lleve una embajada    a mi esposa Leonor:
que me envíe una empanada,    no de trucha, ni salmón,
sino de una lima sorda    y de un pico tajador:
la lima para los hierros    y el pico para la torre.
Oídolo había el rey,    mandóle quitar la prisión.

# 50. Count Arnaldos

If only I could have such good fortune   on the waters of the sea
as Count Arnaldos had   on the morning of St. John's Day!
With a falcon on his wrist   he went out hunting;
he saw a galley coming   that was about to land.
Its sails were of silk,   its rigging of fine silk cord;
the seaman in charge of it   was singing a song
that made the sea calm   and made the winds die down;
the fish swimming in the deep,   it made them come up;
the birds flying about,   it made them perch on the mast.
Then Count Arnaldos spoke up,   you'll hear what he said:
"For the love of God, I beg you, seaman,   tell me that song now!"
The seaman replied,   he made this answer:
"I tell this song   only to him who comes with me."

# 51. Ballad of the Prisoner

It was in the month of May,   when it's hot,
when the lark sings   and the nightingale answers,
when lovers   are servants to love;
"but I, sad and luckless,   live in this prison,
not knowing when it's daytime   or when it's night,
except that a little bird   used to sing to me at dawn.
A crossbowman killed it,   may God punish him!
The hair of my head   descends to my knees,
the hairs of my beard   I use as a cloak,
the nails of my hands   as a cutting knife.
If the good king does this,   he does it as my master;
if the jailer does this,   he does it as a villain.
How I wish someone would now give me   a talking bird,
either a lark,   a little thrush, or a nightingale!
Let it be one raised by ladies   and trained to converse;
let it bear a message for me   to my bride Leonor;
let her send me a pie,   not of trout or salmon,
but with a dead-smooth file   and a sharp pick:
the file for the bars,   the pick for the tower."
The king heard this   and had him released from prison.[26]

---

26. Or: "had his shackles removed."

## 52. Romance de Fontefrida

Fontefrida, Fontefrida,    Fontefrida y con amor,
do todas las avecicas    van tomar consolación,
si no es la tortolica    que está viuda y con dolor.
Por ahí fuera pasar    el traidor del ruiseñor,
las palabras que él decía    llenas son de traición:
—Si tú quisieses, señora,    yo sería tu servidor.
—Vete de ahí, enemigo,    malo, falso, engañador,
que ni poso en ramo verde    ni en prado que tenga flor,
que si hallo el agua clara,    turbia la bebía yo;
que no quiero haber marido,    por que hijos no haya, no,
no quiero placer con ellos,    ni menos consolación.
Déjame, triste enemigo,    malo, falso, mal traidor,
que no quiero ser tu amiga    ni casar contigo, no.

## 53. "Yo me levantara, madre"

Yo me levantara, madre,    mañanica de San Juan,
vide estar una doncella    ribericas de la mar.
Sola lava y sola tuerce,    sola tiende en un rosal;
mientras los paños se enjugan    dice la niña un cantar:
—Do los mis amores, do los,    ¿dónde los iré a buscar?
Mar abajo, mar arriba,    diciendo iba un cantar,
peine de oro en las sus manos    y sus cabellos peinar:
—Dígasme tú, el marinero,    que Dios te guarde de mal,
si los viste a mis amores,    si los viste allá pasar.

## 52. Ballad of Fontefrida

Fontefrida, Fontefrida,   cool fountain of love,
where all the little birds   go for consolation,
except the turtledove,   who is a sorrowing widow.
The treacherous nightingale   passed by there;
the words he spoke   were full of deceit:
"If you wished, my lady,   I'd be your servant."
"Away from here, enemy,   evil, false, cheating,
for I don't perch on a green bough   or in a flowery meadow,
and if I find clear water,   I drink it muddied;
for I don't want a husband,   so that I don't have children, no;
I don't want the pleasure of them   or the consolation.
Leave me, wretched enemy,   evil, false, deceitful,
for I don't want to be your lover   or marry you, no."


## 53. "I Arose, Mother"

I arose, mother,   on the morning of St. John's Day;
I saw a maiden standing   on the seashore.
Alone, she washed and wrung clothes;   alone, she spread them on a rosebush;
while the clothes were drying,   the girl sang a song:
"Where shall I seek my lover,   where my lover, where?"
Up and down the shore   she walked singing a song,
a golden comb in her hands   as she combed her hair:
"Tell me, seaman   (may God keep you from harm!),
whether you've seen my lover,   seen him passing by."

# Alphabetical List of Spanish Titles

# Alphabetical List of Spanish First Half-Lines

A CATALOG OF SELECTED
# DOVER BOOKS
IN ALL FIELDS OF INTEREST

# A CATALOG OF SELECTED DOVER
# BOOKS IN ALL FIELDS OF INTEREST

CONCERNING THE SPIRITUAL IN ART, Wassily Kandinsky. Pioneering work by father of abstract art. Thoughts on color theory, nature of art. Analysis of earlier masters. 12 illustrations. 80pp. of text. 5⅜ x 8½. 23411-8

ANIMALS: 1,419 Copyright-Free Illustrations of Mammals, Birds, Fish, Insects, etc., Jim Harter (ed.). Clear wood engravings present, in extremely lifelike poses, over 1,000 species of animals. One of the most extensive pictorial sourcebooks of its kind. Captions. Index. 284pp. 9 x 12. 23766-4

CELTIC ART: The Methods of Construction, George Bain. Simple geometric techniques for making Celtic interlacements, spirals, Kells-type initials, animals, humans, etc. Over 500 illustrations. 160pp. 9 x 12. (Available in U.S. only.) 22923-8

AN ATLAS OF ANATOMY FOR ARTISTS, Fritz Schider. Most thorough reference work on art anatomy in the world. Hundreds of illustrations, including selections from works by Vesalius, Leonardo, Goya, Ingres, Michelangelo, others. 593 illustrations. 192pp. 7⅛ x 10¼. 20241-0

CELTIC HAND STROKE-BY-STROKE (Irish Half-Uncial from "The Book of Kells"): An Arthur Baker Calligraphy Manual, Arthur Baker. Complete guide to creating each letter of the alphabet in distinctive Celtic manner. Covers hand position, strokes, pens, inks, paper, more. Illustrated. 48pp. 8¼ x 11. 24336-2

EASY ORIGAMI, John Montroll. Charming collection of 32 projects (hat, cup, pelican, piano, swan, many more) specially designed for the novice origami hobbyist. Clearly illustrated easy-to-follow instructions insure that even beginning papercrafters will achieve successful results. 48pp. 8¼ x 11. 27298-2

THE COMPLETE BOOK OF BIRDHOUSE CONSTRUCTION FOR WOODWORKERS, Scott D. Campbell. Detailed instructions, illustrations, tables. Also data on bird habitat and instinct patterns. Bibliography. 3 tables. 63 illustrations in 15 figures. 48pp. 5¼ x 8½. 24407-5

BLOOMINGDALE'S ILLUSTRATED 1886 CATALOG: Fashions, Dry Goods and Housewares, Bloomingdale Brothers. Famed merchants' extremely rare catalog depicting about 1,700 products: clothing, housewares, firearms, dry goods, jewelry, more. Invaluable for dating, identifying vintage items. Also, copyright-free graphics for artists, designers. Co-published with Henry Ford Museum & Greenfield Village. 160pp. 8¼ x 11. 25780-0

HISTORIC COSTUME IN PICTURES, Braun & Schneider. Over 1,450 costumed figures in clearly detailed engravings–from dawn of civilization to end of 19th century. Captions. Many folk costumes. 256pp. 8⅜ x 11¾. 23150-X

STICKLEY CRAFTSMAN FURNITURE CATALOGS, Gustav Stickley and L. & J. G. Stickley. Beautiful, functional furniture in two authentic catalogs from 1910. 594 illustrations, including 277 photos, show settles, rockers, armchairs, reclining chairs, bookcases, desks, tables. 183pp. 6½ x 9¼.                                23838-5

AMERICAN LOCOMOTIVES IN HISTORIC PHOTOGRAPHS: 1858 to 1949, Ron Ziel (ed.). A rare collection of 126 meticulously detailed official photographs, called "builder portraits," of American locomotives that majestically chronicle the rise of steam locomotive power in America. Introduction. Detailed captions. xi+ 129pp. 9 x 12.                                27393-8

AMERICA'S LIGHTHOUSES: An Illustrated History, Francis Ross Holland, Jr. Delightfully written, profusely illustrated fact-filled survey of over 200 American lighthouses since 1716. History, anecdotes, technological advances, more. 240pp. 8 x 10¾.                                25576-X

TOWARDS A NEW ARCHITECTURE, Le Corbusier. Pioneering manifesto by founder of "International School." Technical and aesthetic theories, views of industry, economics, relation of form to function, "mass-production split" and much more. Profusely illustrated. 320pp. 6⅛ x 9¼. (Available in U.S. only.)                                25023-7

HOW THE OTHER HALF LIVES, Jacob Riis. Famous journalistic record, exposing poverty and degradation of New York slums around 1900, by major social reformer. 100 striking and influential photographs. 233pp. 10 x 7⅞.                                22012-5

FRUIT KEY AND TWIG KEY TO TREES AND SHRUBS, William M. Harlow. One of the handiest and most widely used identification aids. Fruit key covers 120 deciduous and evergreen species; twig key 160 deciduous species. Easily used. Over 300 photographs. 126pp. 5⅜ x 8½.                                20511-8

COMMON BIRD SONGS, Dr. Donald J. Borror. Songs of 60 most common U.S. birds: robins, sparrows, cardinals, bluejays, finches, more—arranged in order of increasing complexity. Up to 9 variations of songs of each species.
                                Cassette and manual 99911-4

ORCHIDS AS HOUSE PLANTS, Rebecca Tyson Northen. Grow cattleyas and many other kinds of orchids—in a window, in a case, or under artificial light. 63 illustrations. 148pp. 5⅜ x 8½.                                23261-1

MONSTER MAZES, Dave Phillips. Masterful mazes at four levels of difficulty. Avoid deadly perils and evil creatures to find magical treasures. Solutions for all 32 exciting illustrated puzzles. 48pp. 8¼ x 11.                                26005-4

MOZART'S DON GIOVANNI (DOVER OPERA LIBRETTO SERIES), Wolfgang Amadeus Mozart. Introduced and translated by Ellen H. Bleiler. Standard Italian libretto, with complete English translation. Convenient and thoroughly portable—an ideal companion for reading along with a recording or the performance itself. Introduction. List of characters. Plot summary. 121pp. 5¼ x 8½.                24944-1

TECHNICAL MANUAL AND DICTIONARY OF CLASSICAL BALLET, Gail Grant. Defines, explains, comments on steps, movements, poses and concepts. 15-page pictorial section. Basic book for student, viewer. 127pp. 5⅜ x 8½.                21843-0

THE CLARINET AND CLARINET PLAYING, David Pino. Lively, comprehensive work features suggestions about technique, musicianship, and musical interpretation, as well as guidelines for teaching, making your own reeds, and preparing for public performance. Includes an intriguing look at clarinet history. "A godsend," *The Clarinet,* Journal of the International Clarinet Society. Appendixes. 7 illus. 320pp. 5⅜ x 8½. 40270-3

HOLLYWOOD GLAMOR PORTRAITS, John Kobal (ed.). 145 photos from 1926-49. Harlow, Gable, Bogart, Bacall; 94 stars in all. Full background on photographers, technical aspects. 160pp. 8⅜ x 11¼. 23352-9

THE ANNOTATED CASEY AT THE BAT: A Collection of Ballads about the Mighty Casey/Third, Revised Edition, Martin Gardner (ed.). Amusing sequels and parodies of one of America's best-loved poems: Casey's Revenge, Why Casey Whiffed, Casey's Sister at the Bat, others. 256pp. 5⅜ x 8½. 28598-7

THE RAVEN AND OTHER FAVORITE POEMS, Edgar Allan Poe. Over 40 of the author's most memorable poems: "The Bells," "Ulalume," "Israfel," "To Helen," "The Conqueror Worm," "Eldorado," "Annabel Lee," many more. Alphabetic lists of titles and first lines. 64pp. 5$\frac{3}{16}$ x 8¼. 26685-0

PERSONAL MEMOIRS OF U. S. GRANT, Ulysses Simpson Grant. Intelligent, deeply moving firsthand account of Civil War campaigns, considered by many the finest military memoirs ever written. Includes letters, historic photographs, maps and more. 528pp. 6⅛ x 9¼. 28587-1

ANCIENT EGYPTIAN MATERIALS AND INDUSTRIES, A. Lucas and J. Harris. Fascinating, comprehensive, thoroughly documented text describes this ancient civilization's vast resources and the processes that incorporated them in daily life, including the use of animal products, building materials, cosmetics, perfumes and incense, fibers, glazed ware, glass and its manufacture, materials used in the mummification process, and much more. 544pp. 6⅛ x 9¼. (Available in U.S. only.) 40446-3

RUSSIAN STORIES/RUSSKIE RASSKAZY: A Dual-Language Book, edited by Gleb Struve. Twelve tales by such masters as Chekhov, Tolstoy, Dostoevsky, Pushkin, others. Excellent word-for-word English translations on facing pages, plus teaching and study aids, Russian/English vocabulary, biographical/critical introductions, more. 416pp. 5⅜ x 8½. 26244-8

PHILADELPHIA THEN AND NOW: 60 Sites Photographed in the Past and Present, Kenneth Finkel and Susan Oyama. Rare photographs of City Hall, Logan Square, Independence Hall, Betsy Ross House, other landmarks juxtaposed with contemporary views. Captures changing face of historic city. Introduction. Captions. 128pp. 8¼ x 11. 25790-8

AIA ARCHITECTURAL GUIDE TO NASSAU AND SUFFOLK COUNTIES, LONG ISLAND, The American Institute of Architects, Long Island Chapter, and the Society for the Preservation of Long Island Antiquities. Comprehensive, well-researched and generously illustrated volume brings to life over three centuries of Long Island's great architectural heritage. More than 240 photographs with authoritative, extensively detailed captions. 176pp. 8¼ x 11. 26946-9

NORTH AMERICAN INDIAN LIFE: Customs and Traditions of 23 Tribes, Elsie Clews Parsons (ed.). 27 fictionalized essays by noted anthropologists examine religion, customs, government, additional facets of life among the Winnebago, Crow, Zuni, Eskimo, other tribes. 480pp. 6⅛ x 9¼. 27377-6

CATALOG OF DOVER BOOKS

FRANK LLOYD WRIGHT'S DANA HOUSE, Donald Hoffmann. Pictorial essay of residential masterpiece with over 160 interior and exterior photos, plans, elevations, sketches and studies. 128pp. 9¼ x 10¾. 29120-0

THE MALE AND FEMALE FIGURE IN MOTION: 60 Classic Photographic Sequences, Eadweard Muybridge. 60 true-action photographs of men and women walking, running, climbing, bending, turning, etc., reproduced from rare 19th-century masterpiece. vi + 121pp. 9 x 12. 24745-7

1001 QUESTIONS ANSWERED ABOUT THE SEASHORE, N. J. Berrill and Jacquelyn Berrill. Queries answered about dolphins, sea snails, sponges, starfish, fishes, shore birds, many others. Covers appearance, breeding, growth, feeding, much more. 305pp. 5¼ x 8¼. 23366-9

ATTRACTING BIRDS TO YOUR YARD, William J. Weber. Easy-to-follow guide offers advice on how to attract the greatest diversity of birds: birdhouses, feeders, water and waterers, much more. 96pp. 5³⁄₁₆ x 8¼. 28927-3

MEDICINAL AND OTHER USES OF NORTH AMERICAN PLANTS: A Historical Survey with Special Reference to the Eastern Indian Tribes, Charlotte Erichsen-Brown. Chronological historical citations document 500 years of usage of plants, trees, shrubs native to eastern Canada, northeastern U.S. Also complete identifying information. 343 illustrations. 544pp. 6½ x 9¼. 25951-X

STORYBOOK MAZES, Dave Phillips. 23 stories and mazes on two-page spreads: Wizard of Oz, Treasure Island, Robin Hood, etc. Solutions. 64pp. 8¼ x 11. 23628-5

AMERICAN NEGRO SONGS: 230 Folk Songs and Spirituals, Religious and Secular, John W. Work. This authoritative study traces the African influences of songs sung and played by black Americans at work, in church, and as entertainment. The author discusses the lyric significance of such songs as "Swing Low, Sweet Chariot," "John Henry," and others and offers the words and music for 230 songs. Bibliography. Index of Song Titles. 272pp. 6½ x 9¼. 40271-1

MOVIE-STAR PORTRAITS OF THE FORTIES, John Kobal (ed.). 163 glamor, studio photos of 106 stars of the 1940s: Rita Hayworth, Ava Gardner, Marlon Brando, Clark Gable, many more. 176pp. 8⅜ x 11¼. 23546-7

BENCHLEY LOST AND FOUND, Robert Benchley. Finest humor from early 30s, about pet peeves, child psychologists, post office and others. Mostly unavailable elsewhere. 73 illustrations by Peter Arno and others. 183pp. 5⅜ x 8½. 22410-4

YEKL and THE IMPORTED BRIDEGROOM AND OTHER STORIES OF YIDDISH NEW YORK, Abraham Cahan. Film Hester Street based on Yekl (1896). Novel, other stories among first about Jewish immigrants on N.Y.'s East Side. 240pp. 5⅜ x 8½. 22427-9

SELECTED POEMS, Walt Whitman. Generous sampling from Leaves of Grass. Twenty-four poems include "I Hear America Singing," "Song of the Open Road," "I Sing the Body Electric," "When Lilacs Last in the Dooryard Bloom'd," "O Captain! My Captain!"–all reprinted from an authoritative edition. Lists of titles and first lines. 128pp. 5³⁄₁₆ x 8¼. 26878-0

THE BEST TALES OF HOFFMANN, E. T. A. Hoffmann. 10 of Hoffmann's most important stories: "Nutcracker and the King of Mice," "The Golden Flowerpot," etc. 458pp. 5⅜ x 8½. 21793-0

FROM FETISH TO GOD IN ANCIENT EGYPT, E. A. Wallis Budge. Rich detailed survey of Egyptian conception of "God" and gods, magic, cult of animals, Osiris, more. Also, superb English translations of hymns and legends. 240 illustrations. 545pp. 5⅜ x 8½. 25803-3

FRENCH STORIES/CONTES FRANÇAIS: A Dual-Language Book, Wallace Fowlie. Ten stories by French masters, Voltaire to Camus: "Micromegas" by Voltaire; "The Atheist's Mass" by Balzac; "Minuet" by de Maupassant; "The Guest" by Camus, six more. Excellent English translations on facing pages. Also French-English vocabulary list, exercises, more. 352pp. 5⅜ x 8½. 26443-2

CHICAGO AT THE TURN OF THE CENTURY IN PHOTOGRAPHS: 122 Historic Views from the Collections of the Chicago Historical Society, Larry A. Viskochil. Rare large-format prints offer detailed views of City Hall, State Street, the Loop, Hull House, Union Station, many other landmarks, circa 1904-1913. Introduction. Captions. Maps. 144pp. 9⅜ x 12¼. 24656-6

OLD BROOKLYN IN EARLY PHOTOGRAPHS, 1865-1929, William Lee Younger. Luna Park, Gravesend race track, construction of Grand Army Plaza, moving of Hotel Brighton, etc. 157 previously unpublished photographs. 165pp. 8⅞ x 11¾. 23587-4

THE MYTHS OF THE NORTH AMERICAN INDIANS, Lewis Spence. Rich anthology of the myths and legends of the Algonquins, Iroquois, Pawnees and Sioux, prefaced by an extensive historical and ethnological commentary. 36 illustrations. 480pp. 5⅜ x 8½. 25967-6

AN ENCYCLOPEDIA OF BATTLES: Accounts of Over 1,560 Battles from 1479 B.C. to the Present, David Eggenberger. Essential details of every major battle in recorded history from the first battle of Megiddo in 1479 B.C. to Grenada in 1984. List of Battle Maps. New Appendix covering the years 1967-1984. Index. 99 illustrations. 544pp. 6½ x 9¼. 24913-1

SAILING ALONE AROUND THE WORLD, Captain Joshua Slocum. First man to sail around the world, alone, in small boat. One of great feats of seamanship told in delightful manner. 67 illustrations. 294pp. 5⅜ x 8½. 20326-3

ANARCHISM AND OTHER ESSAYS, Emma Goldman. Powerful, penetrating, prophetic essays on direct action, role of minorities, prison reform, puritan hypocrisy, violence, etc. 271pp. 5⅜ x 8½. 22484-8

MYTHS OF THE HINDUS AND BUDDHISTS, Ananda K. Coomaraswamy and Sister Nivedita. Great stories of the epics; deeds of Krishna, Shiva, taken from puranas, Vedas, folk tales; etc. 32 illustrations. 400pp. 5⅜ x 8½. 21759-0

THE TRAUMA OF BIRTH, Otto Rank. Rank's controversial thesis that anxiety neurosis is caused by profound psychological trauma which occurs at birth. 256pp. 5⅜ x 8½. 27974-X

A THEOLOGICO-POLITICAL TREATISE, Benedict Spinoza. Also contains unfinished Political Treatise. Great classic on religious liberty, theory of government on common consent. R. Elwes translation. Total of 421pp. 5⅜ x 8½. 20249-6

MY BONDAGE AND MY FREEDOM, Frederick Douglass. Born a slave, Douglass became outspoken force in antislavery movement. The best of Douglass' autobiographies. Graphic description of slave life. 464pp. 5⅜ x 8½. 22457-0

FOLLOWING THE EQUATOR: A Journey Around the World, Mark Twain. Fascinating humorous account of 1897 voyage to Hawaii, Australia, India, New Zealand, etc. Ironic, bemused reports on peoples, customs, climate, flora and fauna, politics, much more. 197 illustrations. 720pp. 5⅜ x 8½. 26113-1

THE PEOPLE CALLED SHAKERS, Edward D. Andrews. Definitive study of Shakers: origins, beliefs, practices, dances, social organization, furniture and crafts, etc. 33 illustrations. 351pp. 5⅜ x 8½. 21081-2

THE MYTHS OF GREECE AND ROME, H. A. Guerber. A classic of mythology, generously illustrated, long prized for its simple, graphic, accurate retelling of the principal myths of Greece and Rome, and for its commentary on their origins and significance. With 64 illustrations by Michelangelo, Raphael, Titian, Rubens, Canova, Bernini and others. 480pp. 5⅜ x 8½. 27584-1

PSYCHOLOGY OF MUSIC, Carl E. Seashore. Classic work discusses music as a medium from psychological viewpoint. Clear treatment of physical acoustics, auditory apparatus, sound perception, development of musical skills, nature of musical feeling, host of other topics. 88 figures. 408pp. 5⅜ x 8½. 21851-1

THE PHILOSOPHY OF HISTORY, Georg W. Hegel. Great classic of Western thought develops concept that history is not chance but rational process, the evolution of freedom. 457pp. 5⅜ x 8½. 20112-0

THE BOOK OF TEA, Kakuzo Okakura. Minor classic of the Orient: entertaining, charming explanation, interpretation of traditional Japanese culture in terms of tea ceremony. 94pp. 5⅜ x 8½. 20070-1

LIFE IN ANCIENT EGYPT, Adolf Erman. Fullest, most thorough, detailed older account with much not in more recent books, domestic life, religion, magic, medicine, commerce, much more. Many illustrations reproduce tomb paintings, carvings, hieroglyphs, etc. 597pp. 5⅜ x 8½. 22632-8

SUNDIALS, Their Theory and Construction, Albert Waugh. Far and away the best, most thorough coverage of ideas, mathematics concerned, types, construction, adjusting anywhere. Simple, nontechnical treatment allows even children to build several of these dials. Over 100 illustrations. 230pp. 5⅜ x 8½. 22947-5

THEORETICAL HYDRODYNAMICS, L. M. Milne-Thomson. Classic exposition of the mathematical theory of fluid motion, applicable to both hydrodynamics and aerodynamics. Over 600 exercises. 768pp. 6⅛ x 9¼. 68970-0

SONGS OF EXPERIENCE: Facsimile Reproduction with 26 Plates in Full Color, William Blake. 26 full-color plates from a rare 1826 edition. Includes "The Tyger," "London," "Holy Thursday," and other poems. Printed text of poems. 48pp. 5¼ x 7. 24636-1

OLD-TIME VIGNETTES IN FULL COLOR, Carol Belanger Grafton (ed.). Over 390 charming, often sentimental illustrations, selected from archives of Victorian graphics—pretty women posing, children playing, food, flowers, kittens and puppies, smiling cherubs, birds and butterflies, much more. All copyright-free. 48pp. 9¼ x 12¼. 27269-9

PERSPECTIVE FOR ARTISTS, Rex Vicat Cole. Depth, perspective of sky and sea, shadows, much more, not usually covered. 391 diagrams, 81 reproductions of drawings and paintings. 279pp. 5⅜ x 8½. 22487-2

DRAWING THE LIVING FIGURE, Joseph Sheppard. Innovative approach to artistic anatomy focuses on specifics of surface anatomy, rather than muscles and bones. Over 170 drawings of live models in front, back and side views, and in widely varying poses. Accompanying diagrams. 177 illustrations. Introduction. Index. 144pp. 8⅜ x11¼. 26723-7

GOTHIC AND OLD ENGLISH ALPHABETS: 100 Complete Fonts, Dan X. Solo. Add power, elegance to posters, signs, other graphics with 100 stunning copyright-free alphabets: Blackstone, Dolbey, Germania, 97 more–including many lower-case, numerals, punctuation marks. 104pp. 8⅛ x 11. 24695-7

HOW TO DO BEADWORK, Mary White. Fundamental book on craft from simple projects to five-bead chains and woven works. 106 illustrations. 142pp. 5⅜ x 8. 20697-1

THE BOOK OF WOOD CARVING, Charles Marshall Sayers. Finest book for beginners discusses fundamentals and offers 34 designs. "Absolutely first rate . . . well thought out and well executed."–E. J. Tangerman. 118pp. 7¾ x 10⅝. 23654-4

ILLUSTRATED CATALOG OF CIVIL WAR MILITARY GOODS: Union Army Weapons, Insignia, Uniform Accessories, and Other Equipment, Schuyler, Hartley, and Graham. Rare, profusely illustrated 1846 catalog includes Union Army uniform and dress regulations, arms and ammunition, coats, insignia, flags, swords, rifles, etc. 226 illustrations. 160pp. 9 x 12. 24939-5

WOMEN'S FASHIONS OF THE EARLY 1900s: An Unabridged Republication of "New York Fashions, 1909," National Cloak & Suit Co. Rare catalog of mail-order fashions documents women's and children's clothing styles shortly after the turn of the century. Captions offer full descriptions, prices. Invaluable resource for fashion, costume historians. Approximately 725 illustrations. 128pp. 8⅜ x 11¼. 27276-1

THE 1912 AND 1915 GUSTAV STICKLEY FURNITURE CATALOGS, Gustav Stickley. With over 200 detailed illustrations and descriptions, these two catalogs are essential reading and reference materials and identification guides for Stickley furniture. Captions cite materials, dimensions and prices. 112pp. 6½ x 9¼. 26676-1

EARLY AMERICAN LOCOMOTIVES, John H. White, Jr. Finest locomotive engravings from early 19th century: historical (1804–74), main-line (after 1870), special, foreign, etc. 147 plates. 142pp. 11⅜ x 8¼. 22772-3

THE TALL SHIPS OF TODAY IN PHOTOGRAPHS, Frank O. Braynard. Lavishly illustrated tribute to nearly 100 majestic contemporary sailing vessels: Amerigo Vespucci, Clearwater, Constitution, Eagle, Mayflower, Sea Cloud, Victory, many more. Authoritative captions provide statistics, background on each ship. 190 black-and-white photographs and illustrations. Introduction. 128pp. 8⅞ x 11¾. 27163-3

LITTLE BOOK OF EARLY AMERICAN CRAFTS AND TRADES, Peter Stockham (ed.). 1807 children's book explains crafts and trades: baker, hatter, cooper, potter, and many others. 23 copperplate illustrations. 140pp. $4\frac{5}{8}$ x 6. 23336-7

VICTORIAN FASHIONS AND COSTUMES FROM HARPER'S BAZAR, 1867–1898, Stella Blum (ed.). Day costumes, evening wear, sports clothes, shoes, hats, other accessories in over 1,000 detailed engravings. 320pp. $9\frac{3}{8}$ x $12\frac{1}{4}$. 22990-4

GUSTAV STICKLEY, THE CRAFTSMAN, Mary Ann Smith. Superb study surveys broad scope of Stickley's achievement, especially in architecture. Design philosophy, rise and fall of the Craftsman empire, descriptions and floor plans for many Craftsman houses, more. 86 black-and-white halftones. 31 line illustrations. Introduction 208pp. $6\frac{1}{2}$ x $9\frac{1}{4}$. 27210-9

THE LONG ISLAND RAIL ROAD IN EARLY PHOTOGRAPHS, Ron Ziel. Over 220 rare photos, informative text document origin ( 1844) and development of rail service on Long Island. Vintage views of early trains, locomotives, stations, passengers, crews, much more. Captions. $8\frac{7}{8}$ x $11\frac{3}{4}$. 26301-0

VOYAGE OF THE LIBERDADE, Joshua Slocum. Great 19th-century mariner's thrilling, first-hand account of the wreck of his ship off South America, the 35-foot boat he built from the wreckage, and its remarkable voyage home. 128pp. $5\frac{3}{8}$ x $8\frac{1}{2}$. 40022-0

TEN BOOKS ON ARCHITECTURE, Vitruvius. The most important book ever written on architecture. Early Roman aesthetics, technology, classical orders, site selection, all other aspects. Morgan translation. 331pp. $5\frac{3}{8}$ x $8\frac{1}{2}$. 20645-9

THE HUMAN FIGURE IN MOTION, Eadweard Muybridge. More than 4,500 stopped-action photos, in action series, showing undraped men, women, children jumping, lying down, throwing, sitting, wrestling, carrying, etc. 390pp. $7\frac{7}{8}$ x $10\frac{5}{8}$. 20204-6 Clothbd.

TREES OF THE EASTERN AND CENTRAL UNITED STATES AND CANADA, William M. Harlow. Best one-volume guide to 140 trees. Full descriptions, woodlore, range, etc. Over 600 illustrations. Handy size. 288pp. $4\frac{1}{2}$ x $6\frac{3}{8}$. 20395-6

SONGS OF WESTERN BIRDS, Dr. Donald J. Borror. Complete song and call repertoire of 60 western species, including flycatchers, juncoes, cactus wrens, many more–includes fully illustrated booklet. Cassette and manual 99913-0

GROWING AND USING HERBS AND SPICES, Milo Miloradovich. Versatile handbook provides all the information needed for cultivation and use of all the herbs and spices available in North America. 4 illustrations. Index. Glossary. 236pp. $5\frac{3}{8}$ x $8\frac{1}{2}$. 25058-X

BIG BOOK OF MAZES AND LABYRINTHS, Walter Shepherd. 50 mazes and labyrinths in all–classical, solid, ripple, and more–in one great volume. Perfect inexpensive puzzler for clever youngsters. Full solutions. 112pp. $8\frac{1}{8}$ x 11. 22951-3

PIANO TUNING, J. Cree Fischer. Clearest, best book for beginner, amateur. Simple repairs, raising dropped notes, tuning by easy method of flattened fifths. No previous skills needed. 4 illustrations. 201pp. 5⅜ x 8½. 23267-0

HINTS TO SINGERS, Lillian Nordica. Selecting the right teacher, developing confidence, overcoming stage fright, and many other important skills receive thoughtful discussion in this indispensible guide, written by a world-famous diva of four decades' experience. 96pp. 5⅜ x 8½. 40094-8

THE COMPLETE NONSENSE OF EDWARD LEAR, Edward Lear. All nonsense limericks, zany alphabets, Owl and Pussycat, songs, nonsense botany, etc., illustrated by Lear. Total of 320pp. 5⅜ x 8½. (Available in U.S. only.) 20167-8

VICTORIAN PARLOUR POETRY: An Annotated Anthology, Michael R. Turner. 117 gems by Longfellow, Tennyson, Browning, many lesser-known poets. "The Village Blacksmith," "Curfew Must Not Ring Tonight," "Only a Baby Small," dozens more, often difficult to find elsewhere. Index of poets, titles, first lines. xxiii + 325pp. 5⅝ x 8¼. 27044-0

DUBLINERS, James Joyce. Fifteen stories offer vivid, tightly focused observations of the lives of Dublin's poorer classes. At least one, "The Dead," is considered a masterpiece. Reprinted complete and unabridged from standard edition. 160pp. 5$\frac{3}{16}$ x 8¼. 26870-5

GREAT WEIRD TALES: 14 Stories by Lovecraft, Blackwood, Machen and Others, S. T. Joshi (ed.). 14 spellbinding tales, including "The Sin Eater," by Fiona McLeod, "The Eye Above the Mantel," by Frank Belknap Long, as well as renowned works by R. H. Barlow, Lord Dunsany, Arthur Machen, W. C. Morrow and eight other masters of the genre. 256pp. 5⅜ x 8½. (Available in U.S. only.) 40436-6

THE BOOK OF THE SACRED MAGIC OF ABRAMELIN THE MAGE, translated by S. MacGregor Mathers. Medieval manuscript of ceremonial magic. Basic document in Aleister Crowley, Golden Dawn groups. 268pp. 5⅜ x 8½. 23211-5

NEW RUSSIAN-ENGLISH AND ENGLISH-RUSSIAN DICTIONARY, M. A. O'Brien. This is a remarkably handy Russian dictionary, containing a surprising amount of information, including over 70,000 entries. 366pp. 4½ x 6⅛. 20208-9

HISTORIC HOMES OF THE AMERICAN PRESIDENTS, Second, Revised Edition, Irvin Haas. A traveler's guide to American Presidential homes, most open to the public, depicting and describing homes occupied by every American President from George Washington to George Bush. With visiting hours, admission charges, travel routes. 175 photographs. Index. 160pp. 8¼ x 11. 26751-2

NEW YORK IN THE FORTIES, Andreas Feininger. 162 brilliant photographs by the well-known photographer, formerly with *Life* magazine. Commuters, shoppers, Times Square at night, much else from city at its peak. Captions by John von Hartz. 181pp. 9¼ x 10¾. 23585-8

INDIAN SIGN LANGUAGE, William Tomkins. Over 525 signs developed by Sioux and other tribes. Written instructions and diagrams. Also 290 pictographs. 111pp. 6⅛ x 9¼. 22029-X

CATALOG OF DOVER BOOKS

ANATOMY: A Complete Guide for Artists, Joseph Sheppard. A master of figure drawing shows artists how to render human anatomy convincingly. Over 460 illustrations. 224pp. 8⅜ x 11¼. 27279-6

MEDIEVAL CALLIGRAPHY: Its History and Technique, Marc Drogin. Spirited history, comprehensive instruction manual covers 13 styles (ca. 4th century through 15th). Excellent photographs; directions for duplicating medieval techniques with modern tools. 224pp. 8⅜ x 11¼. 26142-5

DRIED FLOWERS: How to Prepare Them, Sarah Whitlock and Martha Rankin. Complete instructions on how to use silica gel, meal and borax, perlite aggregate, sand and borax, glycerine and water to create attractive permanent flower arrangements. 12 illustrations. 32pp. 5⅜ x 8½. 21802-3

EASY-TO-MAKE BIRD FEEDERS FOR WOODWORKERS, Scott D. Campbell. Detailed, simple-to-use guide for designing, constructing, caring for and using feeders. Text, illustrations for 12 classic and contemporary designs. 96pp. 5⅜ x 8½. 25847-5

SCOTTISH WONDER TALES FROM MYTH AND LEGEND, Donald A. Mackenzie. 16 lively tales tell of giants rumbling down mountainsides, of a magic wand that turns stone pillars into warriors, of gods and goddesses, evil hags, powerful forces and more. 240pp. 5⅜ x 8½. 29677-6

THE HISTORY OF UNDERCLOTHES, C. Willett Cunnington and Phyllis Cunnington. Fascinating, well-documented survey covering six centuries of English undergarments, enhanced with over 100 illustrations: 12th-century laced-up bodice, footed long drawers (1795), 19th-century bustles, 19th-century corsets for men, Victorian "bust improvers," much more. 272pp. 5⅜ x 8¼. 27124-2

ARTS AND CRAFTS FURNITURE: The Complete Brooks Catalog of 1912, Brooks Manufacturing Co. Photos and detailed descriptions of more than 150 now very collectible furniture designs from the Arts and Crafts movement depict davenports, settees, buffets, desks, tables, chairs, bedsteads, dressers and more, all built of solid, quarter-sawed oak. Invaluable for students and enthusiasts of antiques, Americana and the decorative arts. 80pp. 6½ x 9¼. 27471-3

WILBUR AND ORVILLE: A Biography of the Wright Brothers, Fred Howard. Definitive, crisply written study tells the full story of the brothers' lives and work. A vividly written biography, unparalleled in scope and color, that also captures the spirit of an extraordinary era. 560pp. 6⅛ x 9¼. 40297-5

THE ARTS OF THE SAILOR: Knotting, Splicing and Ropework, Hervey Garrett Smith. Indispensable shipboard reference covers tools, basic knots and useful hitches; handsewing and canvas work, more. Over 100 illustrations. Delightful reading for sea lovers. 256pp. 5⅜ x 8½. 26440-8

FRANK LLOYD WRIGHT'S FALLINGWATER: The House and Its History, Second, Revised Edition, Donald Hoffmann. A total revision—both in text and illustrations—of the standard document on Fallingwater, the boldest, most personal architectural statement of Wright's mature years, updated with valuable new material from the recently opened Frank Lloyd Wright Archives. "Fascinating"–The New York Times. 116 illustrations. 128pp. 9¼ x 10¾. 27430-6

CATALOG OF DOVER BOOKS

PHOTOGRAPHIC SKETCHBOOK OF THE CIVIL WAR, Alexander Gardner. 100 photos taken on field during the Civil War. Famous shots of Manassas Harper's Ferry, Lincoln, Richmond, slave pens, etc. 244pp. 10⅝ x 8¼. 22731-6

FIVE ACRES AND INDEPENDENCE, Maurice G. Kains. Great back-to-the-land classic explains basics of self-sufficient farming. The one book to get. 95 illustrations. 397pp. 5⅜ x 8½. 20974-1

SONGS OF EASTERN BIRDS, Dr. Donald J. Borror. Songs and calls of 60 species most common to eastern U.S.: warblers, woodpeckers, flycatchers, thrushes, larks, many more in high-quality recording. Cassette and manual 99912-2

A MODERN HERBAL, Margaret Grieve. Much the fullest, most exact, most useful compilation of herbal material. Gigantic alphabetical encyclopedia, from aconite to zedoary, gives botanical information, medical properties, folklore, economic uses, much else. Indispensable to serious reader. 161 illustrations. 888pp. 6½ x 9¼. 2-vol. set. (Available in U.S. only.) Vol. I: 22798-7
Vol. II: 22799-5

HIDDEN TREASURE MAZE BOOK, Dave Phillips. Solve 34 challenging mazes accompanied by heroic tales of adventure. Evil dragons, people-eating plants, blood-thirsty giants, many more dangerous adversaries lurk at every twist and turn. 34 mazes, stories, solutions. 48pp. 8¼ x 11. 24566-7

LETTERS OF W. A. MOZART, Wolfgang A. Mozart. Remarkable letters show bawdy wit, humor, imagination, musical insights, contemporary musical world; includes some letters from Leopold Mozart. 276pp. 5⅜ x 8½. 22859-2

BASIC PRINCIPLES OF CLASSICAL BALLET, Agrippina Vaganova. Great Russian theoretician, teacher explains methods for teaching classical ballet. 118 illustrations. 175pp. 5⅜ x 8½. 22036-2

THE JUMPING FROG, Mark Twain. Revenge edition. The original story of The Celebrated Jumping Frog of Calaveras County, a hapless French translation, and Twain's hilarious "retranslation" from the French. 12 illustrations. 66pp. 5⅜ x 8½. 22686-7

BEST REMEMBERED POEMS, Martin Gardner (ed.). The 126 poems in this superb collection of 19th- and 20th-century British and American verse range from Shelley's "To a Skylark" to the impassioned "Renascence" of Edna St. Vincent Millay and to Edward Lear's whimsical "The Owl and the Pussycat." 224pp. 5⅜ x 8½. 27165-X

COMPLETE SONNETS, William Shakespeare. Over 150 exquisite poems deal with love, friendship, the tyranny of time, beauty's evanescence, death and other themes in language of remarkable power, precision and beauty. Glossary of archaic terms. 80pp. 5³⁄₁₆ x 8¼. 26686-9

THE BATTLES THAT CHANGED HISTORY, Fletcher Pratt. Eminent historian profiles 16 crucial conflicts, ancient to modern, that changed the course of civilization. 352pp. 5⅜ x 8½. 41129-X

THE WIT AND HUMOR OF OSCAR WILDE, Alvin Redman (ed.). More than 1,000 ripostes, paradoxes, wisecracks: Work is the curse of the drinking classes; I can resist everything except temptation; etc. 258pp. 5⅜ x 8½. 20602-5

SHAKESPEARE LEXICON AND QUOTATION DICTIONARY, Alexander Schmidt. Full definitions, locations, shades of meaning in every word in plays and poems. More than 50,000 exact quotations. 1,485pp. 6½ x 9¼. 2-vol. set.
Vol. 1: 22726-X
Vol. 2: 22727-8

SELECTED POEMS, Emily Dickinson. Over 100 best-known, best-loved poems by one of America's foremost poets, reprinted from authoritative early editions. No comparable edition at this price. Index of first lines. 64pp. 5³⁄₁₆ x 8¼. 26466-1

THE INSIDIOUS DR. FU-MANCHU, Sax Rohmer. The first of the popular mystery series introduces a pair of English detectives to their archnemesis, the diabolical Dr. Fu-Manchu. Flavorful atmosphere, fast-paced action, and colorful characters enliven this classic of the genre. 208pp. 5³⁄₁₆ x 8¼. 29898-1

THE MALLEUS MALEFICARUM OF KRAMER AND SPRENGER, translated by Montague Summers. Full text of most important witchhunter's "bible," used by both Catholics and Protestants. 278pp. 6⅝ x 10. 22802-9

SPANISH STORIES/CUENTOS ESPAÑOLES: A Dual-Language Book, Angel Flores (ed.). Unique format offers 13 great stories in Spanish by Cervantes, Borges, others. Faithful English translations on facing pages. 352pp. 5⅜ x 8½. 25399-6

GARDEN CITY, LONG ISLAND, IN EARLY PHOTOGRAPHS, 1869–1919, Mildred H. Smith. Handsome treasury of 118 vintage pictures, accompanied by carefully researched captions, document the Garden City Hotel fire (1899), the Vanderbilt Cup Race (1908), the first airmail flight departing from the Nassau Boulevard Aerodrome (1911), and much more. 96pp. 8⅞ x 11¾. 40669-5

OLD QUEENS, N.Y., IN EARLY PHOTOGRAPHS, Vincent F. Seyfried and William Asadorian. Over 160 rare photographs of Maspeth, Jamaica, Jackson Heights, and other areas. Vintage views of DeWitt Clinton mansion, 1939 World's Fair and more. Captions. 192pp. 8⅞ x 11. 26358-4

CAPTURED BY THE INDIANS: 15 Firsthand Accounts, 1750-1870, Frederick Drimmer. Astounding true historical accounts of grisly torture, bloody conflicts, relentless pursuits, miraculous escapes and more, by people who lived to tell the tale. 384pp. 5⅜ x 8½. 24901-8

THE WORLD'S GREAT SPEECHES (Fourth Enlarged Edition), Lewis Copeland, Lawrence W. Lamm, and Stephen J. McKenna. Nearly 300 speeches provide public speakers with a wealth of updated quotes and inspiration–from Pericles' funeral oration and William Jennings Bryan's "Cross of Gold Speech" to Malcolm X's powerful words on the Black Revolution and Earl of Spenser's tribute to his sister, Diana, Princess of Wales. 944pp. 5⅜ x 8⅜. 40903-1

THE BOOK OF THE SWORD, Sir Richard F. Burton. Great Victorian scholar/adventurer's eloquent, erudite history of the "queen of weapons"–from prehistory to early Roman Empire. Evolution and development of early swords, variations (sabre, broadsword, cutlass, scimitar, etc.), much more. 336pp. 6⅛ x 9¼. 25434-8

AUTOBIOGRAPHY: The Story of My Experiments with Truth, Mohandas K. Gandhi. Boyhood, legal studies, purification, the growth of the Satyagraha (nonviolent protest) movement. Critical, inspiring work of the man responsible for the freedom of India. 480pp. 5⅜ x 8½. (Available in U.S. only.) 24593-4

CELTIC MYTHS AND LEGENDS, T. W. Rolleston. Masterful retelling of Irish and Welsh stories and tales. Cuchulain, King Arthur, Deirdre, the Grail, many more. First paperback edition. 58 full-page illustrations. 512pp. 5⅜ x 8½. 26507-2

THE PRINCIPLES OF PSYCHOLOGY, William James. Famous long course complete, unabridged. Stream of thought, time perception, memory, experimental methods; great work decades ahead of its time. 94 figures. 1,391pp. 5⅜ x 8½. 2-vol. set.
Vol. I: 20381-6    Vol. II: 20382-4

THE WORLD AS WILL AND REPRESENTATION, Arthur Schopenhauer. Definitive English translation of Schopenhauer's life work, correcting more than 1,000 errors, omissions in earlier translations. Translated by E. F. J. Payne. Total of 1,269pp. 5⅜ x 8½. 2-vol. set.          Vol. 1: 21761-2    Vol. 2: 21762-0

MAGIC AND MYSTERY IN TIBET, Madame Alexandra David-Neel. Experiences among lamas, magicians, sages, sorcerers, Bonpa wizards. A true psychic discovery. 32 illustrations. 321pp. 5⅜ x 8½. (Available in U.S. only.) 22682-4

THE EGYPTIAN BOOK OF THE DEAD, E. A. Wallis Budge. Complete reproduction of Ani's papyrus, finest ever found. Full hieroglyphic text, interlinear transliteration, word-for-word translation, smooth translation. 533pp. 6½ x 9¼. 21866-X

MATHEMATICS FOR THE NONMATHEMATICIAN, Morris Kline. Detailed, college-level treatment of mathematics in cultural and historical context, with numerous exercises. Recommended Reading Lists. Tables. Numerous figures. 641pp. 5⅜ x 8½. 24823-2

PROBABILISTIC METHODS IN THE THEORY OF STRUCTURES, Isaac Elishakoff. Well-written introduction covers the elements of the theory of probability from two or more random variables, the reliability of such multivariable structures, the theory of random function, Monte Carlo methods of treating problems incapable of exact solution, and more. Examples. 502pp. 5⅜ x 8½. 40691-1

THE RIME OF THE ANCIENT MARINER, Gustave Doré, S. T. Coleridge. Doré's finest work; 34 plates capture moods, subtleties of poem. Flawless full-size reproductions printed on facing pages with authoritative text of poem. "Beautiful. Simply beautiful."–*Publisher's Weekly.* 77pp. 9¼ x 12. 22305-1

NORTH AMERICAN INDIAN DESIGNS FOR ARTISTS AND CRAFTSPEOPLE, Eva Wilson. Over 360 authentic copyright-free designs adapted from Navajo blankets, Hopi pottery, Sioux buffalo hides, more. Geometrics, symbolic figures, plant and animal motifs, etc. 128pp. 8⅜ x 11. (Not for sale in the United Kingdom.) 25341-4

SCULPTURE: Principles and Practice, Louis Slobodkin. Step-by-step approach to clay, plaster, metals, stone; classical and modern. 253 drawings, photos. 255pp. 8⅛ x 11. 22960-2

THE INFLUENCE OF SEA POWER UPON HISTORY, 1660–1783, A. T. Mahan. Influential classic of naval history and tactics still used as text in war colleges. First paperback edition. 4 maps. 24 battle plans. 640pp. 5⅜ x 8½. 25509-3

# CATALOG OF DOVER BOOKS

THE STORY OF THE TITANIC AS TOLD BY ITS SURVIVORS, Jack Winocour (ed.). What it was really like. Panic, despair, shocking inefficiency, and a little heroism. More thrilling than any fictional account. 26 illustrations. 320pp. 5⅜ x 8½.
20610-6

FAIRY AND FOLK TALES OF THE IRISH PEASANTRY, William Butler Yeats (ed.). Treasury of 64 tales from the twilight world of Celtic myth and legend: "The Soul Cages," "The Kildare Pooka," "King O'Toole and his Goose," many more. Introduction and Notes by W. B. Yeats. 352pp. 5⅜ x 8½.
26941-8

BUDDHIST MAHAYANA TEXTS, E. B. Cowell and others (eds.). Superb, accurate translations of basic documents in Mahayana Buddhism, highly important in history of religions. The Buddha-karita of Asvaghosha, Larger Sukhavativyuha, more. 448pp. 5⅜ x 8½.
25552-2

ONE TWO THREE . . . INFINITY: Facts and Speculations of Science, George Gamow. Great physicist's fascinating, readable overview of contemporary science: number theory, relativity, fourth dimension, entropy, genes, atomic structure, much more. 128 illustrations. Index. 352pp. 5⅜ x 8½.
25664-2

EXPERIMENTATION AND MEASUREMENT, W. J. Youden. Introductory manual explains laws of measurement in simple terms and offers tips for achieving accuracy and minimizing errors. Mathematics of measurement, use of instruments, experimenting with machines. 1994 edition. Foreword. Preface. Introduction. Epilogue. Selected Readings. Glossary. Index. Tables and figures. 128pp. 5⅜ x 8½.   40451-X

DALÍ ON MODERN ART: The Cuckolds of Antiquated Modern Art, Salvador Dalí. Influential painter skewers modern art and its practitioners. Outrageous evaluations of Picasso, Cézanne, Turner, more. 15 renderings of paintings discussed. 44 calligraphic decorations by Dalí. 96pp. 5⅜ x 8½. (Available in U.S. only.)   29220-7

ANTIQUE PLAYING CARDS: A Pictorial History, Henry René D'Allemagne. Over 900 elaborate, decorative images from rare playing cards (14th–20th centuries): Bacchus, death, dancing dogs, hunting scenes, royal coats of arms, players cheating, much more. 96pp. 9¼ x 12¼.   29265-7

MAKING FURNITURE MASTERPIECES: 30 Projects with Measured Drawings, Franklin H. Gottshall. Step-by-step instructions, illustrations for constructing handsome, useful pieces, among them a Sheraton desk, Chippendale chair, Spanish desk, Queen Anne table and a William and Mary dressing mirror. 224pp. 8⅛ x 11¼.
29338-6

THE FOSSIL BOOK: A Record of Prehistoric Life, Patricia V. Rich et al. Profusely illustrated definitive guide covers everything from single-celled organisms and dinosaurs to birds and mammals and the interplay between climate and man. Over 1,500 illustrations. 760pp. 7½ x 10⅛.   29371-8